The Westside Slugger

WILBUR S. SHEPPERSON SERIES IN NEVADA HISTORY

Series Editor: Michael Green (UNLV)

Nevada is known politically as a swing state and culturally as a swinging state. Politically, its electoral votes have gone to the winning presidential candidate in all but one election since 1912 (it missed in 1976). Its geographic location in the Sunbelt; an ethnically diverse, heavily urban, and fast-growing population; and an economy based on tourism and mining make it a laboratory for understanding the growth and development of postwar America and post-industrial society. Culturally, Nevada has been associated with legal gambling, easy divorce, and social permissiveness. Yet the state also exemplifies conflicts between image and reality: it is also a conservative state yet depends heavily on the federal government; its gaming regulatory system is the envy of the world but resulted from long and difficult experience with organized crime; its bright lights often obscure the role of organized religion in Nevada affairs. To some who have emphasized the impact of globalization and celebrated or deplored changing moral standards, Nevada reflects America and the world; to others, it affects them.

This series is named in honor of one of the state's most distinguished historians, author of numerous books on the state's immigrants and cultural development, a longtime educator, and an advocate for history and the humanities. The series welcomes manuscripts on any and all aspects of Nevada that offer insight into how the state has developed and how its development has been connected to the region, the nation, and the world.

A Great Basin Mosaic:
The Cultures of Rural Nevada
by James W. Hulse

The Baneberry Disaster:
A Generation of Atomic Fallout
by Larry C. Johns and Alan R. Johns

The Sagebrush State, 5th Edition: Nevada's History, Government, and Politics
by Michael W. Bowers

The Westside Slugger
Joe Neal's Lifelong Fight for Social Justice
by John L. Smith

The
Westside
Slugger

Joe Neal's Lifelong Fight
for Social Justice

John L. Smith

UNIVERSITY OF NEVADA PRESS *Reno & Las Vegas*

University of Nevada Press | Reno, Nevada 89557 USA
www.unpress.nevada.edu
Copyright © 2019 by University of Nevada Press
Cover art from Debra Reid
Cover design by Matt Strelecki
Photo Gallery from Neal family collection unless otherwise marked.
Photo gallery background © winning7799/Adobe Stock.

LIBRARY OF CONGRESS CATALOGING-IN-PUBLICATION DATA
Names: Smith, John L., 1960- author.
Title: The Westside slugger : Joe Neal's lifelong fight for social justice /
  John L. Smith.
Description: Reno ; Las Vegas : University of Nevada Press, [2019] | Series:
  Wilbur S. Shepperson Series in Nevada History | Includes bibliographical
  references. |
Identifiers: LCCN 2018037055 (print) | LCCN 2018041048 (ebook) | ISBN
  9781948908047 (ebook) | ISBN 9781948908030 (cloth : alk. paper)
Subjects: LCSH: Neal, Joe, 1935- | Legislators--Nevada--Biography. | African
  American legislators--Nevada--Biography. | Nevada--Politics and
  government--20th century. | Social justice--United States--History. |
  Civil rights--United States--History.
Classification: LCC F845.25.N43 (ebook) | LCC F845.25.N43 S65 2019 (print) |
  DDC 328.73/092 [B] --dc23
LC record available at https://lccn.loc.gov/2018037055

The paper used in this book meets the requirements of American National
Standard for Information Sciences — Permanence of Paper for Printed Library
Materials, ANSI/NISO Z39.48-1992 (R2002).

FIRST PRINTING

Manufactured in the United States of America

Contents

Foreword

Carson City and several early Nevada mining towns embraced boxing as early as 1897. However, it was Las Vegas, which only became a city in the twentieth century, that emerged as the center of the state's boxing culture. Joe Neal, though not a boxer, lived a life that personified the sport at its highest level. Nevada's first African-American state senator is quick, accurate in landing punches, powerful, good on defense and offense, well-conditioned, intelligent, disciplined, and has guts. He is truly the Slugger of the Westside.

From humble beginnings in Mound, Louisiana, Joe Neal migrated to Las Vegas in 1954, the same year that marked the construction of the Moulin Rouge hotel and casino and the arrival of the first black doctor. It was also the same year that the first middle class housing development, Berkley Square, opened for residents. This new neighborhood was financed by African-American attorney Thomas Berkley and featured homes designed by black architect Paul Revere Williams. The burgeoning middle class, composed of people such as Dr. Charles I. West and Joe Neal, joined the movers and shakers of the black World War II migration as the community made ongoing progressive changes. Joe Neal's skill sets were needed, and he fit perfectly into the developing young city.

Even before his first run for office, Joe engaged in the political welfare of the Westside community. He worked on the board of the Economic Opportunity Board of Clark County, enforced the 1964 Civil Rights Act as part of his job at Reynolds Electrical and Engineering Company (REECo), worked with Donald Clark as Clark served as president of the local National Association for the Advancement of Colored People, and helped to pass the 1971 consent decree that stipulated 12 percent of jobs in the resort industry go to black workers. In 1972 Joe ran for the Nevada State Senate. He won.

Indeed, the Slugger had found his place for good rumbles with the best in politics—William Raggio, Joe Conforte, Mel Close, Mike O'Callaghan, and the list goes on and on. Issues over the years included Howard Hughes's discriminatory policies, fair housing, women's rights, reapportionment, increased casino taxes, trade unions, improved fire safety in hotels, and the Lake Tahoe Compact. No issue was too big nor too small for Joe. He tackled the dilemma of pay toilets with the same intensity as the issue of the death penalty for murderers of police officers.

The subject of apartheid and its relationship to tourist dollars for the gaming industry found Joe in a face-to-face meeting with the South African consulate general and then on the Senate floor advocating for a ban on Nevada's investment of public funds in South Africa. "Our state monies should not go to any government to enable it to maintain a system which rejects individuals based on the color of their skin. Our money should not go to any government which uses violence to maintain a system of apartheid, a system which would be illegal under our Constitution."

John L. Smith has written an amazingly comprehensive book of the complex life and times of Joe Neal dealing with matters from Mound, Louisiana, to South Africa. Joe fought the good fight always. He stood alone often. During his first term he became known as "19 to 1." He may have stood alone in the beginning, but the underdog prevailed for 32 years in his work for the State of Nevada and for the African-American communities he represented. Joe Neal was always a fearless contender. He waged and won political heavyweight championship bouts.

— Claytee D. White, Director,
Oral History Research Center
at UNLV Libraries

Preface

An encouraging word from a dedicated teacher, the lessons of a care-worn textbook deemed not good enough for white schoolchildren, a borrowed shirt fit for a bus ride beyond his insular existence. Of such moments was Joe Neal's young life made.

Looking back across the decades, it's clear that his long journey from the sharecropped cotton fields of Louisiana to the halls of the Nevada State Senate turned on such barely recognizable kindnesses. With an uncommon tenacity, Neal knotted those humble lengths of rope and climbed from Madison Parish toward the light of opportunity. In a country that advertised equality, Neal appreciated at an early age what most African Americans of his generation eventually learned: that the fortunate and truly blessed might see a real chance for advancement come just once in a lifetime.

And when a chance came to move west to dusty, segregated Las Vegas in the mid-1950s, he grabbed it. He was quickly reminded that the racism he knew back home wasn't regional, but widespread; not isolated, but institutional. When it became clear that only an advanced education would make a real difference in his life, he joined the United States Air Force, served honorably, and earned the benefits of the G.I. Bill.

He enrolled at Southern University and studied political science and the law at a time of great upheaval in the racial status quo. He helped register the first black voters in the history of Madison Parish. Once he returned to Southern Nevada in the summer of 1963, Neal worked for equal employment opportunity and became one of a small number of activists who pounded away at the door of politics and public accommodation until it opened a crack for African Americans and other minorities.

Once in office as the first black state senator in Nevada history, Neal never forgot why he crashed the party. Fighting for an issue, getting knocked down, rising again, and never quitting: That was Joe Neal. He spent three decades forever calling on his colleagues to consider Nevada's poor, the mentally disabled, and the working class; to see the intrinsic fairness of the Equal Rights Amendment; to invest in job training so that the least skilled might find their own footing; to expand the state's decrepit library system; to seek more funding for public schools. He seldom missed an opportunity to hold up a mirror to the state's most powerful interests, knowing it would brand him not only a rabble-rouser but also that lowliest orphan in Nevada politics, the elected official who is "not a team player."

Joe Neal's life from Louisiana to Las Vegas is emblematic of the greater struggle of so many African Americans to rise from meager means, persevere through racism-driven adversity and Jim Crow venality, and stand up for social justice despite daunting odds.

It all began in Madison Parish.

From Louisiana Soil

JOE NEAL COMES FROM northeastern Louisiana, whose history is a tale of conquest and a trail of tears. The story begins with aboriginal Americans who farmed its lush open spaces, hunted in its woods, and fished its great rivers and streams 3,500 years before Christ. They left their mark in the form of sacred mounds, the first of which predate the Great Pyramids and Stonehenge and are the earliest discovered in North America. Built "to celebrate their bond with the land," they were consecrated high ground, one part burial monument and one part spiritual offering. When the waters jumped their banks and flowed across the land, the rises, some seventy feet high and 200 at the base, survived. Through the centuries, their construction was repeated throughout the Southeast and the Ohio Valley.

Louisiana's Division of Archaeology counts at least 39 "Indian mounds" in the state, some dating back 5,000 years. Through its Office of Cultural Development, the state created the Ancient Mounds Heritage Area and Trails Initiative to celebrate and preserve the "magnificent earthworks." As with so many stories of native culture, the natives were exterminated or relocated by force through a treaty that eventually would not be honored. In time, the remnants of what they left behind were considered worth preserving by descendants of the very people who pushed them out of their birthplaces and living spaces. The state officially began to see the wisdom in saving them for future generations in 1933.

The mound-builder communities were still active in the sixteenth century, when in 1541 they were observed by Spanish explorer Hernando de Soto. By 1682, when René-Robert Cavelier claimed the region on behalf of France's King Louis XIV, the mound people had been eclipsed by myriad tribes, the Chickasaw, Choctaw, Natchez, Osage, Seminole, and Yamasee, to name a few. Although at one time thought to be separate and distinct, the mound builders of the Mississippian culture are considered by most accounts to be ancestral to the better-known Native American tribes in the region.

The tribes warred often, and the Chickasaw took slaves long before the Europeans shipped the first Africans to America in 1619. When the United States purchased Louisiana from the French in 1803 for $15 million—about three cents per acre—slavery culture was nearly a century old. Louisiana was war-torn in 1812, the year it was granted statehood, but life for African slaves and increasingly harassed Native American tribes did not improve with time. In 1830, President Andrew Jackson signed the Indian Removal Act, which, combined with subsequent orders, forced the migration of entire nations of Native Americans from land they'd known for centuries to the comparatively barren territories of Oklahoma and Arkansas.

With the Indians marginalized, Antebellum Louisiana was a slaver's paradise. By 1860, 47 percent of the state's population lived under the lash. During the Civil War, Union troops battered and burned nearby Vicksburg, Mississippi. By the time they reached Tallulah, a town named for a railroad contractor's mistress, beleaguered supporters of the Confederacy offered no resistance. The fighting eventually ceased, but efforts at Reconstruction were no match for the Louisiana legislature. With planters still stinging from defeat and seeking to protect their way of life, lawmakers rewrote laws won with the blood of hundreds of thousands of Americans to create a new constitution that disenfranchised blacks and gave rise to state-sponsored segregation that lasted until more blood was shed in the 1960s civil rights movement.

Northeastern Louisiana's blend of cultures is as rich as its fertile soil with abundant native, African, French, and English influences. Where that diversity ought to have provided strength, Louisiana held fast to its Jim Crow mind-set. In Madison Parish, home to Tallulah, the racial lines were generations old. Named for the fourth president of the United States, Madison Parish had been predominantly black for more than a century. But blacks did not vote, held no public offices, and were allowed only marginal opportunities to trade. In short, it might be said they were relegated to second-class status because no third class was available.

For white residents, Tallulah offered civility amid squalor. For example, few shopping experiences rivaled a trip to Bloom's Arcade, which opened in 1925 and is still touted as America's first indoor "mall." Near Highway 80 (now U.S. Interstate 20), the long, rectangular building was home to many shops and businesses. Officials started to pave the roads of Tallulah in 1938. Eleven miles to the east, the streets of Mound—what locals commonly pluralized as "Mounds"—would remain dirt for another decade.

The farm tenancy system underwritten by the Franklin D. Roosevelt administration during the "second" New Deal brought opportunity and agricultural education to poor sharecroppers, whether black or white, to the Maxwell-Yerger plantation near Mound. It was one of FDR's earliest efforts at fighting the "war on poverty" at the ground level. As long as there was federal oversight, poor farmers received a fighting chance to work fields subdivided on the plantation. Landlords were paid, the people were trained and fed, and when the cotton was harvested and cashed the sharecroppers would have a little money in their pockets.

Joseph Neal and his pregnant wife, Josephine Watson Neal, left Arkansas for that opportunity, their young son, Willie, in tow as they traveled south to Tallulah and Mound. Desperate for work, Joseph hoped to grab a piece of Roosevelt's agrarian American dream. But it was not to be. The popular program was brimming with tenant farmers from the immediate area.

Since a hospital was not an option for blacks, Joseph and Josephine had not been allowed to set foot inside the local health facility. In fact, no blacks could unless they carried a janitor's mop and bucket. The nearest medical clinic that would accept minorities was the Charity Hospital in Monroe, some sixty miles west of Tallulah. So Josephine Neal relied on Missy Luster, an experienced midwife, to help bring her second baby boy into the world. Joseph M. Neal, Jr. was born on July 28, 1935. The midwife Luster would remain as close as an aunt to Neal and his older brother.

The son of the midwife who delivered Neal, Bo Luster, would mentor young Joe, influence his decision to pursue military service and higher education, and remain a lifelong friend. Luster would also provide a strong male influence at a time when Joe was away from both parents, who separated about the time he was born. While Josephine pursued work in distant towns, Joseph severed ties to the family. Neal wouldn't meet his father until age 14, and he gleaned little from the conversation about his family or its breakup.

The elder Neal died of kidney failure in 1963 in Dumas, Arkansas.

"As I looked back on my life during these times," Neal recalled many years later, he didn't really say he knew his father, and "I had not bonded with my mother; but my brother had. I bonded with my older brother and the Prater family who took us in."

With so much work to do, there was little time to dwell on what life hadn't provided. He came to appreciate and cherish the family that had taken him in.

When Josephine found work several months later at an FDR camp in Alexandria, Louisiana, she was forced to rely on friends and family to care for young Willie and Joe. They were a handful. While Josephine worked, the boys were basically left to their own devices with predictable results. Joe ignited his trousers while "popping" bamboo cane on an open fire. Ever the protective big brother, Willie put out the flames with his bare hands, but not before Joe suffered a severe leg burn. Willie carried his brother to a nearby house where the burn was cleaned and dressed. The accident turned out to be fortuitous, for after that the boys were placed in the charge of Mary and Goins Prater—sharecroppers who gave the youngsters guidance and looked after them responsibly.

The burn would heal in time, but it provided lively fodder for brothers who would remain the best of friends throughout their lives. "There was never any conflict between Willie and myself," Neal would recall more than seventy-five years later. "Whenever Willie and I had an argument, he would bring up the fact he saved my life. Which was true. When I was burned at the age of two, Willie, as a four-year-old, put out the fire with his bare hands."

The Praters often told young Joe stories of the Prater family's long history in the area. Mary's tales predated slavery. She firmly believed that her people were in that part of the country when it was tribal land before slavery. Although the white society considered her black, she believed she was part Yamasee. But for those few years there were just hardworking members of one of the great social experiments of the Roosevelt era. As a part of President Roosevelt's New Deal programs, the Farm Security Administration embarked on a far-reaching and not entirely successful plan to assist poor farmers during the Dust Bowl and Great Depression. Through drought, blight, and boll weevil infestations, the FSA and its predecessor Resettlement Administration worked with sharecroppers in the region in an effort to help save their fields and properties and improve their lives. As participants in the La Delta Project at Thomastown, Louisiana, black farm families received training in everything from soil management to home economics in hope that education would lead to independence despite their segregated status and institutional racism. Photojournalist Marion Post Wolcott famously depicted scenes in 1940 of productive black women canning squash in an impeccable test kitchen while paying close attention to the instructor during a meeting of the "Home Demonstration Group." Farmers were depicted disking and plowing fields and admiring a new barn, cotton gin, chicken house, and whitewashed homes. There were also photographs of old slave quarters and the clapboard shanties farmers had been accustomed to inhabiting as sharecroppers on the Yerger plantation.

Against long odds that few would take, the federal government had sent experts to these farmers to aid them immediately while also teaching them to help themselves. Of all the images captured by Wolcott's camera, none had a greater impact on young Joe Neal's life than the freshly painted, one-story Thomastown School. Before its construction, the only education available to black children was to be found at the local church, where Neal received his first school experience at the Shady Grove Missionary Baptist Church from a woman named Minnie Koontz. The classroom was small and full, and the available materials were rudimentary. "She wrote my name on a small blackboard about four feet by four feet: *Joseph Martin Neal Jr.* Then she asked me to copy it," he said. Joe thought that was fantastic in its own right. But when he found out that apples, oranges, and plums were delivered to the school on a regular basis, he was bowled over. "Now that was worth getting up in the morning for!"

It was at the Baptist church that Neal had his first taste of orange juice. In those days, the delivery of the fruits and juices was a mystery. Only later did Neal discover that it arrived courtesy of the political machine created by Louisiana governor Huey P. Long. Dubbed the "Kingfish," Long knew that a little fresh produce in what would be called a "food desert" seventy-five years later in America went a long way in the minds of the poor. Even though the populist politician Long would be assassinated in 1935, his tradition would continue. For years to come, out of respect to the two political figures that embodied their struggle, Louisiana blacks often named their children after the beloved "Huey" and "Roosevelt." Roosevelt and Long engaged in a fierce rivalry to win the hearts and minds of the Depression-era poor. For much of the 1930s their personal and political battle benefited blacks and whites alike. Roosevelt brought federal programs that Long fought, and which he countered with generous handouts. In both instances, America's downtrodden benefited. (Future U.S. Supreme Court Justice Thurgood Marshall himself would recall the story of eating an orange outside a Mississippi courthouse in the 1940s.)

Neal attended his church school until the fourth grade. Then it closed and was replaced by the Thomastown School, with its crisply clean exterior and Roosevelt administration seal of approval. It was tangible proof that the federal government, as harried as it was during the Depression, had its eye on the poor of Madison Parish. The Thomastown School, originally controlled by blacks, was turned over to the local school district, and was soon known for its used books and other classroom hand-me-downs.

That section of the South was a socioeconomic laboratory where experimental programs meant to train and feed the poor in real time were tried out against a backdrop of a veritable American apartheid. While some programs were flawed, others were crushed by political infighting between federal and state agencies.

With millions of acres of previous plantation soil divided and under contract to black families, there was money to be made through both accommodation and exploitation of the new laws of the land. Those fortunate families commonly received up to 100 acres, a plow and mule, a sow, a farmhouse, and even a stove and cooking utensils. A soil conservation expert named "Massengale," and one "Mrs. Nettles" taught the women to can food. Neal recalled that black farmers prospered despite the boll weevil infestations that damaged the nearby fields of white sharecroppers.

"That farm tenancy system was established by the Yergers and Maxwells, who were an inter-married family," Neal described the situation. "The Mound Project was the nation's first war-on-poverty plan by the FDR administration. There were many blacks that owned their farms through the FDR administration, which allowed them to purchase land with government loans. They were given technical assistance from the government in land usage and food planning." Eventually, the federal programs were either discontinued or run to ground by members of Congress from the South who had accrued seniority and wielded great power, especially in the Senate.

The Prater family was kind, but demanding, and the Neal boys sought to contribute to the small farm in any way they could, eager to be useful and unobtrusive. The Praters' fenced slice of the Yerger plantation was less than ten acres, but large enough to grow cotton and a robust vegetable garden. "We had chickens, hogs, and milk cows," Neal would recall. The seven acres of land the Yergers rented to grow cotton were Joe's responsibility. It was his task to plow and grow the cotton crop, and he would never forget working those acres under moonlight. Although the work was hard, it taught Neal the value of manual labor and his calloused hands reminded him daily to pay attention in school if he dreamed of a life away from the fields. At the end of the harvesting season the Praters shared in the proceeds gained from the Neal boys' efforts. "In the 1940s, this amounted to about a hundred dollars each for my brother and me." Joe supplemented that income by selling eggs and butter to neighbors.

The 1940 Census counted 145 residents in Mound. By 2000, the figure had dwindled to a paltry twelve. Neighboring Tallulah's black population had flattened as the result of cross-country migrations to the West from the Great Depression through post–World War II, when an enormous populace sought work on Hoover Dam and other construction sites throughout the West and Southwest. Still, segregation was the law of the land, and real opportunities at home in the South were the stuff of dreams only.

Meanwhile at the Prater homestead, what couldn't be sold could often be bartered for needed dry goods and supplies. And when the Prater family field was in order, Joe and Willie often found themselves working the fields of their neighbors for a portion of the harvest. It wasn't simply a part-time job. "Survival depended upon your skills to prepare for lean times in your life," Neal said. "We never bought food from the store, other than flour. Everything else we made or canned. As to clothing, one pair of pants that was washed at night and hanged by the fire to dry." Willie and Joe were "free spirits" in their Mound childhood. "There wasn't a lot of control, and we went where we wanted to go. As long as we finished our chores, we had the day to ourselves."

During the summers Joe spent his free time cooling off in the bayou, where the children of white sharecroppers, with whom blacks shared a common poverty, often joined him. Neal fished and caught bullfrogs. And although "frogs from Tallulah" were a delicacy, and endless barrels of them were shipped from Louisiana to St. Louis for distribution across the country, Neal wasn't interested in the croaking amphibians for commercial purposes. He just liked eating them the way Mary Prater prepared them.

He also enjoyed reading, but since blacks weren't allowed to check out books at the public library in Tallulah, there wasn't much material available. "We didn't have any books or things in my house," Neal recalled. "We used newspapers for insulation. I'd read the old newspapers that a white guy named Mr. Jones would save for us. He used to subscribe to the newspapers from Vicksburg. Mama would wash his clothes for him every other week at his house, and she'd bring them home. I'd read them, and then they'd be put to use to insulate the house and help keep us warm in winter. Occasionally I'd get my hands on a ten-cent copy of *Jet* magazine, which contained news of the civil rights movement and let you know about racial issues at a time most newspapers refused to cover the issues."

It was in the pages of *Jet* that Neal would learn of the lynching of Emmett Till, the fourteen-year-old African-American boy who was tortured and murdered on August 28, 1955 in Money, Mississippi after allegedly flirting with a white girl. "Through *Jet* you got the sense of who you were in relationship to the larger society."

Mound was 123 miles due south of Money, just a few hours by car, but right next door in soul. In high school, the principal subscribed to the black-owned *Pittsburgh Courier*. Neal read its purple headlines and pages of prose whenever he could get his hands on a copy. It was far more relevant than the books on the shelves of the Mound library, what Neal would remember years later as "a bunch of books, middle-class stuff that didn't fit us." When he needed a reminder about doing the right thing and keeping up with his high school studies, Albert "Bo" Luster was someone Joe looked up to. Bo was focused on getting up and out of Mound, and he planned to use the opportunities provided by the military to achieve his goal. He joined the ROTC at Southern University in Baton Rouge, Louisiana and upon graduation became a career soldier in the United States Army and eventually a helicopter pilot with the rank of colonel. Bo Luster provided a valuable example that, although the playing field wasn't level and institutional racism placed innumerable obstacles in a striver's path, success was possible.

Neal's lifelong friend Richmond Calvin observed, "That was the only environment we were familiar with. We weren't a part of the white establishment. It was probably one of the worst systems you could be a part of, but you enjoyed what you had. As you grew, you understood the social and psychological differences and challenges of being an African American in a white society. It was very much against the Judeo-Christian heritage we talk about. You wonder, 'How could people who profess to believe in Jesus Christ as their Savior, how could they mistreat people in such an inhumane way?' As a youngster it was hard to conceptualize."

In time, Calvin and Neal and others learned the vocabulary of hate even if they did not practice it. "It was very cruel, very cruel," Calvin recalled. "We knew people who were raped, who were murdered. We saw all that. We couldn't get decent jobs. If you got jobs, you got the jobs the whites didn't want. I didn't get angry about it until I was 40 or 50 years old. You look back and get angry, but at the time, well, that's the way things were. We knew no other way.

"What that did for Joe and a lot of us in comparable situations is it gave us a desire to succeed, but it also gave you a desire to bring others along, to take time to motivate others. You become givers, not just receivers. I'm not sure who said, 'I'm not free unless those below me are free,' but it's a pretty good line."

At Thomastown School, participation in the New Farmers of America group was mandatory. "My school had no civics class—teaching civics to blacks was generally discouraged—but the New Farmers meetings served that purpose." The meetings provided important early lessons in the concept of government. "I clearly recall the day I realized one student, Morris Dixon, was more smart than I was. He knew rules I'd never heard of. There was a question in the group, a difference of opinion, and Morris Dixon challenged the leader on the constitution, something I'd never imagined existed. And the [other] kid backed down. Needless to say, I was mightily impressed. I knew there was something about this constitution that made the kid back down."

When the meeting adjourned, Neal mustered the courage to ask Dixon, "What are you talking about? What's the constitution?"

"That's the rules of the organization," his worldly young friend replied. "That's the rules they have to follow."

Neal realized two important lessons that day. First, groups are governed by rules. Second, if you're going to lead the group you had better know those rules. "But, of course, there were rules and then there were rules," Neal recalled many years later. "The only thing I knew with certainty is that the police could come and arrest you and take you to jail. That was the limit of my real-world experience with the rules."

The New Farmers of America group (sometimes called the Negro Farmers) provided valuable experience for Neal. It enabled him to travel outside the confines of Mounds to the early 1950s world beyond. When Neal discovered a meeting would be taking place in far-off Atlanta, he became determined to go. When another young man who had already paid for the trip had to drop out, Neal jumped at the opening. But young Joe Neal's troubles were simple yet profound: no clothes, and no money.

"I had one set of clothes for every occasion," he said. "My mama gave me five bucks for something to eat. That was it. We stayed in people's houses. But I was determined to go, and I made that five dollars last. A group of us from the area drove all the way to Atlanta together, and along the way I met a guy from Tallulah who had an extra shirt. I was very relieved. During the trip I got a sense that I was part of a national organization. There were all these other guys from other Southern states with the New Farmers of America."

Atlanta in those days balanced the Jim Crow realities of the era with its burgeoning reputation as a place where blacks and whites could, on some level, coexist in what would a generation later become commonly known as part of the so-called "New South." Although a rising black working and middle class would cause "white flight" in many areas, as ever, economic disparity kept the classes segregated. All that Joe knew was that it was a place like no other he'd ever seen in his young life. "Atlanta was an incredible metropolis with the tallest buildings I'd ever seen," he recalled. "It was the first time in my life I had ever met a black policeman with a gun. I had to approach this guy and ask him who he was, what he was all about. It might be common now, but it was unheard of in my early experience." In that moment, Neal's Mound-centered worldview changed forever. To see a black man in a position of power in a city dominated by whites was unbelievable to him. That New Farmers excursion broadened the possibilities for this inquisitive black teenager at a time just preceding the landmark *Brown v. Board of Education* case that would crack the foundation of segregated American society.

At the beginning of Neal's fourth grade class, approximately eighty students had been enrolled. By eighth grade, the number had dropped to forty, and by high school graduation only ten had made it. Neal blamed that staggering dropout rate partly on a segregated and financially starved public school system that relied on hand-me-downs and care-worn texts. But the other undeniable fact was that blacks had grown weary of trying to till up a societal mound of institutional racism. Instead, they struck out for opportunities in the West—especially in Las Vegas, Nevada, where residents of Fordyce, Arkansas and Tallulah, Louisiana migrated by the hundreds to work in the defense factories of Southern Nevada.

By 1954, more than a decade had passed since that mass westward migration of black residents from Tallulah and Fordyce to the war-era jobs at the Basic Magnesium Incorporated factory in Henderson—a plant that signaled the founding of that town that, by the twenty-first century, would be the second largest city in Nevada. Some had returned home with tales of success and adventure in the hot, dry desert climate. With her sons Willie and Joe safely with the Prater family, Josie Watson Neal had made the move in 1947 and eventually found work as a housekeeper at a casino hotel. While Joe believed education would be the key to a better life, Willie believed he could rise above Mound with hard work and the right opportunity. He didn't finish high school, but saved enough money working the fields to buy a car. Then he was gone, too.

"Willie was a hard worker even as a child," Neal recalled. "To see Willie operate in later years made me think that my education was a handicap." Willie did not finish high school, but he could maneuver his way in and out of the system. He was not opposed to education, and he would always point out the need for schooling, but he didn't see the personal relevance for a formal education when he was a young man. Willie stayed with the Praters until he was sixteen, and then went to work on the railroad. Joe remained with the Praters until he graduated from high school in the spring of 1954. By then, Willie and his mother were both living in Las Vegas. A few weeks after graduation, Josie sent Willie to Tallulah to get Joe and bring him to join the family.

Even in those early years Joe Neal's indefatigable sense of his future had a positive impact on his classmates, including young Richmond Calvin.

"We went to the same high school," Calvin recalled in a 2017 interview. "In those days, everyone went to the same school. I was a sixth grader, and Joe was a senior. It was a small school. I looked up to Joe. We had a meeting one day, all of us in one room. We talked about who was going to keep time for the basketball team, who would be the scorekeeper. It was a big responsibility. Joe recommended me for scorekeeper and timekeeper even though I was only in the sixth grade. I was very proud of it. I got a chance to know everyone, to learn some basketball skills. Thanks to Joe, my self-esteem was sky high."

Confident beyond his means, Neal provided an example for a teenage Calvin that there was life beyond Mound.

"Joe reminded me to pay attention in school, to take it seriously. When you're a sixth grader and you hear someone saying to go to school, do your work, that was very beneficial," Calvin recalled. "There are events in all our lives when someone pushes you onward. He enhanced my perception of self. He made me feel good, and the interaction enhanced my view."

Neal had been a superior basketball player at Thomastown High, where his jump shot drew cheers. He also showed promise, if not always discipline, in the classroom.

"All the ballplayers had nicknames," Calvin remembered. "Joe was a pretty good basketball player. He was tall, and we had a team with some pretty tall guys. He was an outgoing person who also had one of the most attractive girlfriends on campus. We called him Tommy Chickadee. He had a gift of gab back then, and he still has that."

However humble the grounds, Joe was considered the proverbial "big man on campus." By the twelfth grade, he had realized that he wanted to go to college. "Getting there was another matter. But I remember one day when we had our baccalaureate exercise, a Baptist preacher quoted a verse from Psalms 42, 'Deep calleth unto deep' and the shallow will not answer.' I hungered for learning that only getting a higher education would satisfy." Paying for higher education was an additional obstacle.

Welcome to
"the Mississippi of the West"

WHEN HE ARRIVED in early May 1954 in Southern Nevada with a high school diploma and hands calloused in the share-cropped cotton fields of Mounds, Joe Neal didn't yet appreciate that he was setting foot in an arid land as parched in the spirit of civil equality as it was in water resources. Neal was eighteen years old, tall, athletic, and hungry for work. He burned for more education than the dedicated teachers at Thomastown High were able to provide. The U.S. Supreme Court led by Chief Justice Earl Warren had only days before ruled in *Brown v. Board of Education* that the racial segregation of public school students violated the Equal Protection Clause of the Fourteenth Amendment because separate facilities were inherently unequal. Neal would be reminded many times that "separate and unequal" was the norm in Las Vegas.

He'd left Louisiana a few days earlier in a '49 Ford owned by a friend with big brother, Willie Neal, behind the wheel. The road west was new and exciting, but for the most part the trip was uneventful. By the time they reached Arizona, their meager funds were exhausted and they began watching the gasoline gauge.

"We had very little money to travel on," Neal recalled more than sixty years later. "I remember we passed Kingman, Arizona, and I was a little bit nervous that we might run out of gas in the middle of the desert. Willie had a quarter of a tank of gas, and got across the Hoover Dam, through Boulder City, and I saw that straight road that led all the way to Fremont Street with almost nothing in between. It was one of the most desolate places I'd ever seen. I saw nothing but a dusty road and alkali-type dust."

After two years in Las Vegas, Willie Neal had adjusted to the dry climate, blistering summers, surprisingly chilly winters, and the unwritten racial rules of the town. His little brother would have more trouble. After a lifetime in humid and lush Louisiana, motoring into the "Westside," as the black neighborhood was known in segregated Southern Nevada, was more than a culture shock. Although there were a few nice homes, most of the streets weren't paved and some neighborhoods were little more than tarpaper shacks with dirt floors. While the rest of Las Vegas appeared to be booming, there was no shortage of poverty and squalor on the Westside.

Looking at the clapboard decay, it was hard to believe there was a time in territorial Nevada when blacks actually suffered less discrimination. When trapper and explorer Jedediah Smith crossed the Great Basin in 1826, a black man, John Peter Ranne, was a member of his party. When John C. Frémont, explorer and cartographer, led an even larger expedition through the area in 1843, young black man Jacob Dodson was a member of the group. The region's history noted the contributions of a number of intrepid blacks, including mountain man James P. Beckwourth, who helped establish routes across the Sierra and would have a mountain pass named in his honor. Beckwourth would later be known as a war leader of the Crow Indians.

"Although the number of blacks in Nevada before the 1860s was quite small, they were present at every stage after white Americans began to come into the area," historian Elmer Rusco writes in *Good Time Coming? Black Nevadans in the Nineteenth Century.* Blacks had accompanied John C. Frémont on his early treks, and it was common to see black barbers in Virginia City and other boomtowns, but their population in Nevada according to the 1860 Census was just 44. There was, however, no concerted effort to remove them from society. John Howell was the first black man to own property in Nevada, a family man, rancher, and gold prospector who was first listed in the census in 1880.

Las Vegas, a town since 1905 when railroad man and Montana senator William Clark's representatives auctioned the first lots, had actually started with more promise for racial relations. Some blacks had made the arduous trip to the dusty tent town that held promise of a fresh start. "At the beginning, this semi-integrated setting seemed different from small xenophobic towns throughout the country; nevertheless, a closer look positions Las Vegas in the same category," the Nevada entry in *Black America: A State-by-State Historical Encyclopedia* reads. Like many other whites of their generation, early Las Vegas community leaders made no secret of their desire to keep blacks "across the tracks" from downtown in Block 17, on the far side of the infamous Block 16 brothel district.

"Walter Bracken, the influential officer of the Las Vegas Land & Water Company, tried to segregate blacks in a single section of the town...," James W. Hulse observes in *The Silver State*, his history of Nevada. "However, many businesses, including most places of entertainment and recreation, accepted their trade through the 1920s, and this remained true of the gambling clubs in the early 1930s. While blacks seldom held the better jobs, there was no blatant policy of discrimination in hiring and employment."

Hard-line segregation and outright exclusion was the philosophy during the construction of Hoover Dam, a project that employed thousands of Depression-era men. In the early years, not a single one was black. The Six Companies, builders of the dam, refused to hire blacks to work on their construction crews.

Complaints were ignored, even though blacks had assembled a local branch of the National Association for the Advancement of Colored People and a group called the Colored Citizens Labor and Protective Association of Las Vegas as early as 1926 in an effort to be heard. Six Companies, the dam's contractors led by its president. W.A. Bechtel, downplayed the discontent, arguing that adding blacks to the workforce would cause unrest in the ranks. William Pickens, a NAACP regional representative sent to Southern Nevada to help rally support for black employment at the dam site, was informed that a riot was narrowly averted after Six Companies inserted a foreman of Mexican descent to lead white workers.

As the months passed, Bechtel promised to begin hiring blacks on the massive job. But by 1933, as the dam neared completion, just twenty-four blacks had been hired. It was less than one percent of the total. Not a single black lived in Boulder City, and the distance on the dusty and rutted road from the Westside made it certain relatively few

Las Vegas blacks would have access to work. A small group of blacks wound up mucking in gravel pits across the Colorado River a few miles into Arizona. Another group assembled a top-notch "drilling" team.

One effective way of ensuring blacks would never become part of the burgeoning Boulder Dam construction workforce was to compel them to live in the tent and shanty squalor of the newly created "Westside," at the end of the long, dusty road that led back to Las Vegas. Only white families lived in Boulder City during the dam's construction. Westside living conditions surely made some residents long for the tarpaper shacks of the South back home. Canvas and clapboard were the predominant building materials available. Outhouses and scarce running water complicated sanitation needs.

"Employment and housing became a focal point for the civil rights movement in Nevada," one historian would observe. "...At first blacks were denied employment due to race, and it was only through the intervention of the Las Vegas NAACP branch that they were allowed to work at Hoover Dam. Even then, blacks were systematically excluded from certain types of jobs and housing, and it was during this time that the Westside began to develop as the primary black residential and business community in Las Vegas."

Those who were lucky enough to find work ate separately from whites and drank from separate water buckets. As a U.S. Bureau of Reclamation report observed, and somehow managed to understate, "The construction of Hoover Dam was proof of human progress on many levels....Progress on civil rights and race relations, however, could not be counted among them."

"Before 1931 Negroes were welcome in Nevada society," Ed Reid and Ovid Demaris wrote somewhat simplistically in their groundbreaking exposé, *The Green Felt Jungle.* "There was no discrimination or segregation. The hardy pioneer was interested only in his fellow man's character and ability—not in his color, race, or creed. Then the poor whites from Texas, Louisiana, Florida, and other points south moved into the state with their gaming devices and bootlegged money and took over not only the gambling but the social and political life of the state as well. They were thugs and thieves and murderers, but they were white, and segregation set in overnight. When the eastern and northern gangsters arrived they were quick to protect the status quo. They didn't want any Nigrahs upsetting their high-rolling southern gentlemen, who had more oil wells than the gangsters had slot machines. And besides, many of the mobsters had been brought up in teeming slums where they had rumbled against the colored gangs, and they had not forgotten their own prejudice and hatred."

If the authors overestimated the freedom blacks enjoyed in Nevada's early years—it's likely that discrimination against blacks and other minorities wasn't widespread in early Las Vegas only because there were so few of them—the writers were on the mark about the decades following the dam's construction. Incidents of Ku Klux Klan activity, including a public protest downtown, were noted in the Las Vegas newspapers. (Although Reno and Elko were considered hotbeds of Klan activity and support, a rally of the white supremacy group took place in Las Vegas in 1925.) Segregation wasn't the law of the land, but local police enforced it at the end of a nightstick.

Although the dam construction experience could hardly be called a success for blacks longing to join the rest of the "'31ers" in building the great concrete edifice, it could only have tempered their mettle as America ground through the Great Depression and into World War II.

When Basic Magnesium, a plant that processed materials to be used for ammunition and airplanes, opened in Henderson, a concerted effort was made to recruit black mill workers from Fordyce, Arkansas and Tallulah, Louisiana. A shortage of available personnel because of the war effort necessitated what otherwise might have been a continuation of the job segregation of the day.

In no time, the race was on to Southern Nevada in 1942, where blacks often found their treatment by white society every bit as discriminatory as it was back home. Movie theaters separated the audiences on the basis of race, and restaurants did not serve blacks. While blacks had been invited to gamble on Fremont Street in the 1930s, they weren't welcome after World War II. Gambling halls such as the El Morocco Club sprung to life on the Westside and, depending on the economy, did a lively neighborhood business. The El Morocco closed the year Neal arrived and was later reopened by Oscar Crozier, one of the few blacks in Las Vegas whose gambling background enabled him to not only serve as a civil rights leader but also communicate with the white casino establishment.

"Overt discrimination became a way of life in the forties," University of Nevada, Las Vegas historian Claytee White observed. "Industrial mobilization during World War II not only stimulated additional black migration, but also contributed to increased racial tension and resulted in widespread segregationist policies in the Las Vegas Valley."

"The inhabitants of the Westside lived behind what they call the 'Concrete Curtain'—so named because of the railroad underpass that separates their community from the commercial section of downtown Las Vegas," Reid and Demaris wrote. "Though some dusty streets have been paved and some new homes built, much of Westside still qualifies as slum."

In the mid-1950s, two versions of Las Vegas tended to rule the popular press. The most prevalent was the tale of the glittering oasis filled with acceptable sin. Las Vegas was a sunny playground for movie stars and world-class entertainers—and millions of tourists. The other Las Vegas, depicted mostly through the lens of the post-Kefauver era by a handful of investigative journalists, was the flashy storefront for Murder, Inc. and transplanted bootleggers and racketeers such as Cleveland's Moe Dalitz and Dallas's Benny Binion.

Few journalists attempted to contrast Nevada's reputation as a "tax-payer's paradise" with its increasingly obvious deficits: health care, public education, incarceration, and civil rights. An often-quoted study by Albert Deutsch published in 1955 in *Collier's* magazine peeled away the hype and revealed a quality of life and government service "below those of many of the poorest states."

With a nod to Deutsch, historian Hulse observed in his highly critical look at the state, *Forty Years in the Wilderness: Impressions of Nevada, 1940–1980*, that civil rights was a key area in which the state was an abject failure and an embarrassment to the nation.

"Nevada was slow to recognize and join the involvement toward more equitable civil rights that transformed American history in the 1950s and early 1960s," Hulse wrote. "Although the citizens of the state had not officially endorsed 'Jim Crow' policies as some of the states in the Old South had done, they had equally acquiesced in patterns of

discrimination that effectively denied black citizens any places of opportunity or dignity in the trade unions or professions, had encouraged
them to live in distinct regions of Reno and Las Vegas, and had denied
them most places of public accommodation and entertainment."

The community had few black professionals and no minority political influence. It was, Hulse observed, "virtually impossible for a black
person to get a job as a waiter, cook, or barber in Reno—although all of
those fields were open to blacks in the South and East. Nevada's reputation as the 'Mississippi of the West' was not totally deserved, because
the state had no official policy of segregation in the schools and on the
buses....But the image was not entirely undeserved, because of the de
facto segregation in housing and the quiet discrimination in employment and in most places of public accommodation."

It was in the entertainment field that the sins of Las Vegas segregation
were most obvious. The city's burgeoning casino entertainment machine
provided opportunities for big paydays for the era's greatest artists of
the stage, but the wealth and headliner status came with a catch.

Tales are plentiful of black entertainers such as Sammy Davis Jr.,
Lena Horne, Billy Eckstine, and Ella Fitzgerald packing Strip show-
rooms night after night and then being forced to slip out the backdoor
and sleep in humble quarters on the Westside. The efforts of white
entertainers such as Frank Sinatra risking lucrative contracts to lobby
casino owners on behalf of Davis and others are also the stuff of legend—and have often been blown out of proportion. The fact is, there
were no progressive casino operators in Las Vegas. Jewish and Catholic
gaming bosses who had faced plenty of discrimination in their own
lives were more than happy with the status quo of 1950s segregation.

"The hotels we passed in downtown Las Vegas looked awful compared to the El Rancho, but even they were out of bounds to us," Davis
recalled in his memoir *Why Me?* "In Reno we could stay at the Mapes.
But Vegas was a different Nevada for us. The cab continued to the
Westside. 'There's a woman name of Cartwright takes in you people.'
It was Tobacco Road. A child, naked, was standing in front of a shack
made of wooden crates and cardboard." And when Davis and other entertainers got off work after the late show, longtime Strip publicist Mort
Saiger remembered, "I had to take them back after midnight, right after

the second show, because there was no other transportation to the Westside…It was unfortunate, but that was the law; they could not stay in this hotel or in any other. I remember Eddie Anderson, 'Rochester' from Jack Benny's fame. I was so hurt that I couldn't see straight, because this is the way I was treated in Poland, as a Jew, so I just ached."

When Horne broke through at the Sands and persuaded its mobbed-up frontman Jack Entratter to let her stay in one of the hotel's bungalows near the back of the property as long as she promised to keep a low profile, the order went out to burn her bedsheets as soon as she vacated the premises, according to *The Money and the Power* authors Sally Denton and Roger Morris. (Other sources attribute the location to the Flamingo during the time of Bugsy Siegel.)

The opening of the Moulin Rouge in May 1955 on West Bonanza Road at the edge of the Westside featured cancan dancers and a full casino. With heavyweight boxing legend Joe Louis greeting customers and a late-night show that drew white customers and entertainers from the Strip, the Moulin Rouge generated national headlines and even a photo on the cover of *Life* magazine. But for all the excitement it appeared to generate, it failed to turn a profit, was riddled with mismanagement and suspected skimming in the casino, and closed after just five months. At a time when the Strip was entering the largest expansion in its history, casino bosses declined to throw the Moulin Rouge a financial lifeline. "The full story of its closure will likely never be known," historian Frank Wright observed. "Claims of insufficient capitalization and mismanagement were countered by charges that Strip operators tried to prevent their employees from patronizing the Moulin Rouge and urged creditors to bring suit for payment of overdue bills."

Efforts to integrate the Las Vegas hotel-casino industry predated the opening of the Moulin Rouge by more than a decade. During World War II, nightclub promoter and bandleader Horace Heidt saw money to be made catering to black servicemen and their families in the region, but his integrated Shamrock Hotel downtown drew immediate catcalls from whites in the area, and the all-white Las Vegas City Commission denied its business license application. Although it was reported an estimated one hundred blacks assembled to question the fairness of the decision, their political strength was far outweighed by white hotel and casino operators who had no interest in the subject of integrating their gambling halls and rooming houses.

Increased enforcement of Jim Crow laws and segregation during the war years and beyond had an unexpected impact on the Westside. Down on Jackson Street, a bustling gambling and nightclub trade rose along with the black population. The Brown Derby, Cotton Club, and Harlem Club offered entertainment and alcohol to servicemen of color and workers in Henderson's Basic Magnesium and Titanium Metals plants. A decade later, the El Morocco and Carver House provided late-night entertainment, gambling, and something like a hedonistic hope for a young Sammy Davis. The Hotel Biltmore tried to desegregate in the late 1940s, but the city thwarted its efforts.

It can safely be said that Davis first felt the real buzz of Las Vegas not on the Strip but at the Westside's El Morocco. In West Las Vegas, he said, "There were no streetlights, the shacks did not have electricity. Then, in the distance, there was a little patch of light and my father said, 'That must be the Cotton Club and the El Morocco. Hey, driver, how 'bout dropping us there'...I had the sudden realization that we were all colored people and we were all there because that was the only place they 'allowed' us to be."

About the time the Moulin Rouge made national headlines, the Westside welcomed its first medical professionals, dentist James B. McMillan and physician Charles West. Entertainer and businessman William "Bob" Bailey, who had come for the opening of the Moulin Rouge but stayed for the potential for commerce, rose to prominence in the community. Their business practices and political philosophies aside, all three men took it upon themselves to participate in the Westside's slow-to-boil civil rights movement with a variety of ministers, teachers, and businesspeople.

For Neal and a generation of blacks who moved from places of codified segregation to Southern Nevada seeking an equal opportunity, the impact of those unwritten laws was more cruel than much of what they experienced in places such as Tallulah, Fordyce, and Mounds. At least there they knew the onerous rules. But from its earliest days Las Vegas has always been good at selling an image to the outside world that didn't match the reality of local life.

Few of the indignities were widely reported. Many were exceedingly petty, some downright mean-spirited. Blacks, for instance, were allowed to use the skating rink on West Charleston Boulevard, but only on Monday. The Westside's all-black Boy Scout troop was invited to the local Jamboree, but wasn't allowed to camp with the white children. Instead, the scouts were forced to pitch tents across the street from the event.

Other insults were more widely observed. When blacks were finally allowed access to El Portal Theater on Fremont Street, they were limited to seats on the far-left side and in the balcony next to the clacking projection room. The El Portal played an important role not only because it was a popular and air-conditioned meeting place in a young desert community, but because it was opened in 1928 by insurance man and Las Vegas mayor Ernie Cragin, who would play an integral role in the development of the community and also enforce largely unwritten segregationist policies.

Cragin's "failure to include black people undercut his dream" of a brighter Las Vegas, longtime Southern Nevada reporter A.D. Hopkins observed in *The First 100*. "Neglecting the needs and the rights of a growing minority generated social problems that have plagued Las Vegas ever since."

The boomtown mayor wielded outsized clout, but political survival, his close ties to powerful U.S. senator Pat McCarran, D-Nevada and the health of his insurance business made it a certainty he'd follow the whims and wishes of the local business community.

But young Joe Neal had it better than many. His mother's housekeeping position enabled the family to live in a home with a floor and indoor plumbing. If it might not have measured up to most houses in white neighborhoods, in the mid-1950s there was no appreciable groundswell of civil rights to argue the case for integration and equal public accommodation.

Arriving on the Westside from Mississippi just a year after Neal, Mary Wesley would recall to author Annelise Orleck in *Storming Caesars Palace: How Black Mothers Fought Their Own War on Poverty*, that "People mostly lived in tents. The house they had me live in when I first came had no floor. Just rugs. And a carpet hanging for a wall. The desert wind blew in. All you could see was desert for miles around. I didn't see how anybody could live here for long. I knew I was gonna go home to Mississippi. I missed the green and all the gardens so much. I couldn't imagine staying here."

Rosie Seals left Tallulah in 1951, but when she entered the Westside she considered turning the car around: "It was so hot and it looked so dead. They didn't even have no paved streets when I came here." She thought Las Vegas looked "all right at night" thanks to its glittering lights and neon. "But then I found out they wasn't allowing black people to go into those hotels. They wasn't *[sic]* allowing us to sit or eat in all those pretty restaurants. It was upsetting. I knew back there they didn't allow blacks to eat in restaurants. But I thought it would be different when I came here." When she found out all the things she couldn't do, Seals replied, "Well, hell I could've stayed where I was instead of coming all the way over here."

Still, change was coming. And strong personalities, some motivated by the greater public good and others on behalf of themselves foremost, were moving the black community forward. Detroit physician Charles West, who had served in the United States Army and with the U.S. Public Health Service in Liberia, fought his way through the closed system of medicine in 1954 to become the first black physician in modern Nevada. The political victory in a segregated system helped vault West into an important position in Southern Nevada's civil rights movement. Being the only black physician in the entire state also wasn't bad for his medical practice, as a feature in a 1954 issue of *Jet* magazine would attest.

West's business boomed, and he immediately reached out to a dentist friend, Dr. James McMillan, whom he'd met while practicing medicine in Detroit. Born in Aberdeen, Mississippi, McMillan saw deep-rooted racism up close in the South before moving with his family to Chicago. After attending the University of Michigan and University of Detroit, McMillan graduated with a doctorate in dental surgery from Meharry Medical School in Nashville, Tennessee. He served in the United States Army Dental Corps in World War II and the Korean War, and then returned to Detroit, where he was invited by West to come out to Las Vegas and open a practice. In 1955, McMillan became Nevada's first black dentist and had no shortage of patients waiting when he opened his office doors. McMillan, too, would become known even more for his role in Southern Nevada's civil rights movement and the NAACP than for his ability to perform root canals and dental implants.

McMillan and his wife, Mickie, were married poolside at the Moulin Rouge not long after it opened. Affable entertainer Bailey booked acts at the Moulin Rouge and parlayed the contacts he made into everything from real estate sales to his own radio show. He teamed up with Alice Key for Southern Nevada's first television program hosted by African Americans, *The Talk of the Town.*

Neal's mother came to Las Vegas after World War II with no delusions of finding equal rights or making it as an entertainer. She was grateful to land a maid's job, and when Moe Dalitz and his Cleveland syndicate friends opened Wilbur Clark's Desert Inn in 1950, she jumped at the chance to become a housekeeper in a sparkling new hotel on the Strip. Dalitz would see the good business sense of maintaining positive relations with the black community, members of which made the beds and kept his resort clean. He would help fund a day care center for black workers, and in the late 1950s, when other casino bosses were still dragging their feet, he provided niceties such as Christmas parties for the children of all his employees.

"I recall that my mother, who came to Las Vegas in 1947, at that time was living on C Street right across from the Variety Club Child Care Center and just northeast of the old Westside Elementary School," Neal said. "The home was simple, but in an area where some streets had no lights, electricity, or indoor plumbing, we counted ourselves among the fortunate."

Neal's job search began almost immediately after he arrived. Although Las Vegas was growing rapidly, work for minorities, especially young black men, outside the confines of the Westside was nearly impossible. Neal would fill in idle hours playing basketball and shadowing his childhood friend Ernest Douglas, who had landed a job watering the lawn at the newly constructed Cadillac Arms apartments. On days Douglas didn't feel like working, he turned the duty over to his friend Joe. The job didn't last long, and Neal was soon once again searching for work that would put a little change in his empty pockets.

Segregation hadn't followed him from Louisiana. It was an entrenched and zealously enforced way of life when he arrived. At 18 years
old, he began to experience its sharp edges in a town that felt far more
segregated than the place he'd left. He would find little opportunity for
either employment or education during his first sojourn to fabulous
Las Vegas, the garish gambling oasis located in a state openly chided
in those days as "the Mississippi of the West." But the early experience
would never leave his mind.

Another friend from the Tallulah and Mound area, A.J., had picked
up work at Polar Ice, which supplied the casinos. Neal began traveling
with him on his morning rounds, which took him to the back entrances
of every casino on Fremont Street and Las Vegas Boulevard, which was
only beginning to become widely known as the Strip. It was another
part-time job with few prospects, but at least he was able to see what
Las Vegas looked like away from the Westside.

While making a delivery to the El Rancho, Neal transferred the load
of ice and had a few minutes to kill. He wandered around to the hotel's
swimming pool, which was as blue as a sapphire and splashing with
tourists and plenty of young women in bathing suits bronzing under
the summer sun.

"Hey, boss, come back here," A.J. called, rousing Neal from his rev-
erie. "You don't belong there."

He obviously didn't. The only people of color poolside were the
ones catching suntans.

Although he'd smile at the youthful memory, he'd also recall the
moment as the first time he'd ever seen a swimming pool. "We went
swimming in the bayou," Neal said. "I was fascinated with the vision of
a swimming pool in the desert."

The ice-delivering job gave him a few dollars, but it was no way to
earn a living. As the summer wore on, his boredom grew and his private dream of going to college was threatened. He talked about his goal
to Willie, who was in no position to help him financially. But he did
know a way out and up: Joe Neal could join the military.

"You keep saying you're wanting to go to college," Willie said. "Go
into the military. They'll pay for your college when you get out."

He visited an armed services recruiting office on Fifth Street and learned all branches of the military were open. The United States Army and Marines demanded eighteen-week basic training and two-year enlistments.

"I didn't like that idea, so I decided to give the Air Force a try," Neal recalled. "They had an eleven-week basic training with a four-year enlistment. At the end of four years, I'd be free to use the G.I. Bill and pursue what I really wanted—a college education."

When the local recruitment office informed him that it had met its quota, it was suggested by a uniformed officer that Neal travel to Los Angeles and apply there. He'd made some friends in the few months he'd been a Las Vegas resident and been playing basketball at the recreation center thanks to Jimmy Gay. He'd almost forgotten about filling out those recruitment papers when he received a knock at the door one day. It was a uniformed recruiter with a bus ticket in his hand.

"I wanted to back out right then," Neal recalled years later, laughing at the memory. "The white guy said, 'You're supposed to report to Los Angeles tomorrow.' I had to catch the bus at midnight. It got there at seven in the morning. They were expecting me."

Full Service, Full Citizenship

JOE NEAL DREAMED of college, and would eventually see that dream realized. All he had to do was fulfill a four-year commitment to the United States Air Force. Much later in life he would laugh and recall, "I signed on for four years not knowing at the time that I could have received the same benefits if I'd signed on for two years in the Army."

The Air Force opened a new world. The physical part of boot camp training was eleven weeks long and conducted at Lackland Air Force Base in San Antonio, Texas. It wasn't overly taxing for a teenager raised plowing fields and chopping cotton. Neal didn't mind the military regimentation, and was intrigued by the ongoing experiment in integration. Whites, blacks, Hispanics, and Asians might not have mixed at all in their previous lives, but they would be thrown together under a common banner and were expected to act professionally.

The military demanded much, but provided opportunities impossible to otherwise imagine for poor boys from small towns and inner cities alike. He might have been the only representative of Mounds, Louisiana, at the air base, but Neal would discover there were many Mounds across America. And there were other perquisites of military life—free clothes, enough food, a chance to learn new things and rise through the ranks—the more fortunate take for granted.

"Until I joined the Air Force, I'd never been to a dentist," Neal would recall. "Or a doctor." Nor had he actually thought much about racism, or his place in a changing world. That worldview, defined by the Southern tradition of racial and economic segregation, began to change in the Air Force.

"In Mound, we had sharecroppers who were black and white," Neal said. "We all worked the fields together. So I never did think much about race until I got into the military. Then I was never confronted with it until I finished basic training in 1954, and I was on my way to Alamogordo, New Mexico. Myself and another black guy on the bus. There were about eighteen of us going to this particular base, Holloman Air Force Base. After a while the bus stopped outside a diner and all the whites got off and went inside. The few blacks stayed on the bus. Well, I got off and went inside and sat at the counter because this was the thing. We were coming from San Antonio, Texas, going to Alamogordo, and in between we had this one little stop where we could eat. And I got off along with the other white guys. I went into the restaurant, put my cap down on the counter, and all of a sudden this Hispanic girl appeared in the doorway. She got my attention and waved for me to come to her. I looked around, at first not understanding that she was looking at me, because there were all these other guys around. I got up and walked behind the counter and back into what was a storage room. There was a table there.

She said, "Have a seat. What do you want?"

It hadn't dawned on Neal that in order to be served he'd have to sit by himself in the storage room, the space set aside for his kind.

"A sandwich, a ham sandwich," he said as the picture began to focus.

When the waitress returned in short order with his sandwich, he took one look at it, picked up the plate and slammed it on the table. He turned and walked out of the diner. "I got back on the bus," he said. "I guess that might have affected me for the next couple years because I was in the service. I thought about that greasy spoon and that damned ham sandwich. When I lived in Mound I was not aware of real discrimination. This was the first experience I'd ever had of really being discriminated against."

Neal thrived under the military routine and occasionally witnessed history in the making at Holloman Air Force Base. In the years immediately following the 1947 separation of the U.S. Air Force from the U.S. Army Air Corps, Holloman outside Alamogordo, New Mexico played an integral role in the early development of the space program and was home to some of the world's greatest scientific minds. By 1954, Holloman was a hotbed of research and home not only to former Nazi

V-2 rocket engineers, but also to Lieutenant Colonel John P. Stapp, "the fastest man alive," who on December 10 had traveled 632 miles per hour in a rocket-propelled sled named "Sonic Wind No. 1." It was all heady stuff for a teenager from Mound and clearly made an impression on Neal that would inform his perspective on future political issues.

"They had all these German scientists working for them," he recalled. "Wernher von Braun and many others were there. So I got a chance to observe the rudiments of the space program, how it was developed, the ejection seats and so forth. They were testing G forces on sleds then. The intercontinental ballistic missile was being tested there. We became the security force that tried to protect those secrets. It worked well for me."

Neal filled some of his spare time with correspondence courses in law enforcement, criminal identification, and forensic science. He learned the basics of criminal investigations, firearms, fingerprinting, and handwriting analysis, and in the process learned to type. The long-term plan was a possible entry into a career in law enforcement, but in the short term the extra training enabled him to become a military policeman. That led not only to advancement at Holloman, but to passing background checks that gave him a United States Department of Energy top-secret Q clearance.

For the first time he also made friends from a variety of cultures. Of course, not everyone was willing to break bread in brotherhood. Incidents involving Southern servicemen were common, and after a fashion Neal tired of the snubs, the groans, and the whispers. One refused to sit at the same table with him. Whenever Neal approached, he picked up his plate and moved away.

Coming off duty one day, Neal entered the mess hall and sat down directly next to him.

"I was still strapped down with a .45," he said. "When he tried to get up I said, 'Sit down.' He got scared, really nervous. I kind of felt sorry for the guy. But he got the message."

With his family's history and its native ties to the land of Mound often on his mind, he soon became conscious of the Native American presence in Alamogordo and the surrounding region. He saw the dysfunction, but also met unlikely kindred spirits far from Madison Parish.

"While I was at Holloman, I noticed that the white airmen would get into fights with the Indians from the Mescalero Reservation almost every weekend," he said. "These were Apache Indians. The Indians accepted me, and I would stay overnight on the reservation. I remembered that there was a sign at the entry of the reservation that stated you traveled at your own risk.

"It was not until I enlisted in the Air Force that I became keenly aware of what those early conversations with Mama may be about. This Mexican airman kept referring to me in Spanish as 'Primo.' I did not know what the hell he was talking about. So, I decided to look up the word. I found that its general definition was 'first.' I approached this fellow one day and asked him what he meant by calling me 'Primo.'"

The Hispanic airman answered with a question: "You don't know your heritage, do you?"

After Neal left Thomastown for Las Vegas and then the United States Air Force, childhood friend Ernestine Madison kept in touch with Josephine Neal, who remained interested in her progress in school and continued to hope that her son Joe would pursue his college degree. "It gave her a thrill to know we were succeeding despite the obstacles in our way." Madison, having excelled in school, wanted to push on to college but was daunted by the expense. In search of tuition money, Madison made the trip west to Las Vegas, where she was reunited with Josephine Neal.

"At Joe's mother's house, I told her I was there to work to be able to go back to school. Joe called her Ma'dere, and I got to where I called her that, too. She was just like my mother. She kept me there that summer, and I made my money in the laundry pressing sheets for all the hotels," Madison recalled. "She had me save all my money by sending it back to my mom each time I got a paycheck. She fed me and clothed me. When I got ready to leave, she gave me things I could wear from her closet. She packed it in my luggage."

Madison went on to earn her bachelor's degree from Southern University, a master's from the University of Mississippi, and a doctorate in administration from Mississippi State. "All of us have succeeded, I think, and done well," she said. "Calvin has done well in his area. Others have also done well. The three of us have held it together and remained friends a long time. Calvin, Joe, and I were very close, like brothers and sisters. We supported one another. All these years later we have each other's phone numbers, and we call and check on each other and offer support."

Throughout her life she would remain grateful for the Neal family's generosity and beam with pride that three friends from the diminutive Thomastown School had risen so far.

In the Air Force of the 1950s, basic racial issues were strictly controlled. It was when Neal traveled off base that he discovered the snarling edge of segregation. "I was in the military, serving my country, and after I got to my duty station I did come back home one time. This is after I'd made rank and knew the ropes. I was coming on the bus some little place in Texas. I've forgotten the name. Everyone stopped to eat, and I just wanted some water.

"I walked up to the counter and asked the lady. I said, 'Give me a glass of water, please.' She acted like she was ignoring me. I repeated myself. You have to understand. I'd been sleeping on the bus. I didn't have my cap on. My hair was kinky. I lost my temper and said, 'Give me a glass of water!'"

Neal later found that the place was near Beaumont, Texas, where they'd had race riots. "I think the woman thought I was going to tear up the place. All I wanted was a glass of water."

Returning from leave once, Joe stopped in El Paso at a restaurant with a long counter and a long row of chairs. In the corner was a small table with a sign that said 'colored' that he hadn't noticed upon entering the restaurant. "I sat down in one of the booths, and the woman waitress kept walking by me. She said, 'You can't sit here,' and kept walking. She wouldn't stop. So after a while I just stood up and walked out. On my way out I noticed the sign on the far table that I'd missed initially."

The experiences, common to most blacks of Neal's generation, seared into his memory.

"I was in uniform," he said. "But what was the uniform worth? I didn't know how I would succeed, but I was determined not to let that happen to anybody else." When Neal earned some leave time, he spent it back in Las Vegas, where in the summer of 1955 the Moulin Rouge made national headlines. Headlines to the contrary, most Las Vegas blacks weren't hanging out late at the Moulin Rouge. They were struggling to find work in a community that was anything but welcoming. After two years in uniform, Neal was approached by a superior officer and informed he qualified for a temporary duty transfer closer to home. With his security experience and Q clearance, he transferred to Indian Springs Air Force Base north of Las Vegas, the field closest to the Nevada Test Site and its active nuclear weapons testing program and super secret Area 51. "All that was good duty for me," he said. "After I came here we were kind of like the force that helped secure Area 51. We did that from Indian Springs Air Force Base. In those days there weren't too many people there. I was at the test site in the 1950s when they bussed people up to the mountains to watch the mushroom clouds.

"On the test site, one of the requirements we had was, we had to wear those dose meters. I had to take them from Indian Springs up to the test site and have them read. You'd get a reading on them."

Give or take a dose of radiation, it was indeed good duty, for being stationed at Indian Springs enabled Neal to increase his local contacts, see his mother and brother, and network with members of the Westside who were beginning to make names for themselves as professionals, businessmen, and civil rights activists. Neal wasn't yet out of the service and there was talk of entering law enforcement as a career.

His investigative training served him well after a fatal auto accident involving an Air Force serviceman in the desert not far from a Pahrump brothel west of Las Vegas. Neal conducted the accident investigation, wrote up his findings, and submitted them to the Nye County Sheriff's Office. In pursuit of the facts, Neal was forced to drive north to Beatty to interview the sheriff at 2 a.m.

Suffice to say that in 1957, a sheriff from rural Nevada wasn't accustomed to being awakened by an armed black member of law enforcement.

"He was shocked seeing me at his door," Neal said. "I expect it was the first time he had seen a black in authority, and that commanded his attention. I always got a kick out of that."

Neal investigated auto accidents, theft, and even a fatal shootout involving a pair of drunken airmen. Although he wanted to go to college, law enforcement seemed to be calling. When he mustered out of the service in 1958 and returned to Las Vegas, he was approached by black community leaders who thought it imperative to add to the sparse lineup of black police officers in Southern Nevada. Neal briefly put his education plans on hold and went down to the Las Vegas Police Department to fill out an application.

"I had real experience and training," he recalled. "Not only did I have experience in the Air Force with the military police, but I also had taken correspondence courses in investigation, fingerprinting, and so forth." He took his credentials to the local police department.

The personnel officer looked up and replied, "You better go to Los Angeles. They need your skills there."

In other words, there would be no openings for him anytime soon in a department that lacked a sophisticated crime forensics bureau and whose roster was larded with political appointees and the relatives of the local good ol' boys.

"I didn't have those contacts," Neal said, and locals could count the number of black officers on one hand. He was again searching for work as he applied for acceptance at Southern University with a push from his mother and his childhood friend, Ernestine Madison.

Madison recalled, "I know she wanted him to go to college. We both did and we kind of did that behind his back, picking up the forms from Southern University in Baton Rouge and sent them to him in North Las Vegas. She got him to fill out those forms and got him to send them off. I had confidence in him."

Neal, meanwhile, was stitching together the finances.

"I tried a couple times to get a job, and that was kind of difficult," he said. "I worked at the Stardust for a short period, then left and went to college on the G.I. Bill."

As with so many areas of Louisiana's racial history, educational advancement for blacks came only after overcoming steadfast resistance from white majority lawmakers—and often only after help of the federal government. Southern College opened with a dozen students in 1880 in New Orleans as a concession in the post-Reconstruction era and even held classes in a former Jewish temple. When it fell short of meeting federal requirements for land grant college status, the tiny outlet found its way to a hill, Scott's Bluff, on the edge of Baton Rouge overlooking the Mississippi River. It was there in 1914 that Southern University was formed in earnest, first as a mechanical school and teachers college, then as a full university that also included the State School for the Negro Deaf and Blind. Because the segregated state did not allow blacks to enroll in the law school at Louisiana State University, Southern added a law school following litigation by black students. The Southern University Law Center opened in 1947 and would become popular. When he got the chance, Neal studied the Constitution with a focused fever, and for good reason: "That was the only way blacks could win a case in the South."

The struggle to literally and metaphorically maintain an educational foothold in Louisiana helped raise Southern University as a place of political thought and civil rights among its student population. Neal's own worldview, so narrow during his youth in Mound but greatly expanded thanks to his travel to Southern Nevada and his service in the Air Force, continued to evolve.

"I wanted to get a law degree and become a lawyer," he recalled in an interview many years later. "That meant studying politics and government. Doing so gave me a different perspective and helped me learn how things were connected in the country. I think it was the best decision I ever made because it opened my mind up to a lot of stuff."

It wasn't all books and lectures. It was at Southern that Neal met the person who truly changed his life. Estelle Ann DeConge had grown up in New Rhodes, Louisiana, and graduated from high school in Baton Rouge. She took classes at Xavier University in New Orleans, then transferred to Southern University, where she worked part-time in the library to help put herself through school.

"I came in to check out a book," Neal would recall.

And, as they say, that was all she wrote. Joe and Estelle would eventually marry, but both were focused first on getting an education.

Neal also got reacquainted with his friend, Richmond Calvin, whom he'd influenced and mentored just a few years earlier. This time, however, Neal's time in Las Vegas and Air Force service put him behind Calvin in class. "I was a junior, and he came in as a freshman," Calvin recalled in 2017. "We'd see each other all the time. I felt a little different about the relationship. I wanted him to become a junior like I was! After graduating from Southern, we kept in touch on a regular basis. Whenever I got to Las Vegas to visit relatives, I'd check in with Joe. From the time I was eleven or twelve years old until today, we've been friends. We've talked on a regular basis for about sixty years, and of course I followed his career. We've talked often about the obstacles and events that occurred to us to make us what we are today. Being at Thomastown, we knew what the stakes were and knew how to support each other and how to form a community. We sort of knew we had to depend on each other, friends, neighbors, and relatives, when people needed help—especially when it came to education, to go to school and to college."

Southern University was a cauldron of political activity in the push for civil rights, much of it roiling almost clandestinely. The names of Rev. George Lee and Lamar Smith, murdered in 1955 during sepa-rate attempts to organize and register voters in Mississippi, were well known to politically active blacks in 1960. The murder of fourteen-year-old Emmett Till in Money, Mississippi, had even made national headlines. The toll of martyrs would continue to rise like crosses on the roadside in the long march toward civil rights equality.

Neal's decision to enter the fray started, of all places, in a freshman French class at Southern. It's there he met J.K. Haynes, an older student and the director of the all-black Louisiana Teachers Association for the state of Louisiana. Learning that Neal was born and raised in Madison Parish, Haynes would laugh and say, "You can't vote." Time after time, the two would talk on a range of issues, but when it came time to dis-cuss politics, Haynes would crack, "You can't vote." Neal was getting hot under the collar.

"He kept telling me this," Neal said. "I never had voted, but I'd served in the military. He was kidding me. He asked me what I was studying, and I told him political science. He said, 'For what? You can't vote.' And so he finally bugged me enough that I decided to go and see what he was talking about, and whether it was true."

After his freshman year, with Haynes' chiding voice still ringing in his ears, he spent time back in Madison Parish. In 1957, during his stint in the Air Force, Neal had read the news of the Little Rock Nine, black students prevented from enrolling at Little Rock's Central High School by order of Arkansas governor Orval Faubus. President Dwight Eisenhower sent troops to the school to enforce the constitutional tenets of the *Brown v. Board of Education* decision. The inability of blacks in Madison County to register and vote gnawed at Neal with each passing day.

"The thought of it was starting to bug me," he said. "I'd served in the military. So I went up to Tallulah and met with a group of people who were talking about what was going to happen, 'When we get the vote.' I was shocked to hear the words. I said to them, 'No one is going to give you the vote. You're going to have to make an effort. You can't just sit down here and wait until somebody gives you the vote.' My cousin owned a store in the area, and he sat on the grand jury. It was a trusted position. They would pick him out and put him on the grand jury, but he couldn't vote for the sheriff or the mayor or anybody in the town."

It had been that way from the start in Madison Parish. And it wasn't just racism or a philosophy of segregation that moved whites to refuse blacks the vote. It was also a matter of political survival. Blacks had held a large majority of the parish population from its earliest census taking. With as much as 90 percent of the population black, whites might easily be swept from public office.

Determined to prevent that from occurring, in 1898 the Louisiana Constitution was amended to include various ways to keep blacks off the voter rolls. As a majority of blacks were illiterate, an education requirement made an applicant's ability to read and write mandatory. But even literate blacks were likely to have difficulty navigating the "traps for the unwary" contained in the forms.

Requiring voters to provide proof of property ownership of at least $300 in assessed value was another way to deter an unlanded majority. But demanding prospective voters offer proof that they had a grandfather already registered to vote was the highest wall for blacks to climb.

The U.S. Supreme Court invalidated the so-called "grandfather clause" in the early twentieth century, but by 1921 a Louisiana constitutional convention was convened that resulted in prospective voters being required to pass an "interpretation test." In order to successfully register, a citizen had to be able to not only read and write, but also interpret sections of the Louisiana and United States constitutions.

When the federal government again recoiled, Louisiana concocted a voucher system for new voters. All a prospective voter had to do was to get two registered voters to vouch for his residency and literally admit knowing the applicant. Blacks could be kept off the voter rolls in any town or parish in which white voters refused to vouch for them. The law kept black political activism well watered down throughout the state, but Madison was one of four parishes in Louisiana where blacks were shut out of voting entirely until the early 1960s. The local political system was "so darn tight, there wasn't any way in the world you could get two white people to go up there," Neal's old Tallulah acquaintance Martin Williams recalled.

As with Neal, Zelma Wyche's worldview had also been shaped by military life. Wyche served in the heavily segregated U.S. Army during World War II. "And here you are fighting and you can't vote," Wyche recalled. "A man without a country, but you're fighting for a country." Wyche was a member of an NAACP-organized voter registration attempt in the 1940s that met with grinding opposition. The minority resolved the challenge to its power by outlawing the NAACP in Madison Parish. In the years before the rise to national prominence of the Rev. Martin Luther King Jr., parish ministers worked side-by-side with Wyche and other civil rights foot soldiers.

James Sharp Jr., by multiple accounts the only practicing lawyer of color in that part of Louisiana, took on the constitutionality of the identification requirement with a 1954 lawsuit that appeared to have merit, but the case was dismissed on a technicality when the plaintiffs were told they arrived late for a hearing in the courtroom of U.S. District Judge Ben Dawkins Jr., who soon would rule against racial segregation in Shreveport.

Cracking the legal system was too difficult for one attorney, but the Civil Rights Acts of 1957 and 1960 provided enabling language that empowered the Department of Justice to litigate any jurisdiction suspected of depriving citizens of the right to vote. Madison and East Carroll parishes in Louisiana were ideal early testing grounds.

During one trip, Neal met with more than a dozen Tallulah residents at the black Elks Lodge. Some of the men he'd known since childhood. "I sat and listened to them a while and finally spoke up and said, 'How many of you want to get the vote?'" Neal recalled. "They raised their hands. Then I said, 'How many of you are willing to meet me Monday at City Hall so we can kick this thing off?' All fourteen raised their hands."

When Monday morning came, the group was scheduled to meet at Martin's Cleaners. William Martin was among the fourteen who raised their hands. I asked him, 'Martin, are you coming with us?' And he said, 'I just discovered I have something over in Vicksburg I have to do.'" Neal was irritated, but when he thought about it later, watching Martin demur and deflect was understandable. He had a hard-won business to protect. For blacks, registering to vote in Madison Parish was unheard of and nothing short of revolutionary, not to mention dangerous, in 1960.

Of the fourteen who had raised their hands, Neal would recall years later, several others failed to show up entirely. Some surely wondered whether stirring up all that trouble might be worth whatever satisfaction they eventually received as second-class citizens. The vote was guaranteed by the Constitution, but it was anything but assured in Louisiana.

"Three showed up," Neal said. "There was a fellow by the name of William Butler, an elderly guy who walked with a cane, Wyche, and a fellow named Harrison Brown. That made four of us. I really only needed one beside myself. But all of us walked downtown to City Hall and walked in. We met with Miss Ward, the registrar of voters. You have to understand. This was a time when there was an emphasis put on blacks registering, in the late 1950s and early 1960s, and invariably they put white women in charge of the voter registrar's office in towns across the South. This lady, we called her Miss Ward."

Miss Ward looked up from her work and politely inquired, "What can I do for you fellows?"

"We are here to register to vote," Neal replied.

"That's unusual," she said.

"Why is that unusual?" Neal asked.

"You have to have two people to identify you," she said.

"Two people?"

Wyche said, "Miss Ward, you know me. I used to cut your lawn."

"If the mayor comes over and identifies us," Neal said, thinking quickly, "will you let us register to vote?"

Obviously appreciating the realities of Tallulah better than young college man Neal, she agreed. The four men went to see the mayor,

William Putnam "Buck" Sevier Jr., a local banker who had served in his public capacity since 1932 and would continue as mayor until 1974—a record in Louisiana. There had been a Sevier in public office in Madison Parish almost without interruption since the Civil War era, and that tradition would continue into the mid-1980s. Buck Sevier was a member of one of the most historically and politically entrenched families in the region. As a banker, he was the man to know in Tallulah on many levels.

Sevier was unflappable and unperturbed by the approach of four black men he'd known in one capacity or another for many years. In a moment, they explained what was needed. All Sevier had to do was cross the street and admit he knew Wyche, Butler, Brown, and Neal. He smiled in feigned astonishment and said, "You know I can't go over there and help you. People will take all their money out of my bank if I go over there."

Having made multiple unsuccessful attempts to register to vote, the four men left the bank. They weren't discouraged. They hadn't anticipated being allowed to do so. But they had become corroborative witnesses to the denial by the registrar and the refusal of the mayor to render assistance.

"I was satisfied we had done all we could do," Neal said many years later. "There was enough to contact the Department of Justice Civil Rights Division and file a lawsuit. I sent a coded telegram to J.K. Haynes, and he sent me a coded telegram back."

It read, "Okay. You did your job. Now get the hell out of there."

Pressing the civil rights issues on behalf of the U.S. Department of Justice was a young attorney named Frank Dunbaugh, who would go on to a storied legal career. He'd already worked on official misconduct, prison guard brutality, and a lynching case—one in which a grand jury failed to indict—before working on a strategy to register African Americans to vote. In Louisiana, lawmakers had duly noted the *Brown* decision by passing protectionist legislation with an official "goal of retaining the Southern way of life."

In an era of bus boycotts in Montgomery, Alabama, the murder of innocent black organizers and protesters, and the rise of White Citizens' Councils intent on purging the voter rolls of blacks in areas in which the minority was actually in the majority, Dunbaugh searched for residents willing to step into the breach and request to exercise their right to vote. A generation of African-American soldiers had returned from World War II and the Korean War to an America that accepted their loyal military service but rejected one of the most basic rights of citizenship.

Dunbaugh notes with a sense of irony that each February, the month in which black history is celebrated, the same legendary figures are discussed. From Dr. Martin Luther King to Rosa Parks and John Lewis, the stories are repeated in an endless loop.

"All of those people made wonderful contributions to the movement," Dunbaugh said, "But in my mind the real heroes are people like Joe Neal who put their lives on the line."

Each Louisiana parish had its hometown heroes, and some paid terrible prices for their courage.

"These people weren't just foolishly out there standing up for their rights," Dunbaugh said. "They knew perfectly well that they were endangering their lives and the lives of their families. Their churches and homes could have been burned down." They lost jobs. Black farmers lost their crops when whites suddenly stopped doing business with them.

Neal, Dunbaugh said, was actually among the fortunate ones in Madison Parish because he was young and decided to move to Southern Nevada. Before Neal said goodbye to his hometown, he joined Wyche and Harrison Brown in testing the new law and, in doing so, would make history.

As the Department of Justice began assembling its civil rights case in Madison Parish, as it was in so many other jurisdictions throughout the South, student life returned to something approaching normal for Joe Neal. His interest in the law seemed unlimited, but his G.I. Bill was not. After 36 months, he amassed more than enough credits to graduate and had put in 30 hours of law under an arts and sciences program at Southern. He would crack as many books as time and money allowed.

"I wanted to stay and complete my law degree, but after three years my money had run out," he said, and two precious scholarships at the law center were taken. "I needed one class to finish my bachelor's degree in political science with a block of law studies."

Culture shock once again greeted him when he returned to Las Vegas, where blacks had the ability to register and vote but were unlikely to see a familiar face among the legion of candidates for local and statewide office. As of 1961, a black had yet to be elected to a local government office.

Neal took a job as a porter at downtown's Fremont Hotel not far from the edge of the Westside. In those days, the Fremont was operated by Meyer Lansky business representative Eddie "Lights Out" Levinson, a fellow considered notorious to federal law agents. However, he had managed to ingratiate himself with local law enforcement and government in a well-established Las Vegas tradition while the FBI conducted surveillance and wiretapped the casino's phones—a controversial technique in those days. Despite his brand-new college degree Neal was among the joint's nearly invisible black employees hired for menial labor. He was inquisitive by nature with powers of observation honed in the military, and it wasn't long before he learned the lay of the land at the Fremont—and spotted a telephone line where one didn't belong. As it turned out, it was part of a crude FBI listening strategy, one later exposed and soundly ridiculed by Nevada governor Grant Sawyer.

Sawyer's lament over the federal government's heavy handedness with Nevada's gambling fraternity was still in the news when a fellow employee approached Neal.

"Joe, there's a judge out there looking for you."

Neal had been to law school, but few people in his Las Vegas circle knew that. When another employee repeated that someone associated with a federal judge was looking for him, he started to panic. A third approach clarified the request further: The FBI wanted to talk to him.

"'Oh, shit,' I thought," Neal recalled. "I didn't know what it had to do with me. Was it that damn wire I saw? I didn't want any trouble with the casino guys or the hoodlum element."

But the FBI was simply delivering a message from Dunbaugh. The DOJ's Civil Rights Division was ready to go to court on the Madison Parish voter registration case, and Neal's presence was being requested. Afraid the Fremont's suspicious casino bosses would think him a government snitch, Neal knew then that he'd need to find a different job.

Dunbaugh explained that Neal would receive a check for $500 to be used to cover his plane travel and expenses prior to his testimony. Neal's thoughts were immediately directed to that single English class he lacked for graduation from Southern. That $500 would more than cover the tuition, but he'd have to find a different way to get to Monroe, Louisiana, sixty miles west of Tallulah, in time for the court hearing.

A check of the available bus service showed he could get there in time, but he had to hurry. Sleeping all night on a crowded bus was nothing compared to the taste of becoming a college graduate. And so he bought the bus ticket, put the $500 check in a briefcase with other paperwork, and arrived in Tallulah in time to rest up and prepare for the busy days ahead.

In the fatigue of the trip, he departed the bus and forgot the briefcase. By the time he remembered his error and returned to the bus station, a white ticket agent was rifling through it.

Neal knew the written and unwritten law: if he approached him aggressively, he'd wind up arrested. No one would believe a black man would come into possession of a $500 check legally.

Instead he added molasses to a drawl and said, "I'm heah to pick up a briefcase fo' Mistah Neal." Neal would recall, "He handed it to me because he thought it was a white man's. But the check was gone." Neal called the federal marshal's office in Las Vegas, put a stop on the check and had it reissued and resent. It arrived in time to pay for that last pesky class."

Neal's first foray into politics was dangerous, and years later his closest friends remained impressed.

"After I got out of college, Joe was very active in Louisiana when it came to organizing for voting rights," Calvin said. "Even though I thought he was a damn fool to challenge" the restrictions that prevented African Americans from voting, "I admired his effort and courage."

Ernestine Madison observed, "It wasn't safe, but he was able to enter into it and stay with it," Madison said. "I just appreciate him being able to pave the way for the rest of us because that's what he did."

At the hearing, the absurdity of keeping blacks, whether literate or unlettered, from registering to vote became abundantly clear. One white farmer, a longtime voter, was called to testify to discuss the process. He was shown his voter registration application and was certain of its authenticity.

"Are you sure this is your signature?" Dunbaugh asked.

"Yeah, that's my X," the farmer replied.

The illiterate signed with an X, but Neal and other members of the community weren't allowed to register without jumping through multiple hoops.

In an attempt to remain one step ahead of the federal hounds, Louisiana abandoned its voucher system in favor of a literacy test that included a challenging interpretation of the state and federal constitutions for prospective voters. Those already registered, specifically the white population, were grandfathered in. Only blacks were made to take the tests and many turned away from examinations that, Wyche would recall, "You have to be a little old lawyer to pass."

But, give or take a few hours and an official sheepskin, Joe Neal was the closest thing to a little young lawyer they were likely to find. And when the voucher system was brushed aside, Neal was the first to take the so-called literacy test. He had help in the tutoring department in the form of several sample tests purloined by housekeepers with access to the residences of the whites who were working so hard to prevent blacks from voting.

"I passed with 100 percent," Neal said years later, laughing at the memory. "The lady registered me. But I knew I could not vote there because I was already registered in Nevada."

The literacy test was thrown out following the passage of the Civil Rights Act of 1964. By then, Wyche had begun to emerge as not only a civil rights activist but also a future police chief of Madison Parish. He later appeared in an *Ebony* magazine feature, titled "Black lawman in KKK territory."

Although Neal's life was back in Southern Nevada, and others involved in the struggle gave many newspaper interviews and in the process tended to assume ever-expanding roles in the march toward equality, the *Madison Journal* chronicled the historic moment in a 1975 article: "Joe Neal was the first black registered after the identification requirement was lifted; in fact, he was the first black voter in the parish since Reconstruction."

With violence increasing against civil rights workers and voting rights activists, Neal took the good advice of Dunbaugh and Haynes and returned to Las Vegas, where he soon took his push for equal access and participation in the political process to a higher level.

From Photo Opportunities
to Real Opportunities

A T THE TIME, the irony was unacknowledged but inescapable: there were the much-publicized Moulin Rouge Agreements in 1960 between black leaders and the influential and image-sensitive white business and gaming community. This ended with a gentlemen's agreement to improve hiring practices inside the casino industry. By then a green-felt ghost on the edge of the Westside, its six-month "heyday" already blending into Las Vegas legend, the Moulin Rouge provided an ideal backdrop for the photo opportunity the gathering created. Photographs of the meeting, which resulted in the cancellation of a scheduled march by blacks on the Strip—an act that would surely be bad for business and once again remind the outside world that the Strip's casino kings were far behind the curve when it came to civil rights—were widely circulated. The meeting itself cemented the reputations of local black leaders and some vocal whites such as *Las Vegas Sun* publisher Hank Greenspun as champions of the cause of social equality.

Some important strides were being made, and the efforts of those on the ground ought not to be discounted, but the agreement was as symbolic as substantive. It would take more than the agility of the Las Vegas News Bureau to change the ugly course of racial history in Southern Nevada. The so-called Moulin Rouge Agreement would make big headlines, but generate only small gains for blacks on the Strip. Without dedicated representation in local or state government, they were relegated to taking to the streets and making threats of insurrection in order to get the attention of the press and business bosses.

"The people who came out here from Fordyce and Tallulah where I came from just came here for jobs in the magnesium plant, and some came out a little bit earlier to work on Boulder Dam and were unsuccessful finding a job," Neal said. "People came out here and were confronted with prejudice. With the exception of voting, they had no real rights no matter what they agreed to at the Moulin Rouge. They were able to vote, but the public accommodations were not open to them."

Born of the desperation that accompanies high unemployment, poor living conditions, and the lack of a voice in the seats of political power, the rhetoric of the NAACP and Westside clergy was destined to increase in volume. Leaders such as Dr. James McMillan, Dr. Charles West, attorney Charles Kellar, and radio and television personality Bob Bailey were quoted often. But Kellar and McMillan especially were sometimes characterized in the media more in terms of their militancy than their advocacy.

In the wake of the Moulin Rouge Agreement, the real fight for equal treatment in the workplace had just begun. Neal followed the developments closely. In his eyes, the pattern of placation over progress was once again repeating itself.

Officially, the Nevada Equal Rights Commission (NERC) was created in 1961 out of the Moulin Rouge Agreement to oversee the state's equal rights and equal opportunity programs, handling employment discrimination complaints relating to race, national origin, color, religion, and sex. It was positioned to receive complaints and attempt to settle them. Failing that, it would then send the complaints on to the applicable state and federal agencies.

Although former Nevada governor Grant Sawyer would be lauded deservedly for his courageous stance in support of civil rights in the Silver State, and he made his personal philosophy on the subject clear as far back as his first State of the State speech, in a candid moment he admitted he was essentially dragged into the position he took.

"Even though I was highly motivated to extend civil rights to Nevada's black citizens, without constant urging from people who were directly involved in the movement I might not have been as committed as I was to advancing the cause," Sawyer said in his oral history, *Hang Tough! An Activist in the Governor's Mansion*. "We got as far as we did in such a relatively short period of time due in large measure to help—not just help, but 'forceful' help (laughter)—from members of Nevada's NAACP, whose leadership kept things moving. Their initiative, energy, and resolve enabled us to pass civil rights legislation before Congress or Jack Kennedy had taken any position on the issue, putting Nevada in the forefront of a social reform issue on which it had long trailed the nation."

Sawyer credited Kellar, McMillan, Bailey, West, and Reno political activist Eddie Scott for staying the course. Joe Neal's friend Kellar was the best-versed in the law and arguably the most courageous of the group of activists who were also trying to manage their own business careers in a society where it was essential to maintain contacts in the white community. Keller was "perhaps the most aggressive member of the group, very impatient and demanding. He certainly kept the Legislature's attention focused on civil rights, but he could sometimes be abrasive." He came about his irritation with the status quo honestly. Born in Barbados, with a law degree from St. John's University in New York, he moved with his family to Las Vegas in 1959 and fought for acceptance in the legal community. Kellar not only played an integral role in the historic Moulin Rouge meeting, but he battled to desegregate public schools and jousted in court on behalf of blacks wrongly accused of everything from loitering to homicide. Kellar's undaunted courage—one cowardly critic fired gunshots into his home—earned him the reputation as a rabble-rouser, but also the respect of his community.

Sawyer's legacy, meanwhile, was intertwined with his important role on the civil rights issue. In his oral history he took care to praise the Westside leaders. "All were on the same team, working for the same objective," he said. "Each in his own way was very forceful, but while they were not equals in status and influence, and their efforts sometimes followed divergent paths, these men respected one another. I don't recall ever looking to one specific guy and thinking, 'This person will be able to dictate their position.'"

For his part, Sawyer rose swiftly through the political ranks in the 1950s in a state still shaking off the dust of its frontier heritage. A son of patronage, he was considered one of Nevada powerhouse U.S. Senator Pat McCarran's "boys," and he became integrally involved in the state's political machinery as Elko County district attorney. When the time came to challenge two-term incumbent Charles Russell in 1958, Sawyer fought the weight of the Democratic Party machine in the primary, overcame the candidate it had chosen instead of him, and brought it to bear in the general election. He won handily.

But if anyone believed Sawyer might attempt to mimic the anti-Communist zealotry of the late McCarran, they would be sorely disappointed. Sawyer was an unabashed progressive who pushed to regulate the gangster-infested casino racket and pushed for equal rights. He angered conservatives in the state when he signed a proclamation designating "Black History Week" in February 1959 at a time the state's own racial history left much to be desired.

When the opportunity came to press the casino crowd to pay more than lip service to its business and working relationships with blacks, Sawyer was a politically pragmatic progressive. Thanks in large part to the efforts of Democratic assemblywoman Maude Frazier, Sawyer surprised even himself by the watered-down success of the Nevada Equal Rights Commission enabling legislation. He'd been aided in his campaign efforts by grassroots organizing in the black communities in Washoe and Clark Counties, and upon election he was true to his word, adding civil rights to his first State of the State speech. Although it was a truly far-reaching bill, it would die in the state Senate as far too progressive.

The weaker version that was eventually signed into law did much to drag Nevada forward into the latter half of the twentieth century. Frazier was fearless, introducing Assembly Bill 122 and spending endless hours shoring up support. Although Sawyer recognized "there was little sympathy for civil rights, and I had difficulty even finding someone to introduce the bill (on the Senate side)," he had Frazier in the Assembly. She forwarded an admittedly less comprehensive bill during the 1963 session, "which proposed to outlaw discrimination in public employment and forbid all contractors who did business with the state to discriminate on the grounds of race, national origin, religion, sex, whatever. There was some resistance, particularly in the Senate, but the bill eventually passed and I signed it into law in March."

Actually enforcing the law, of course, was entirely another matter. Nevada's skeletal state government had no ability to police recalcitrant businessmen and even outright racists from denying blacks public accommodations in hotels and restaurants. But it could oversee its own contracts. Again, the symbolism outweighed the substance.

On paper, Nevada appeared to have emerged as a progressive state on civil rights. Sawyer was successful in creating the Nevada Equal Rights Commission in 1961, but it provided more theater than protection for blacks.

"The commission came after a lot of pressure from the NAACP at the time," Neal recalled. "Its first chairman was Bert Goldwater, a white progressive guy. His selection upset a lot of people, and that's when Bob Bailey was chosen. Bob was, to put it politely, a safe choice for the state's bosses." In the end, Neal was of the opinion that the commission produced a lot of reports without curtailing many practices, but it was also true that Bailey's style and emphasis on opportunities for minority businesses made him more acceptable to the prevailing political power structure.

Opponents knew the best way to defeat the commission's mission was to make sure it lacked the ability to investigate, and for two years it did little more than collect complaints. By 1963, however, NAACP leader Kellar and progressive Democratic assemblywoman Flora Dungan took it upon themselves to press for changes that would strengthen the commission, including greater investigative powers and a working relationship with the Legislature. The reaction to their efforts provided Neal a lesson in Nevada legislative politics: in a part-time "citizen's Legislature" that in the early 1960s met for just 120 days every two years, delaying a bill was as effective as defeating it. So it was with a pair of bills in the 1963 session that sought to strengthen the state's anemic Equal Rights Commission that Sawyer proudly considered so progressive.

With Dungan doing the ramrodding, the Assembly bill appeared to have an honest chance of gaining passage. But then the delays began. Civil rights progress was being made in major cities across the nation in 1963, but progress has never been the strong suit of the Nevada Legislature. Press accounts show the process gaining ground, but then running into difficulty not only with conservative Republicans, but with equally conservative Democratic leaders, including several influential Mormon legislators. The outspoken Kellar pointed to what he considered the obvious influences at work and, when that wasn't enough, set up a picket line in an attempt to call attention to the stalling tactics.

New civil rights legislation would follow the same tumultuous course in the state Senate, where Lieutenant Governor Paul Laxalt made several promises and talked of compromise, with the only impact being a delay in the process. Improvements to the Tinkertoy Equal Rights Commission failed in both houses.

Casino bosses had little interest in being hurried toward integrating their joints, or their workforces. There was substantial pushback from Mormon legislators, and during the height of the debate Democratic House Speaker Ty Tyson simply stopped coming into work. A vote in the Assembly drew scant Republican support, and lost 23–13, but more importantly conservative Democrats were deaf to the appeals of Sawyer and the NAACP.

The comments of Senate Majority Leader Charles Gallagher of White Pine County were typical of Republican rhetoric on the bill in hand and the issue generally. "It is too late now to introduce a bill of this importance," he said. "At this late date, we would prefer to amend the present law rather than introduce new legislation." Besides, he added, his colleagues weren't about to take "dictation" from Sawyer. When pressed, Gallagher reflected the viewpoint of his colleagues: the fact they promised to stop any attempts to strengthen the state's civil rights laws didn't mean they were necessarily opposed to civil rights as a general proposition, but only that the Legislature lacked the time to do the job right.

Meanwhile, scribbling skeptics in the press noted, other bills were moving through the process without incident.

Kellar lamented, "This is a strange type of logic. No doubt they think we are too ignorant to understand such a thing. We are now going to start demonstrations to let the world know what is going on in Nevada."

Placards reading "Democrats wreck civil rights," "Gamblers deny civil rights," "Mormons are against civil rights," and "Republicans wreck civil rights" hung from the necks of adults and children in a nearly silent protest.

The reaction was almost immediate. Blacks were promised action by Laxalt, the president of the Senate, from the Legislature's Republican-dominated upper house. He said senators would amend legislation to carry forward where the Assembly bill had foundered.

Laxalt and his fellow Republicans were apparently motivated in part by the Kellar's picket line. Laxalt publicly said he believed the bill would work "if we get the right people appointed" to the commission, which lacked the power to accomplish anything of substance.

"We reiterate that regardless of personal sympathy, it is too late to take a second try," Gallagher told a reporter. But Dungan scoffed at the notion. "There's talk of a gambling tax being introduced at this late date," she countered.

Senate Democrats, rarely lionhearted in the best of years, were in the narrowest minority in the seventeen-member upper house. Some were vocal about being willing to introduce civil rights legislation, but they noted the obvious: without some Republican support, their efforts were doomed.

Given an opportunity to lead, Nevada again chose to placate when necessary, obfuscate and obstruct when possible. The passage of the Civil Rights Act of 1964 and the U.S. Supreme Court's decision in the *Heart of Atlanta Motel, Inc. v. United States*, which upheld the right of Congress, in its duty to control interstate commerce, to pursue methods to abolish racial discrimination in areas of public accommodation, would give the state the opportunity to change.

Neal returned to Las Vegas full-time in the summer of 1963 armed with a political science degree, training in law enforcement and criminal science, a top-secret clearance from the Department of Energy, and four years of experience in the Air Force. He scoured the community for work that might challenge him, but like most blacks in Southern Nevada was told he wasn't quite right for the available white-collar jobs. He landed at Titanium Metals Corporation, a World War II–era plant in Henderson's industrial district, and went to work as a janitor. He was not amused, but undeterred, he wisely kept his disappointment to himself.

He also immersed himself in Southern Nevada politics, working on campaigns and becoming an active member of the NAACP. In his mind, Governor Sawyer had more than stepped up on behalf of Nevada's black population. But Neal also noticed progress was painfully slow. At the local level, life for working-class blacks was largely unchanged. They weren't getting hired for front-of-the-house jobs in the casino business, were never quite "right" for government assignments, and were marginalized politically by splintered districts that all but assured a black candidate could not get elected.

He was also quickly learning the ugly underside of the local civil rights scene. Others were running for office, and clearly taking personal advantage of their higher profiles in the community.

"Most black people who came to Las Vegas from Tallulah, Louisiana, in the forties into the early sixties, had not participated in the political process, including myself," Neal said. "Politically, they were prime targets to be taken advantage of." The same could be said for those migrating from Fordyce, Arkansas, and small towns in Mississippi.

Neal thought that McMillan, a groundbreaking civil rights leader, was not shy about promoting himself, his business, and his allies while calling for historic racial change. A supporter of U.S. Senator Howard Cannon, McMilllan used the soft-spoken former fighter pilot's need for a spokesman on the Westside to help young Robert Archie receive patronage jobs in Washington, D.C., and entrance into Howard University. Archie eventually graduated from law school and worked for several years as a member of Cannon's Senate staff.

The mercurial McMillan's relationship with Cannon cooled considerably in the run-up to the federal passage of the Civil Rights Act of 1964. As recounted in former Cannon staffer Michael Vernetti's portrait of the senator, McMillan complained that his former political ally "was just one of the 'good old boys' and he never did do anything for civil rights or black people that was visible." Vernetti added, "Sometimes gratitude is fleeting." Neal would recall McMillan years later complaining that Cannon hadn't done enough to help him salvage a business investment that had soured.

Not yet thirty years old, Neal found himself pulled by several forces into Southern Nevada politics. He was active in the Democratic Party, which had begun to appreciate the advantages of a registered black population motivated to go to the polls. He volunteered for the '62 Sawyer and '64 Cannon campaigns and appreciated their rhetoric on civil rights. Shaped by his upbringing, education, and participation in the historic Madison Parish voter registration lawsuit, Neal was also seeking real change.

All those things informed his decision to run for elected office in 1964, but in a quiet moment it was the righteous, chiding voice of J.K. Haynes from the Louisiana New Teachers Association that put him over the top: "You can't even vote where you are from."

Westside community leaders such as Charles Keller and James McMillan wanted to see a qualified black run for every open active seat. As McMillan would recall in his oral history, "Joe Neal also ran for an office at that time, his first stab at politics. We had a big old wagon on the Westside, and all our politicians came up on the thing and made speeches, and people came to hear them." Although Neal would choose to run for the state Assembly, he also considered taking a shot at a North Las Vegas City Council seat.

Behind the scenes, more than one political expert whispered, "Just don't put your face on your campaign material."

"As if white people would not know if they were black," Neal recalled of his first legislative campaign. "I thought this was a ridiculous idea. I met an older gentleman whom I called Mr. Jackson. He owned a building on Jackson Street. Many years later it would be converted to a barbershop. I do not recall how or why Mr. Jackson became involved with me in my campaign. He took me down to Marc Wilkinson Printing and had fifty posters made. I tacked these posters up across town. I remembered putting one of these posters out near the Joe W. Brown Racetrack (near the current site of the Las Vegas Country Club). At the time, I believe Sahara might still have been called San Francisco Street. This action of putting up posters with my picture on them across town caused those persons who claimed to be the overseers of the black community at the time to run a person by the name of Leo Johnson. They put his picture on posters with the same color as mine, and made Leo's posters a little bigger than my posters. This was supposed to have the effect of overshadowing me. Neither one of us won, but I had made my point.

"There was no need for any of us to hide."

But in frank retrospect, it might not have helped him win many white votes. The good news for black residents in 1960 was the election of fellow African American Helen Lamb Crozier to the State Board of Education.

How did she do it? In part, due to her politically potent middle name. Lamb was a well-known name in Nevada politics, with brothers Floyd, Ralph and Darwin Lamb all holding office within a few years of each other. Helen Crozier chose not to have her image depicted on her political placards, and she prevailed.

"At the time of the election of Helen Lamb Crozier, other than her immediate family, no one in the community, as I recall, knew that she was black," Neal said.

Neal took out a small advertisement in the *Las Vegas Sun* spotlighting the need for a public defender in Clark County and a law school for the state. Until 1963, becoming a lawyer in-state was a matter of apprenticing under an established attorney and readying for the bar exam. Clark County district judge John Mowbray, with funding from the Ford Foundation, helped create the local public defender's office. A young attorney named Richard Bryan, who would go on to become a governor and U.S. senator and one of Nevada's most beloved and respected political figures, was named the community's first public defender.

The early years of Neal's political activism were punctuated by the April 1964 visit to Southern Nevada by Dr. Martin Luther King Jr., who spoke before a large crowd at the Las Vegas Convention Center on the topic of the nonviolent pursuit of civil rights. The racially blended crowd was enthusiastic, and few noted the irony of a black man speaking in a place that had not so long ago been as segregated as Selma. With the local NAACP chapter playing host, and Bob Bailey reminiscing with King about their time as classmates at Atlanta's Morehouse College, the event was an undeniable success.

Like so many positive moments that made inspiring headlines, it was hard to measure the lasting impact of King's visit. Neal remained inspired not only by King, but by Ella Baker and her organization of the increasingly assertive Student Nonviolent Coordinating Committee, which engaged in college campus sit-ins. Like many others of his generation, Neal was angered by racial injustice and drawn to the action-oriented SNCC with its impassioned speakers Julian Bond, John Lewis, and Stokely Carmichael.

He was also an admirer of U.S. Senator Hubert H. Humphrey, a liberal Democrat from Minnesota, after first reading about him during his military service. By 1964, Neal joined an army of Southern Nevada volunteers in support of the Lindon B. Johnson-Humphrey ticket. Neal said he was further impressed after meeting Humphrey at New York's Waldorf Astoria that same year and a decade later after hearing him speak at a pharmaceutical convention in Las Vegas. "I saw Hubert as a man willing to fight for the rights of black folks when they were not able to fight for themselves," he reflected many years after that first meeting.

Neal participated in the political process, but he also had a living to earn. In the wake of the passage of the Civil Rights Act of 1964, he decided to seek a better job than janitor at Titanium Metals Corporation in Henderson.

After opening Neal's work file and noting the résumé, the personnel officer said wryly, "Your degree is not working for you."

A few days later, he received word that he'd been promoted to "ingot inspector," a brutally physical job involving quality-testing titanium blocks weighing several tons. The position in the Engineering Division paid better, but it wasn't exactly challenging. But Neal became proficient, and not long after was hired by Reynolds Electrical and Engineering Company (REECo), as the company's equal rights compliance officer at a time when many employers and supervisors throughout the community were blocking hiring for blacks and other minorities.

If the casino bosses could be outed for their segregationist practices, so could officials in the building trades and construction industry. And REECo was also a major player at the Nevada Test Site.

Neal began to hit his stride at work, and he found his life partner in Estelle Ann DeConge, whom he'd met in the library at Southern a few years earlier. The couple was wed in a brief ceremony on the morning of May 29, 1965, at historic Saint Columba Catholic Church in Oakland, California. The church itself provided inspiration to the newlyweds: it was founded in 1898, and through the decades, according to its website, had seen its congregation transition from Irish and Italian to black and Hispanic. In the decades to come, the Neals continued to attend regular services at Saint James the Apostle Catholic Church on H Street.

Joe's job at Titanium was in transition, and Estelle was busy completing her internship as a dietitian at the VA hospital in Long Beach,

California. After completing her internship, she returned to Southern Nevada, where the couple took up residency on Alwill Street. Estelle had the distinction of being Nevada's first black dietician, and she continued her career while eventually juggling the duties of a mother of four.

Estelle and Joe's first child, Charisse Marie, was born November 17, 1965, at a time of great tumult in the Southern Nevada civil rights movement. It was all pretty confusing for a youngster.

"I remember there was a time when Dad had to hide us downstairs because someone had thrown a rock in the yard or tried to burn up the yard. It was frightening," Charisse recalled. "We had to go down to the lower level. All we heard was a lot of noise and yelling." Other times she remembered her father receiving phone calls late at night, then putting on his overcoat and announcing, "I'll be back."

Often as not the political disputes into which Neal was drawn weren't legislative, but party oriented. He was giving pain to the local building trades unions by demanding they open up real opportunities for minority apprentices. He was pushing the Democratic Party into being more inclusive of persons of color not just on the ground but in the county and state hierarchy.

At home, "He was always loving, my dad, but he taught us that education was the thing," Charisse said. "I remember asking him for a toy and him saying, 'No, why don't you get a book?' At school we got the Scholastic book list and had to pick out and order a book. Instead of buying us an expensive toy, he'd take the amount of that toy and buy us ninety-nine-cent books. I was always the one in class with the most books when it was time for them to be delivered to the classroom.

"Now, of course, I'm glad my dad put education in our home. God was first, and then it was education. He'd say, 'You put your friends last. They'll be there for you. You have to build you up first. He taught us how to love, in spite of the hatred and the prejudices that were out there in the world. He taught us how to love past it."

Charisse thought her parents were very brave in a world that at times seemed to want nothing more than to see them quit fighting. "We were taught to get your education and always face fear head-on," she said. "Trust God. What you're going to do is going to come to pass. My dad, he lived that in front of us. We had a chance to see him face hatred, not only in the news articles and later at the Legislature, but even in our home. We all have that fight of my dad in us."

Joe Neal knew that the only real way out of poverty for blacks and other second-class citizens was through education, workplace opportunity, and political clout.

A change was coming to the casino industry that would write a new chapter in Las Vegas history and help lead Joe Neal to the decision to try again for political office.

Change arrived by train on Thanksgiving 1966, not long after Sawyer lost his bid for reelection to Paul Laxalt, who never appeared to lose much sleep over civil rights. Billionaire Howard Hughes, and agent of change, could have helped usher in a new era of racial accord in the casino industry, but instead his racial paranoia and political intrigues helped set back blacks a decade.

Not every battle generated banner headlines and community outrage. Some of the toughest fights were at the micro-political level in an attempt to get the black community a public recreational facility taken for granted in better neighborhoods.

In the late 1960s, Neal was part of a group of citizens that managed to push approval for the Reverend Prentiss Walker Memorial Pool, in tribute to the dedicated leader of the Greater Faith Baptist Church. The North Las Vegas City Council had little difficulty approving the project in concept, but when it was time to fund its construction, there never seemed to be enough cash on hand. Neal fought with little success to augment the funding through the Legislature as the North Las Vegas council dragged its feet.

"We've been patient, but we're getting tired of asking for that pool," Neal told council members, who rose in offense at his abrupt manner. "We're well aware of our numbers in this community, and if we have to use these numbers, we will."

After a decade, the ground was finally broken. The pool was built. Children in the predominantly black neighborhood would have a place to swim. All it took was ten years and overt political threats from Joe Neal.

Meet the New Boss

JOE NEAL'S DUTIES AT REECo kept him busy, but also gave him insight into the local building trades unions, which bustled along in growing Southern Nevada but rarely hired minorities. In addition to participating in the Clark County Democratic Party, the NAACP, and his politically active Catholic church, he helped plot what would eventually become Southern Nevada's first minority jobs program in the construction industry. It wouldn't come without a fight, and more than a few threatening stares from business agents already battling to keep nonunion workers from Utah and other states from undercutting local tradesmen. But Neal knew civil rights weren't worth the paper they were printed on without equal opportunity in the workplace.

Participating in politics, campaign volunteering, and mustering votes for candidates was part of the process. In the spring and summer of 1966, he campaigned in the Westside and North Las Vegas on behalf of Governor Grant Sawyer's reelection campaign and several down-ticket Democrats. By fall it was clear the state Assembly candidacy of Woodrow Wilson, a Westside businessman, Republican, and former NAACP chapter president, was boosting Paul Laxalt's bid to unseat Sawyer in Southern Nevada's minority neighborhoods. Although Neal saw Sawyer as far more evolved on civil rights issues, he also understood that Laxalt—a Northern Nevada attorney who was rarely vocally supportive of minority equality issues in the lieutenant governor's office—was well aware of the advantage of having a credible surrogate work voters in poor neighborhoods. And Woody Wilson was a well-liked fellow.

Although they rarely saw eye to eye politically, in later years Neal would get to know Laxalt and consider him a friend. Laxalt told Neal privately he believed a lack of minority inclusion, what others would later call the "big tent," was one of the Republican Party's greatest failings. But in the mid-1960s Laxalt couldn't approach Sawyer on issues of race and equality. The foundering of the "Sawyer in '66" campaign signaled to some a return of the status quo.

But Sawyer's defeat wasn't even close to the most damaging thing that happened to Nevada blacks that November. It was the month that also signaled the arrival in Las Vegas of the eccentric billionaire Howard Hughes. Obscured in the breathless ballyhoo surrounding Hughes's sudden appearance as mogul-in-residence was a troubling fact that remained hidden in plain sight from average Southern Nevadans. Among Hughes's many maladies, mental and physical, was an unrealistic but undeniable fear and loathing of black people. Not merely the poor and downtrodden Southern blacks, whose plight in a segregated society by 1966 was playing out nightly on the national news, but representatives of the elite in black society as well. Hughes hated "negroes," believed them to be unclean, a menace to mainstream society—and bad for his business bottom line.

Muckraking investigative columnist Jack Anderson observed that, behind the façade of the Hughes publicity machine, the billionaire was in fact "a bigot, a political fixer, a greedy baron who tried to turn Nevada into his personal fiefdom, a man who considered his own accumulation of wealth paramount to the interests of the United States, a self-appointed savior with a profit motive." But that brand of salvation didn't include empathy for American blacks. Although Anderson noted that even Hughes admitted his opinions weren't "politically correct," he landed just short of calling on the resurgence of the Ku Klux Klan, writing in a memo to his alter ego, former FBI man Robert Maheu, "But I am not running for election and therefore we don't have to curry favor with the NAACP either."

His feelings about race might never have surfaced or been fully appreciated had it not been for his fear of germs, a phobia which kept him walled off from all but a few handpicked servants and physicians after he was embedded on the ninth floor of the Desert Inn. He had arrived by train on Thanksgiving eve to avoid publicity and disguise the fact that he was a heavily medicated shadow of his former self. His behavior was increasingly erratic, but Hughes still wanted to keep a handle on his empire, and the day-to-day transfer of wealth and assets to Las Vegas. To that end, Hughes wrote hundreds of memos to Maheu. Those communications, which later surfaced in a nasty civil suit aimed at the shadowy Maheu, provide an insight into the ugly feelings Hughes harbored.

His fears not only informed his worldview, but also had a substantial trickle-down philosophical impact on his Mormon management team. Their attitude toward equal opportunity employment reflected his, and Las Vegas blacks just breaking out of the prejudices of the old mobbed-up ownership regime found a new ogre with which to contend. The difference was, they didn't have newspaper publishers or the governor in their corner.

Las Vegas press baron Hank Greenspun played the media maitre d' to Hughes, and governors Laxalt and Mike O'Callaghan, Laxalt's successor, both catered to the billionaire's eccentricities. They were rewarded for their willingness to bend state gaming regulation to please the new boss of Las Vegas. Greenspun in 1968 sold KLAS TV-8, the local CBS affiliate, to Hughes at a handsome profit. Las Vegas legend has it that Hughes bought the station to control its selection of late-night movies, but he also took time to critique its coverage of the black community.

When equal employment opportunity, fair housing, and school desegregation bills were drafted at the Nevada Legislature, Hughes ordered his political fixers to undercut them at the highest levels. Through Maheu and attorney Thomas Bell, the campaign cash flowed and the phones rang immediately with demands for action. When the press ought to have been investigating, it was reduced to cheerleading. Racial progress in Las Vegas had never had such a formidable enemy.

"Many casino owners fiercely resisted civil rights legislation in Nevada," Annelise Orleck wrote in *Storming Caesars Palace: How Black Mothers Fought Their Own War on Poverty*. "But none was more adamant, or freer with invective, than aviation and film mogul Howard Hughes. In the 1960s, he was buying hotels on the Strip as if they were pieces in a Monopoly game. State officials, who hoped that he could wrest control of the Strip from unsavory organized crime figures and make Las Vegas tourism respectable, welcomed Hughes's buying spree. Hughes promised to give Nevada gambling 'the kind of reputation that

Lloyd's of London has, so that Nevada on a note will be like Sterling on silver.'"

Las Vegas was noted for its lapdog press beholden to casino bosses, but the muckraking Greenspun led the parade at a time he ought to have been more circumspect. He made no secret that he believed Hughes's presence in Las Vegas could help the city's casino industry shake its notorious reputation as a haven for organized crime front men and facilitators. What went unstated was the fact that Hughes's acquisitions of mobbed-up casinos such as the Silver Slipper, Frontier, Sands, and Landmark did nothing to dilute the presence of mob connections at the Stardust, Tropicana, Dunes, and Riviera, or the shadowed rise of the influence of the hoodlums behind labor boss Jimmy Hoffa and the Teamsters Central States Pension Fund.

Hughes was no savior. He did, however, come along at precisely the wrong time for Westside blacks struggling to rise from the grip of poverty and ignorance.

"The deeply racist Hughes didn't believe African Americans were good for business," Orleck observed. "He even fought against improving housing conditions on the Westside, because that might encourage more black migrants to settle there. Flexing his muscles in the state capital, Carson City, Hughes blocked open housing and school integration bills during the late 1960s. As one of the largest employers in the state, he fought fiercely against equal employment legislation. And he handed out staggering amounts of cash to curry support for his views."

Laxalt was arguably the most duplicitous of Hughes's many Nevada courtesans. As he had just a few years earlier with equal rights legislation, Laxalt publicly supported the state's fair housing bill at a time when incidents of discrimination in home buying, apartment renting, and lending were commonplace. Nevada's overrated reputation for civil rights progress following the Moulin Rouge accords and Sawyer's push for an Equal Rights Commission had been eclipsed by a grim reality for blacks: with some exceptions, they still weren't welcome in predominantly white neighborhoods. (And the occasional press account of housing discrimination bore this out.)

Thanks to the loyalty Hughes purchased with a few thousand dollars, the fair housing bill failed by a 4-3 vote in the Senate Finance

Committee. Its most ardent critic, James Slattery, a state senator representing Washoe and Storey Counties, received $2,500 and conservative Democrat Jim Gibson of Henderson, where Neal had worked for Titanium Metals, accepted $1,500 from Hughes's Silver Slipper political slush account—large contributions in those days. Privately, Maheu made little secret that Hughes was getting what he paid for. The aide wrote to Hughes: "I do not claim one iota of credit for the foresight you had when you instructed me to make political contributions to 'worthy' public servants.... Without 'our friends' we would not have had a prayer." It helped that Tom Bell, Hughes's legal operative, was close with Governor Laxalt, who Maheu said, "delivered to Tom the critical vote which enabled Bell to kill it in committee."

Laxalt secretly dumped his own fair housing bill, in part to appease the racially paranoid Hughes. Although the press attached the governor's name to the legislation—it was officially his plan and came in the wake of similar measures already passed in other states—privately he helped to defeat it by ensuring it never escaped the Senate Finance Committee. He could tell the press he'd done all he could, and Hughes and other segregationists on the Strip and in Nevada's business community could quietly celebrate. A watered-down version would eventually pass that the next administration would be compelled to amend.

Contrast the action behind the scenes with Laxalt's lofty rhetoric during his January 21, 1969, State of the State address, in which he was more than willing to hold up Assemblyman Woodrow Wilson as an example of the state's progress on race relations.

"Let me say in the field of equal rights, Nevada's record has been one of basic harmony and responsibility when compared to the inflammatory situations in other states," Laxalt said. Although he name-dropped his legislative ally Wilson and repeatedly mentioned the need for a fair housing act and an equal rights commission "with an increased budget and enlarged staff," he stressed the need for a solution by the state and not the federal government. It was a familiar dodge other reluctant leaders used when attempting to stand on both sides of a contentious issue. But, Laxalt added, "This would enable Nevadans to deal with our own problems rather than facing the heavy hand of the federal government." Although he called for respect and acceptance "of the rights and human dignity of minorities," he allowed Hughes's paranoia and political pressure to prevail.

The truth about the death of the fair housing bill didn't emerge until years after the fact when the voluminous Hughes-Maheu memos were discovered and published in Michael Drosnin's 1985 book, *Citizen Hughes*.

Hughes's paranoid racism manifested itself in many ways and pathologies. Unlike some of the more obviously mobbed-up operators on the Strip, who had instructed security guards to simply stop blacks when they entered the building, Hughes damaged the progress of civil rights in Nevada in other ways. His fears, supposedly stoked by a race riot in 1917 during his pampered early life in Houston, manifested themselves in active discrimination that defied state and federal law with impunity.

"However, now, a half century later, the well-guarded recluse was besieged not by armed mobs but by phantoms of his own creation. Consumed by a nameless dread, he projected his fears onto a variety of unseen enemies," Drosnin wrote. "Sometimes they paraded before him in blackface—a minstrel show of his subconscious mind."

He referred to revered actor James Earl Jones as a "repulsive gob of grease" after watching him kiss a white woman during a television broadcast of the Tony Awards. Jones was being honored for his portrayal of Jack Johnson in *The Great White Hope*.

Hughes not only feared blacks as a group. He also feared their "germs" and the "contamination" he believed they carried.

After Hughes bought KLAS TV-8, he noticed that CBS carried a *Black Heritage* program each morning. This discovery sent him into a rage.

He complained to Maheu, "As you know, this program commenced without my permission....Since then I have been forced to squirm under the intense displeasure of watching this program every morning—I have to watch and listen every morning while the only academic program on KLAS pours out such propaganda as: 'Africa is the mother and the father of the world.'" He wasn't interested in compromise, eventually offering, "We do not want any programs involving negroes."

Nor was he interested in his Desert Inn, which had established a national reputation as a place for PGA golf events and professional tennis matches, featuring groundbreaking African-American tennis star Arthur Ashe on its courts for a Davis Cup event. Hughes was fretful that "hordes of negroes" would converge at courtside and contaminate his resort. Although Ashe eventually appeared at the Desert Inn, Hughes used his alter ego Maheu to scrap a plan to place a heavyweight fight featuring Muhammad Ali at the resort. It was yet another example of Hughes's maniacal racism hurting his business, but he had money to burn.

Hughes wasn't just another racist casino boss or ignorant security guard trying to please his supervisor. He was the key figure in the transition of the mob-owned Las Vegas casino racket to the new and supposedly corporate and modern gaming industry. He purchased exclusively mobbed-up casino resorts, ones that had been under investigative scrutiny by the Department of Justice for skimming and organized crime connections. His views on race, not widely known publicly, ought to have been of substantial concern to gaming regulators in an era in which the state found itself woefully behind the curve on the subject of civil rights. But it didn't matter to authorities, who catered to his every eccentricity.

On the Westside, a new generation of leaders pushed for change from the inside against formidable odds in a political system suddenly dominated by a new moneyman. For his part, Neal weighed in with essentially unfunded campaigns for the state Assembly in 1964 and for state Senate in District 3 in 1966. His second attempt came against legislative powerhouse B. Mahlon Brown.

Neal's political activism was getting noticed throughout the state. The bishop for the Church of God in Christ for Nevada predicted to his congregation that "if there is ever going to be a black fellow in Carson City in the Senate, it is going to be that Joe Neal," according to Bernice Mathews, who would become the first black woman state senator more than two decades later. "My father said there is a young man running for office, and he encouraged everyone to listen to him speak," Mathews recalled. She traveled from her home in Northern Nevada to Las Vegas "to hear this mighty man" speak. "I shall never forget it."

Neal's fledgling runs for office were noisy and served to help organize and develop voter registration. But at no time did Neal entertain the thought of pulling off a political upset—not with the district lines that catered to incumbents who resided, in community consciousness, far from Southern Nevada's poorest neighborhoods.

While Hughes hid under the covers from the question of race, the nation was changing before his eyes. Although Las Vegas didn't erupt in violence after the April 4, 1968, assassination of Dr. Martin Luther King in Memphis, Tennessee, a racially charged riot did break out a few months after the fair housing fiasco. On October 5, 1969, the Westside was torn by violence that led to two deaths, numerous injuries, and a number of arsons. Police poured into the community and rounded up more than two hundred people.

The black community, rife with many problems, suffered largely self-inflicted wounds. The greater Las Vegas area, and especially the well-guarded Strip, was never in danger. But that didn't prevent police from placing snipers on school rooftops and the governor gearing up the National Guard.

At the Desert Inn, Hughes seethed with misguided rage mixed with unfounded fear. He relied on the assurances of Sammy Davis Jr., who was politically conservative and rarely seen on the front lines of the civil rights movement, that "his people" would never harm the Hughes empire. At the time, Davis was the only highly visible black in Hughes's employ and was celebrating a new five-year performance contract.

In private memos, Hughes made his feelings about bringing racial progress to the Strip undeniably clear.

He said he knew "there is tremendous pressure on the strip owners to adopt a more liberal attitude toward integration, open housing, and employment for more negroes. Now, Bob, I have never made my views known on this subject. And I certainly would not say these things in public. However, I can summarize my attitude about employing more negroes very simply—I think it is a wonderful idea for somebody else, somewhere else. I know this is not a very praiseworthy view, but I feel the negroes have already made enough progress to last the next 100 years, and there is such a thing as overdoing it.

"I know this is a hot potato, and I am not asking you to form a new chapter of the K.K.K. I don't want to become known as a negro-hater or anything like that. But I am not running for election and therefore we don't have to curry favor with the N.A.A.C.P., either."

At the time, no member of standing in the Nevada press dared criticize Hughes's racism—indeed, *Las Vegas Sun* publisher Greenspun would do substantial business with him through Maheu. Hughes held sway over Republican governor Laxalt and later made peace with his Democratic successor, Mike O'Callaghan. Hughes was untouchable. And Las Vegas blacks paid the price.

On Thanksgiving Day 1970, as mysteriously as he'd arrived, Hughes vanished from Las Vegas. He wasn't finished with the place—his empire had invested heavily there, and soon questions were raised by the O'Callaghan administration about his suitability to hold a license. It was only after Hughes departed that local press barons and politicians appeared to begin to recognize the error of allowing the eccentric cart blanche. Greenspun, who had helped perpetuate the Hughes mythology, guarded the billionaire's privacy, and made a score off his profligacy, had started to criticize his largely empty gesture at Las Vegas development.

"With Hughes, it was never a question of building, only of buying so he could be the biggest in the state," he wrote in an October 6, 1971 "Where I Stand" column in the *Sun*. "...In a way, it is fortunate the Hughes matter has come to a head so the people could know what forces make contribution to the growth of the area and what forces tend to keep it small so they could dominate it." He neglected to mention his own role in creating the mythos of the man in the Desert Inn penthouse. "It is also fortunate the new state administration has taken the stand it has, because this new growth will help dilute the hold of one group, which controls one-sixth of the state's economy." Perhaps feeling the weight of his own hypocrisy, Greenspun later admitted he'd prostituted his newspaper in Hughes's interest.

Ruby Phillips Duncan had a few questions for the casino bosses herself. Like Neal, Duncan rose from extremely humble roots. She was born June 7, 1932, in Tallulah to poor sharecroppers. Duncan grew up with relatives after her parents died and spent most of the year working in plantation cotton fields. She attended a segregated school eight miles from Tallulah, and after hearing of opportunities way out west in Las Vegas, in 1953 she jumped at the chance to leave.

She found a Westside awash in poverty worse than anything she'd known in Tallulah. Opportunity for a young black woman, if she was lucky, was defined by a shift as a hotel maid. And when she lost that meager wage and was injured on the job, she survived with her young children on Nevada's notoriously penurious Aid to Families with Dependent Children. The state had no food stamps program, offered no job training, and wasn't motivated to change its Spartan philosophy toward the poor.

Duncan considered herself ignorant, but she knew enough to recognize when she was being victimized by the state. Thus she began her lifelong quest for a better life for her children, herself, and welfare mothers such as her. And she understood the politically powerful imagery a group of poor mothers projected.

She developed a strong voice calling out government functionaries for their unwillingness to assist the neediest members of the community. She eventually turned her calling into a full-time career, earning a living, picking up allies, and gaining a national profile for standing up to casino bosses and even the governor himself.

She witnessed Nevada's unwillingness to embrace federal changes in the Aid to Families with Dependent Children program, saw the afterthoughts and handouts that passed as an approach to the welfare system, and became enraged. With a group of welfare mothers, many of them originally from Tallulah and Fordyce, she created the Clark County and Nevada Welfare Rights groups, calling for the creation of a food stamp program and a newborn nutrition program known as Women Infants and Children (WIC).

With allies Mary Wesley, Alversa Beals, Rosie Seals, Essie Henderson, and Emma Stampley, Duncan cut inroads through grassroots activism, plying astonished local media outlets with high-volume criticism and threats of greater protests and boycotts to come. What began as rabble-rousing and the threat of larger protest—a card played a decade earlier, prior to the Moulin Rouge agreement, and threatened at the state Legislature in 1963—gathered energy day by day.

After the civil rights debacle of the Laxalt administration, Duncan and the black community at large hoped for improved recognition and treatment from Democrat Mike O'Callaghan, a Korean War hero and former director of the State Department of Health and Welfare under

Grant Sawyer who won election in 1970 as a champion of the working class and public school teachers. But O'Callaghan was also a fiscal conservative, and when state revenues flagged as he took office he responded with steep cuts in the state's rock-ribbed welfare assistance to women and children.

Duncan had allies in O'Callaghan's administration, but she also had progressive activists with national political contacts who were willing to use Nevada as a test case for the country. Duncan's small organizations provided a template for two mass marches down Las Vegas Boulevard that not only stopped traffic, but also disrupted business in Strip casino-resorts.

More than 1,500 people gathered for the first march on March 6, 1971, with Dr. Ralph David Abernathy by Duncan's side and Jane Fonda, Donald Sutherland, and Dr. Benjamin Spock among the white celebrities walking in solidarity. Neal was a face in the crowd, observing the march and entering each casino. Although Duncan was the undeniable spokeswoman and driving spirit of the local movement, behind the scenes Nevada progressive Maya Miller provided thoughtful strategy and national contacts.

Deputies from the Clark County Sheriff's Office and casino security heavily monitored the marches. Although Sheriff Ralph Lamb's men had a reputation for brutality on the Westside, they spared the baton. Surely those who remembered Laxalt placing the National Guard on alert following the assassination of Dr. King were relieved by the restraint shown. Some activists attributed the officers' reserve more to the increased media presence than to a sense of empathy.

Most casino bosses understood that it was better to let the wave flow by than to put up barriers or display a show of force. The welfare mothers' march became a walk in the park.

The Hughes properties remained on a high alert that, by comparison, bordered on paranoia. What might have been a publicity debacle, or even a bloody riot, went off without major incidents. And after U.S. District Judge Roger Foley ordered that the women and children dumped from the assistance roles be restored, the O'Callaghan administration toed the line and repositioned itself as leading the battle for progress. Behind the scenes, O'Callaghan seethed. He didn't take being embarrassed lightly, but he slowly appeared to realize he'd been receiving poor counsel from his Northern Nevada advisor, Chris Schaller.

After a fashion, the welfare mothers and the Westside's working poor found a genuine ally in O'Callaghan thanks in part to the efforts of civil rights activists Jan Smith and Harriet Trudell, who served as his executive assistants in Clark County. It was Smith who, years earlier as a member of the local NAACP chapter, helped bring order to the group in the chaotic days following the assassination of Dr. King. The NAACP's tribute vigil in honor of the slain civil rights legend helped part of the community grieve while assuaging some of the fears in another segment of Southern Nevada. Trudell's relationship with Duncan helped O'Callaghan secure a legacy as a champion of Nevada's poor.

Duncan, once ragged and uneducated, became a professional activist and, Neal would observe, managed to do well for herself. She joined Operation Life shortly after it was founded in 1972 with the help of Jack Anderson and B. Mahlon Brown, son of the veteran Nevada legislator. With an ever-widening circle of political contacts, she expanded Operation Life's mission on the Westside to include providing not only assistance to welfare mothers and their children, but medical aid, childcare, and residential assistance as well. She eventually would earn a decent living with a salary coming from the Ford Foundation and other ancillary income associated with Operation Life programs. She also taught the white establishment that even the lowliest members of the minority community, when so motivated, could disrupt the action.

Orleck's generous assessment was tempered with a reality check: "Operation Life was a success, but only for a short time," she wrote. "There would be more cuts and restorations in the years to come. So when the cameras and celebrities left Las Vegas, Ruby Duncan and her band of welfare mothers set their sights on a more ambitious and, they hoped, more lasting goal: upgrading life on the black Westside of Las Vegas, a Jim Crow shantytown that lacked paved streets, telephones, even indoor plumbing into the 1950s and 1960s."

Neal served on the Operation Life board for several years during the 1970s, fought for it at the Legislature and within the political community, and helped steer funds in the nonprofit's direction. Duncan's energy and willingness to act, sometimes quite spontaneously, had its advantages and helped move forward the local cause of equality. But Neal also thought she sometimes fiercely defended her growing power base and income sources at the expense of other opportunities for the entire Westside.

Operation Life existed until 1990, just after its fiery founder's health began to fail. Ruby Duncan won some and lost some, but she could always say with certainty that she was chiefly responsible for one of the precious few times in Las Vegas history when the Westside's grass roots prevailed over the Strip's green felt.

6 Breaking Into the System

THE CIVIL RIGHTS MOVEMENT was forging historic change across America in the 1960s, but change came ever so slowly to Las Vegas and the Westside. Neal was changing, too. He'd spent nearly two decades in local politics, and had run unsuccessfully. Along the way he'd built sweat equity organizing voters and rallying for Nevada gubernatorial candidate Grant Sawyer and Democrats up and down the ticket. He played integral roles in helping to create job opportunities for blacks and Hispanics at REECo, the local construction trades, and inside the casino-hotel industry. He was known as a fighter who wasn't afraid to crack a law book and challenge authority.

The Westside's community leadership was often fractured by self-interest, but during the march toward civil rights the black population emerged as an important voting bloc. While many African Americans had been raised with a soft spot for the Republican Party, the "party of Lincoln," the Democrats were clearly perceived in the press as being more pro–civil rights in the modern era. Neal had experienced what passed for community involvement and later recalled, "Of course, the culture here is a little different, although we were yet still known here in Las Vegas as the 'Mississippi of the West' because we still had a lot of racial issues, a lot of prejudices going on. But then there were opportunities to do some things to make a change. So I saw this happening in the communities."

James Anderson, who had courted controversy and gained political experience as a grassroots organizer with Senator Alan Cranston of California before moving to Nevada in the early 1960s, influenced Neal. With his understanding of the labor movement and the importance of good jobs in poor communities, Anderson became the labor and industry chairman of the Las Vegas office of the NAACP. He built connections, hustled work opportunities. And once jokingly told the less experienced Neal, "You have Communist tendencies." Through Anderson Neal realized blacks would have to be willing to leave their community in order to improve it. One day Anderson told him, "Look, son, the way you change things for the best, you can't always change it from the outside. So you need to get involved."

Neal knew Anderson was right, but even with voting rights and improved registration and participation the odds were stacked in favor of the mostly white political machine. Neal attended rallies and studied the issues and players—"getting myself educated," he would call it—and decided to run for the state Assembly.

The process was frustrating with each county receiving one Senate assignment and the Assembly races run "at large," which heavily favored candidates with name recognition, money, and organization. There weren't many opportunities for community activists, no matter how motivated. He made three attempts to win a seat in the state Legislature. The early efforts generally went this way: "I'd get fifty posters and just tack them up around town because at that time all of the Assembly people ran at large. So I tacked up signs—the fifty posters."

With the ink still drying on federal civil rights legislation in 1964, and the intrepid legislator and civil rights activist Flora Dungan pitching a legal battle against the state, Neal had displayed the courage to do something previous black candidates had been loath to attempt: put his picture on those posters, and in doing so making an undeniable statement. And "people just went wild over this person who was so brave and brazen to put his picture on a poster."

Neal was welcomed in Dungan's home and came to admire her courage and energy. Although he didn't make the cut, Neal put forward pertinent issues in the campaign that generated attention from the legal establishment. He had cards printed stating his platform and passed them out everywhere he went, even in groups made uncomfortable by the approach of an imposing black man. Neal, an avid student of the law, believed in the importance of creating a law school for the state and a public defender position for Clark County, where minorities and indigents accused of crimes found themselves facing an imbalanced system whenever they set foot in a courtroom.

The lines had to be redrawn if minorities were ever going to receive representation at the Legislature, and progressive assemblywoman Dungan, a Clark County Democrat, decided she was just the person to do it. Born in 1917 in Minnesota to Russian immigrants, Dungan was a social worker and an accountant who in a long career distinguished herself as a tireless advocate for civil rights, the poor, and public education. She was also a Democratic Party mechanic, working her way up through the central committees and the county and state levels on the way to winning election to the Assembly in 1962. That same year the U.S. Supreme Court ruled in *Baker v. Carr* that redistricting issues weren't "political questions" and not subject to judicial review. Federal courts for the first time had an established right to review apportionment issues. In 1964, in *Reynolds v. Sims*, the court threw out the "little federal plan" in which states set up their legislative districts in imitation of Congress. "One man, one vote," it would be, the court decreed.

Beginning in 1964 with Dr. Clare Woodbury, Dungan brought a lawsuit against the state (*Dungan v. Sawyer*) that eventually forced reapportionment at the Legislature and fractured the timeworn borough system. Rapidly growing and multi-ethnic Clark County, for decades starving for votes at the Legislature, would finally begin to see relief.

The fight to redraw the lines dragged through the 1965 Legislature, which ended without a compromise. The U.S. District Court took up the matter, and the state's tradition was ruled unconstitutional. Although it took several bitter weeks and a special session of the Legislature to set the change in type and bring it into law, Clark County eventually added seven seats in the Senate and four more in the Assembly. (Dungan's relentless effort also resulted in an expansion of the University Board of Regents with more-populous Clark County receiving a majority of seats for the first time.)

This didn't ensure balance and fairness. The Legislature was apportioned based on population, but still relied on an at-large system that heavily favored incumbents and high name recognition. But it did lead to more opportunity.

Neal made a second attempt at state office, this time in the Senate, but took on a local political heavyweight and incumbent, B. Mahlon Brown. It was a long shot, and Brown won easily, but it once again put Neal's name before the public in the position of feisty underdog scrapper. The political establishment, and political parties, could no longer ignore blacks, and elected officials who did so courted upset.

Running against an incumbent Democrat was no way to make friends inside the local political machine, but Neal was listening to Anderson, not to those who implored him to wait his turn. When the political lines were once again drawn to impede minorities and split the black vote, in 1970 he moved his family to North Las Vegas, where Democratic Party loyalist Paul May Jr. appeared to be ensconced on his way to a long career highlighted by the Assembly Speaker's position in 1979.

The Neals' arrival at a then-new housing development called Regal Estates was just across the city line in the place locals called "Northtown." Neal had his sights set on getting the attention of the party and the mild-mannered May, whom Governor Mike O'Callaghan would describe as "a low-key leader who seldom, if ever, raised his voice."

Best of all for O'Callaghan and Nevada's Democratic leadership, May was a team player who never rocked the boat—just the opposite of Joe Neal.

"I decided to run for Assembly," Neal said. "Keep in mind I was not thinking about winning—that was never my thought. It would have been a miracle if I had won. There were other people in this state who needed to be represented and who could be represented if given the opportunity, and those were members of the black community," which was then Southern Nevada's largest minority population. Neal pushed May and generated support from the district's minorities.

"In that election, I only campaigned in the black community—purposely!—because I knew that we had a sufficient amount of votes that could really, really push Paul to do some things," Neal recalled. "One of the things I wanted him to do was create a district that blacks could be elected from and cut back on the status quo...I was campaigning for reapportionment. I stayed strictly in the black community, and when the vote came, I almost beat Paul May."

It may have improved his profile in the local community, but it did him no good with O'Callaghan and the state's top Democrats. Neal had lost in the primary, but not long afterward he received a phone call from a relieved and somewhat perplexed May. Why had he run against a fellow Democrat? Wasn't he concerned about repercussions? Didn't he want to work within the system?

No, it was all about reapportionment. If substantive change in representation was going to come, it wouldn't arrive by going along and getting along.

May asked to meet Neal and drove to his office at REECo. Neal was waiting for him and, as those who knew him would have guessed, was prepared for his visitor. On a blackboard, Neal took chalk and wrote a political schematic that pointed toward the future as he envisioned it: a state senator, two assemblymen, a school board trustee, a university regent, a county commissioner, and a member of the hospital board of trustees.

"These are the offices that I'm looking for in terms of reapportionment," Neal said.

May was a machine man, but he also was a devoted public servant. He respected the cause of civil rights, and he also knew he'd been fortunate to prevail in the primary against an opponent with few dollars in his campaign coffers.

"Okay," May replied to Neal's surprise. "We will help you get this."

From there it was necessary to round up enough votes to push through the historic changes. Neal turned to Frank Young, a Republican who, in addition to having a background in science as defense contractor and Nevada Test Site manager at EG&G, was an active and pragmatic Republican who'd been elected to the state Assembly in 1966. Young saw reapportionment as a question of fairness—one person, one vote. When Republicans took control of the Assembly in 1969, Young rose to become Elections Committee Chairman, and Neal and others had an inside advocate willing to act not only on behalf of party but also in the name of fairness for bustling Southern Nevada. Neal's motivations were layered: his party interest was subsumed by the knowledge of the importance of bringing political balance south from Carson City. He also knew it was the only way Westside's underclass would ever be heard in the halls of the Legislature.

With Democrat May and Republican Young carving a trail, Neal traveled to Carson City during the 1971 session and met privately with Young, who showed him a draft of the working reapportionment map.

"Is this it? Is this what you want?" Young asked.

"Yes, that's exactly what I want," Neal replied.

But that wasn't everything the O'Callaghan administration was looking for. A Republican-majority Assembly made O'Callaghan's battles during the 1971 session more difficult. When the reapportionment bill passed, the Democrats sued. Neal found himself at odds with his own party.

"I had to get some Republicans to come on my side to fight this in court," he recalled. "Mike O'Callaghan was the governor and was very popular. Of course, he could have stopped the lawsuit if he wanted to, but he didn't say anything about it. The Legislature had to defend what they'd done."

Legislative Counsel Frank Daykin was being pressured from both sides of the issue, and conservative Democrats who weren't known for their support of civil rights in the state were up in arms over the proposed changes.

The Democrats tried to protect some of the old guard, and in doing so protected only the imbalance. They were on the wrong side of history. "They had created a couple of single-seat districts," Neal told an interviewer in 2008. "One was a district in the black community, and one was in (conservative Democrat) Jim Gibson's district. I think they might have had a couple single seats up north, but the rest of them were dual seats. So we filed a countersuit to create all single seats for the Senate and the Assembly. We couldn't lose because now we had the Legislature on our side who had passed the bill that we thought was good."

It was good enough for a three-judge panel at the U.S. Ninth Circuit on December 13, 1971, to rule in favor of the Legislature's action and put an end to a rare embarrassment by the O'Callaghan administration. As 1972 began, backward Nevada suddenly had a new political playing field—one on which Joe Neal could find traction.

At first, Neal appeared to have the 1972 state Senate campaign for newly minted District 4 all to himself. "I would like to see the community in which I'm running recognized as a place to be somebody."

He might have been somebody, but his then-controversial platform of no-fault insurance and increased medical services was almost certain to get him treated like a nobody in Carson City. "No one should be evicted from their homes because they don't have the ability to pay their rent. The state takes no responsibility for adequate housing." Nor, he would soon discover, did it have any intention of doing so without being dragged unwillingly from its libertarian pretenses.

But perhaps Neal should have anticipated what would come next when he received a challenge for the state Senate from Woodrow Wilson, who at that time was the only black in the Legislature. Born in Morton, Mississippi, on August 28, 1915, Wilson joined the migration of Southern blacks to Southern Nevada in search of work in 1942 and found it at Henderson's American Potash Chemical Corporation and later Kerr-McGee plants. A former president of the local NAACP chapter and chairman of the Nevada State Advisory Committee for the U.S. Commission on Civil Rights, Wilson had tried to push through an early version of the state's Fair Housing Act. He had a hand in starting the first black-owned bank and was active in the Westside's chamber of commerce.

The Republican also was receiving plenty of help behind the scenes from friends in the Democratic Party who seethed at the idea of being one-upped by uppity Joe Neal. With an estimated $50,000 in cash on hand, Wilson had more than enough campaign funds at his disposal, and be also benefitted from a sudden change in Neal's working hours at REECo.

A respectful and professional atmosphere suddenly was defined by clockwork precision where Neal's hours were concerned. He was ordered to come in at 8 a.m., take a lunch hour at noon, and leave at 5 p.m. No exceptions. It was, of course, intended to interrupt his campaigning. Neal responded by working late into the evening going door to door. He met anyone who answered a door in his district in a classic shoe-leather campaign that would define his style for years to come.

"They tried to pull some things at my job because the people I worked for had connections with the wider white business community," he said.

Neal spearheaded the Greater Las Vegas Plan that sought to break the color barrier in the local trade unions. It generated mixed results.

He used his increasing understanding of procedural rules to best benefit, but was no favorite of the Associated General Contractors, who tried unsuccessfully to oust him from his chairmanship for pleading his views in the press. At one point, the contractors managed to generate a 10–2 vote to remove Neal, only to be reminded they had failed to win over any minority members. Neal remained adamant in the face of foot-dragging by business agents and presidents of local craft organizations. Although they would eventually relent under the threat of a U.S. Department of Justice order, and saw the results Neal had generated in integrating the Nevada Test Site, they weren't about to politically reward the candidate or any Democrats who sidled up to him.

For its part, at one point the O'Callaghan administration sought to slip $1,500 into the struggling Wilson's coffers to bolster his sagging campaign. Neal discovered the move and, with help from his longtime friend and onetime Clark County district attorney George Foley, he filed a suit that threatened once again to embarrass the proud governor.

Actual proof of the donation was tucked inside a local bank and out of reach of the civil suit, but Neal and Foley knew that Wilson, who started the Westside's first credit union, kept his campaign account at First National in the Twin Lakes area. A white female friend of the campaign volunteered to enter the bank with the simple request of a harried secretary.

"Where do you keep the cancelled checks?" she asked. The teller was happy to show her the way, and even assisted in the photocopying.

The lawsuit was eventually resolved, but bygones were not yet bygones.

"I was not running without name recognition, and that's why, I think, that I was able to beat Woody so badly," he recalled to an interviewer. "All of a sudden, the white establishment, including O'Callaghan, was faced with a Joe Neal coming to the Legislature.... I spent $500 on that race."

In the wake of the historic 1972 election, Neal was 36 years old and determined to make the political groundbreaking more than a token victory. Not only had his Senate win been a first for blacks in Nevada, but it also represented one of a handful of times the state's voters had sent a progressive to the upper house. The Senate had long been a bastion of Nevada's business class riddled with attorneys and insurance men seeking to strengthen their positions in their home districts.

"We never have been districted to the point that black people could elect their own representative before," he told an Associated Press reporter, adding that his simple goal was to be "a protector of poor folks and black folks."

The spirit of FDR and Louisiana's Long brothers was strong. He couldn't resist openly envisioning further reapportionment that gave blacks a chance to enter the judiciary. At the Legislature, he'd seek funding for medical scholarships for minorities, encourage large businesses to provide daycare facilities, and mandate that banks loan to minority businesses.

Such goals were considered outlandishly liberal, even socialist, in Nevada. Neal's awakening at the first session would at times be rude, but his colleagues would soon find where he stood.

Neal, meanwhile, was building his own network and constituency, one that didn't always include allies from the predominantly white Democratic Party. He was active on the central committee, but was known as much for his pugnacity as his team play.

One feature writer for the *The Valley Times*, struggling for the best words to describe his controversial subject in a 1972 profile before the election, offered, "The name 'Joe Neal' is widely known around North Las Vegas, as well as around the state, but it is not always thought of in the best light." Neal "is frequently spoken of in political terms. He is often called a 'radical.'"

Neal's credentials were pigeonholed. Although he was the chairman of the Equal Opportunity Board and the Las Vegas Plan, an active member of the Catholic Welfare Board and the Clark County Democratic Central Committee, and "has considerable influence in the black community," he was also considered a volatile rabble-rouser, a "Thoughtful Radical," who used "Confrontation Technique to aid NLV blacks," as the headline trumpeted. A photo of Neal, his wife, and their young children, Charisse and Tania, accompanied the surprisingly positive piece that—unlike others—included his hard-fought civil rights accomplishments in Louisiana, his military service, education, and even his success in forcing black hiring and apprenticeship in the long-segregated local building trades. For an activist used to backhands from the press and low blows from columnists such as Paul Price of the *Las Vegas Sun*, it was a journalistic breakthrough.

Although Neal would tone down his rhetoric as the 1970s wore on, his references to confrontation and the controversial young civil rights leaders of the day were considered alarming in the Democratic Party. "My philosophy is about the same as Martin Luther King's, but I lean toward confrontation techniques," Neal said. "Like (H.) Rap Brown and Stokely Carmichael, I started out nonviolent. But when I saw my friends' heads broken, I felt I had to fight back."

It was not the kind of rhetoric likely to endear him to party bosses, but Neal was already showing a lack of concern for the party line.

If he saw life filtered through a racial lens, the image wasn't necessarily out of focus.

"There are racists on the city council," he said plainly. "The fact that the council imposed a curfew on North Las Vegas black areas during the 'riots' in the fall of 1969, when any rioting which occurred was in Las Vegas, indicates segregationist thinking."

Then he said something that made hearts skip in North Las Vegas City Hall, which had long enjoyed federal funding to address issues of minority housing, poverty, and education and had relatively little to show for it. If officials weren't willing to roll up their sleeves, Neal and a new generation of black leaders would be glad to take their places. "We who live in this area cannot put up with that for long. We could build our own city. North Las Vegas gets so much federal funds because of the black people. We could take those funds ourselves."

If Neal saw the world through his unapologetic black experience, his eyesight was 20-20. Of the efforts of Aaron Williams, the first black elected to the North Las Vegas City Council, Neal offered a plaudit and a reality check about conditions in black and white neighborhoods: "There are common needs of both communities, but there are also specific needs of the white and black communities alone."

Addressing society's inequities in unambiguous terms would become a Neal trademark in the years to come. Doing so in the Southern Nevada press in the early 1970s made him nothing less than a radical.

Interrupting the Party

ALTHOUGH IN ENSUING YEARS Joe Neal would be recognized as a fiercely independent and outspoken senator and for his knowledge of the Nevada Legislature's rules, written and unwritten, on January 15, 1973, when he first set foot in Carson City as an elected representative of the people, he couldn't help but be filled with emotion. Accompanied by his wife and two daughters as well as a sister and brother-in-law, who had traveled from Oakland, California, to the Nevada capital for the occasion, Neal had come a long way from the sharecropped fields of Mounds. If his story had ended there, he would have been able to call his journey a success. Reflecting on that time, Neal's childhood friend Ernestine Madison recalled, "I was excited for him. I just felt like, to me, this was just a victory. Because I knew where we came from."

He was just getting started.

A slight drizzle fell on the overcast day, but the weather was mild for Carson City, then a town of slightly more than 16,000 residents. With an elevation of 4,800 feet in the Carson Range and in the long shadow of the Sierra Nevada, the town was named for frontiersman Christopher "Kit" Carson and began in 1851 as a stage stop before becoming the territorial capital in 1861 and gaining its loftier title once Nevada was granted statehood in 1864. Beginning full-time in July 1862 as a reporter with the *Territorial Enterprise* of nearby Virginia City, a young Sam Clemens covered three sessions of the territorial legislature and the state's raucous Constitutional Convention in a satirical style that would help gain him fame as Mark Twain. It might easily be said that the Nevada Legislature, with its history of biennial meetings of citizen lawmakers buffeted by the powerful political fixers and kingmakers of the day, was especially designed for the satirist. It was a place where Comstock barons, stock-swindling bankers, and real estate–rich ranchers played checkers with lawmakers and crowned each other king. By the 1970s, the casino kings of Las Vegas and Reno held prime seats at the table.

"No man's life, liberty, or property are safe when the Legislature's in session," Twain once quipped. During a speech in Hartford, Connecticut, several years after leaving Nevada, he observed, "I think I can say, and say with pride, that we have some legislatures that bring higher prices than any in the world."

It was, in short, no place to keep one's hard-fought reputation, and Neal wouldn't have been blamed if he'd turned on his heel that first day. He was the first African American to stand in the building as a member of the Senate. Thanks in great part to the reapportionment battle plan he'd helped to carry out, the 1973 session included black Assembly freshmen the Reverend Marion D. Bennett Sr. and Cranford L. Crawford. Bennett would hold the seat a decade, Crawford just a term, and Lonie Chaney would join them two years later in what for the Nevada Legislature was a veritable invasion of color.

Neal arrived with a sense of pride and ached to get started.

"I was mostly thinking about what I was going to do—the type of issues that I was going to tackle," he recalled. "Being the first person of African-American descent to serve in the Senate, I felt that it was going to be difficult to do the things that I wanted to do because the other legislators who had been part of the process for some time wanted me to have a waiting period to learn about the process and sit back and be quiet. I was aware that I only had two sessions in a four-year period, and that if I wanted to do anything, I had to start from day one."

It wouldn't be easy for many reasons, not the least of which was the hushed and conservative tradition of the Senate, the upper house that was known to stand closest to the state's power brokers. That is, a full step to the right of center politically.

Future Nevada attorney general, governor, and U.S. Senator Richard Bryan was elected to the state Senate in 1972 after two terms in the Assembly. It became very clear to Bryan in the earliest days of the

1973 session that his fellow freshman from North Las Vegas wasn't in Carson City to win any popularity contests.

"Four of us that year were new, and Joe was the first African-American state senator in Nevada," Bryan reflected. "The Senate was a different institution. In some ways, it may have been better. It was certainly far more collegial. There was very little partisanship."

The important points of division were geographic, not party-driven. For instance, Senator Cliff Young, a Northern Republican, was much more socially moderate than Democrat Jim Gibson. And Senate Majority Leader Mahlon Brown and Finance Committee Chairman Floyd Lamb, both Democrats, would have been labeled right wing elsewhere.

On the other end of the spectrum was Neal, who was clearly an outsider and appeared quite comfortable in that position. "He was absolutely fearless and uninhibited in terms of expressing his views," Bryan said. "In other words, what you saw with Joe Neal is what you got. He was not ingratiating himself with leadership, and sometimes, quite frankly, it irritated folks. Later in his career I think Joe earned a measure of respect. He proved that he was not just a guy who was a bomb thrower. But Joe was not hesitant to stir the pot."

That included butting heads with former Washoe County district attorney William Raggio, a Republican rising star on his way to carving out a legendary legislative career. While Raggio was "recognized as a team player and very, very smart," Bryan observed, "let me say that Joe's style was abrasive, and it didn't serve him well initially, and I think Joe would acknowledge that. As people got to know Joe better, they realized that he was not just a so-called troublemaker. He had deep-seated feelings. Even though he was not often popular with leadership or the group that ran the Senate in those early years, I think Joe was not reluctant to be the only dissenting vote, and he deserves credit for that."

Bryan recalled Neal's early efforts to raise the issue of highway safety when it came to long-haul truckers pulling a third trailer, which was legal in several Western states. Neal went on the attack. "Joe was uninhibited, unhesitating in terms of when he saw something that was not right, he'd raise questions about it."

The Legislature was predominantly made up of what Bryan called "the old Nevada," and in general was a body that went out of its way not to call out either members or the governor. Outside Nevada, legislator Warren "Snowy" Monroe might have been considered backward and even racist, but up north the *Elko Independent* editor was understood as a well-meaning "real curmudgeon type." Helen Herr might have been celebrated in some circles for becoming the first female state senator, but it was also true she was a conservative who was outspoken against feminist issues and the Equal Rights Amendment. Both were Nevada Democrats in good standing.

Although modern reapportionment had first passed through the Legislature in 1967, it took until the 1973 session to leave the judicial arena. That made the 1973 session easily one of the most important in state history. Where the Senate had been historically filled with one person for each of Nevada's seventeen counties, after reapportionment, for the first time booming Southern Nevada had increased representation—and its minority population gained genuine footing in politics for the first time. "Clearly reapportionment had a dramatic change," Bryan observed. "But basically many of the senators who survived that reapportionment represented the old school from the South."

And Neal? "Joe was cut out of a different bolt of cloth," Bryan said. In a body in which it was considered "bad form" for senators to debate a matter on the floor—differences were to be settled privately and in committee—Neal was not shy about expressing his view of legislation. What made him doubly devilish to the Legislature's veterans was his insistence on actually reading the bills and invoking rules of order. Some felt disrespected, but journalists and historians might be left to wonder whether Neal's skin color was as off-putting to some as his political manners. "Joe's position was, with all due respect, 'I got elected by the same group of folks you did,'" Bryan said.

"The Senate was conservative in 1973," Neal recalled. "There was no difference between Democrats and Republicans in the Senate. There was one woman in the Senate, Helen Herr, and she was opposed to the Equal Rights Amendment. Ideologically, you would think that there would have been a difference, but there was not a difference. You couldn't tell them apart. You might say that I was the only true Democrat that was there."

Neal's ability to go along and get along lasted approximately three days. On the afternoon of January 18, Governor Mike O'Callaghan gave his State of the State speech at the outset of the fifty-seventh session of the state Legislature. There was much to admire about O'Callaghan's heartfelt emphasis on improving Nevada's bedraggled mental health system and care-worn welfare, public education, and higher education programs. Like most of those who had come before him, he was longer on compassion than on calling for a substantive tax increase, but he used his broad brush to paint in bright colors: "Our State, then, is in excellent health. We continue to prosper; we continue to grow."

Sitting quietly in his place on the floor, almost anonymous in a room where everyone would eventually know his name, Neal considered the economic status of the citizens he represented. He knew O'Callaghan, as a fellow Catholic, was an advocate of civil rights and a man who kept a hand out to the downtrodden, but he also wondered whether the governor was talking about the same state his neighbors lived in. A call for no new taxes and a lament about the failure of the federal government to make good on its annual promises to financially assist programs for the poor and mentally ill sounded more like the status quo than a bold new direction.

Then O'Callaghan tossed a bouquet to the tough-on-crime contingent by calling for the death penalty for the killers of cops and prison guards. Although the governor had been a dedicated advocate for the state's beleaguered penitentiary officers, to Neal it smacked of a cop-out at a time the headlines were full of frightening tales of violence perpetrated by groups such as the Weather Underground and the Black Panther Party. Neal knew that Las Vegas blacks had far more to fear from Sheriff Ralph Lamb's deputies than the other way around.

"I'm sitting there as he gave his State of the State address, knowing, of course, that someone from the press will ask me about this particular statement," Neal recalled in a 2008 interview. "So when they asked me about that, I said, 'Why give the death penalty to one who kills policemen? Why not give the death penalty for killing a janitor? Life is life. It's just as important to a janitor as it would be to a policeman.'

"The press just took that and ate it up."

And *Las Vegas Sun* columnist Paul Price, a friend of the sheriff and a fierce bulldog in the employ of firebrand publisher Hank Greenspun, immediately placed Neal on his editorial radar. It was the start of an ugly relationship.

"O'Callaghan was angry over the fact that I had kind of upped him on that particular issue," Neal would remember. "So our road would become a little rocky from that going on during that particular session."

When Senate Bill 545 came to the floor, Neal went further still.

"I will submit further, Mr. President, that killing a police officer shouldn't be any different than killing any other ordinary citizen," he said to stunned silence. "By giving this type of coverage to a police officer who is armed with a lethal weapon, I tremble at the consequences that might develop with the passage of this law. By the passage of this particular bill, we are elevating the police officers to a status, which we haven't seen since the storm troopers in Nazi Germany.

"The question should be whether or not the police officer is more essential to the maintenance of society than, say, a doctor, a farmer, a carpenter, who gives us shelter. I think that he is not.

"This bill predisposes [sic] that a peace officer is and always will be a just and kind individual who needs this type of protection. I would submit that this could not be further from the truth. As I have stated, the police officers, particularly in the State of Nevada, are armed individuals and they don't always administer justice to our Nevada citizens.... I would like to say, also, that we as elected officials should be concerned not to exploit the fear and anger that has been generated in discussion of this particular matter."

Neal's rhetoric was written off in some quarters as overheated and riddled with bias, but even in his hyperbole he was expressing a view of the world few of his colleagues had considered. For a black man in a society of white police officers, it was rarely a relief to encounter a cop on the beat.

By 1973, the state-by-state battle to forge an amendment to the U.S. Constitution spelling out equal rights for women was the talk in capitals from Tallahassee, Florida to Olympia, Washington. In Carson City, Nevada lawmakers were moving with trademark slowness when it came to progressive causes. A joint resolution had passed in the Senate

Judiciary Committee and was being maligned with nonsensical rhet-oric—the ERA will force Nevadans to use a unisex bathroom!—and outright fear-mongering. The simple truth was the conservative white men, some of them of equally conservative religious beliefs, had no intention of embracing the changes in society despite growing support for the measure in the political and activist communities. The "Battle of the Sexes" between Billie Jean King and Bobby Riggs that year might have been entertaining on television, but in the Nevada Legislature anti-ERA senators were playing tennis without a net.

The ERA's grassroots support, exemplified by its statewide coor-dinator Kate Butler and political activist Jean Ford, had been unsuc-cessful in garnering much vocal support in Carson City. Senators Tom Wilson and Richard Bryan coauthored Nevada's first attempt at pass-ing the Equal Rights Amendment for women during the 1973 session. Neal offered impassioned testimony and attempted to shoot down the "fallacious" arguments against the amendment, which received public support from conservative organizations that included the Church of Jesus Christ of Latter-day Saints and the John Birch Society. Even Herr, a Democrat and the only woman in the Senate, came out against the legislation, claiming the act would deliberately undermine the family. "This will be a great day in history for rights of women if we vote to reject the ERA," she said.

"Until I made this speech, nobody knew where I stood on equal rights—not even the women who were pushing it," he recalled. Neal left no confusion on the issue in one floor speech given on the last day of February.

"Mr. President, as a black man, my appreciation for equal rights for any citizen is as equal or greater than any senator present here today," he began. "Yes, I can understand the hopes and aspirations in attempt-ing to forge a declaratory principle as encompassed in the Equal Rights Amendment. I can also understand the despair that is generated when one sees this amendment come from the Judiciary Committee with a recommendation of 'Do Not Pass.' Who says or gives you the right to deny to your sisters that which we will not deny ourselves?

"Women have played a major role in the development of this coun-try. They were with you when you landed on Plymouth Rock. They were with you when you moved westward; yes, they were with you when you took up the mantle to repel Nazi Germany. They were with you on the Bataan Death March, yet all her noble acts in service to mankind have been overlooked by you because you do not consider her an equal."

Neal assailed the fomented fears of restroom privacy and the fracturing of the American family. He knew the ERA was especially anathema to the senators of the Mormon faith, including top Democrat Jim Gibson, but he refused to return to his seat.

Then he hit them where it really hurt—right in their windy expressions of faith and patriotism.

"For the past several weeks in the Senate, I have watched with great concern how each morning at the convening of the Senate we pay homage to God and extol the virtues of a 'free society,'" he said. "I have seen the President of this Senate each morning turn and say proudly 'will you follow me in the Pledge of Allegiance to the Flag.' I always flinch with amazement when we come to that portion of the Pledge of Allegiance that says 'one nation, under God, indivisible, with liberty and justice for all.' With liberty and justice for whom? Certainly not for women, certainly not for Blacks and certainly not for Indians. It is liberty and justice for the white Caucasian male, who by his pride is willing, by his vote against Equal Rights for Women, to make the Senate Chamber a den of inequity instead of a place for liberty and justice for all."

He implored his perturbed colleagues not to exercise a power "buttressed by fear. Whatever the American has and will become will be a reflection of your action here today."

Neal had spoken his piece and in doing so further distanced himself from the collegial club to which he'd just gained entry. But his speech was a reminder to his critics that he had no intention of sitting silent while aggrieved minorities were trying to be heard. The measure, which had passed in the Assembly for the first time, lost 16–4 in the Senate but had at least come to a vote. The ERA's proponents would have to wait two more years to try again.

In Reno, the *Nevada State Journal* opined, "The defeat of the Equal Rights Amendment places Nevada in the august company of Arizona,

Georgia and Utah, all states which vetoed the amendment this year. The defeat does not speak well for the general level of reason or compassion in this state.

"It does indicate that sexism is firmly ingrained in the minds of many Nevada legislators (not necessarily in their constituencies)."

One of Neal's memories from his earliest days in the Senate was a meeting with Leola Armstrong, who served as secretary of the Senate from 1958–1981 and was renowned for her knowledge of politics and procedure. She was also married to influential *Las Vegas Sun* columnist Bryn Armstrong. She called Neal into her office and chatted with him privately, then handed him a heavy tome. It was *Mason's Manual,* the rules of order used at the Nevada Legislature. Some lessons only experience could teach Neal, but for the rest *Mason's Manual* was the definitive source.

"Leola Armstrong, who was the secretary of the Senate for a long time, called me when I first got elected," he recalled. "She gave me her *Mason's Manual* and said, 'Learn this book. If you learn this book, you're going to be able to represent yourself very well on the floor of the Senate.' And I studied that sucker—studied it and studied it. It became very handy to me because many years later I was able to do things to them that set them back on their heels and beat them at their own game when they tried to do things. I found great delight in doing that."

Neal had generated headlines and, thanks to Armstrong's sage advice, already had shown a skilled understanding of the rules of the process. But he also had a lot to learn about the Legislature's real players, and the lawmakers who acted on their behalf. It was a lesson he learned after drafting a bill to restore the rights of ex-felons, something enormously controversial at the time, but an issue that affected Southern Nevada's poor and minority neighborhoods, places in which families were one breadwinner from the welfare line.

"This whole trend had started, and they were sending a lot of blacks to prison," Neal said. "The difficulty they were having once they got out was getting a job. So my first piece of legislation was to restore the rights to ex-felons once they had been out for a period of time and had no greater offense than a traffic ticket and to allow them to enter the workforce, to get a job, and not have that crime or whatever it was being held over them. I introduced this bill, and I had some opposition."

In the Nevada Legislature, no one ever went wrong being tough on crime. In 1973, lawmakers on both sides of the aisle were eager to follow Governor O'Callaghan's lead. Opposition to Neal's legislation bordered on fierce. Then, one day a stocky older fellow ambled up to him and offered him an outstretched hand. It was the rather infamous mitt of former Storey County senator James "Slats" Slattery, who was known as the go-to guy for Northern Nevada's casino crowd and those who operated in the shadows of mainstream business.

"I didn't know Jim Slattery from Adam, but I did know that he had been a senator," recalled Neal, who prior to the '73 session could count his trips to Northern Nevada on one hand. "He came to me and asked if I needed any help with that bill. I said yes, and he took that bill, and he ran it through the Legislature. That was the only piece of legislation that I was able to pass in 1973."

Neal was proud of the success, but the issue was much more complicated than he'd imagined. Slattery was no friend of civil rights. He'd worked hard against civil rights legislation in the early 1960s. He was, however, on close speaking terms with Mustang Ranch brothel baron Joe Conforte, an ex-felon whose wife, Sally Conforte, had managed to be introduced to Neal early in the session through the Northern Nevada activist and reverend Willie Wynn.

Weeks after the end of the session, when Neal was home with his family and back on the job at REECo, he nearly choked on his morning coffee. Slattery had been no Adam, all right. Far from it. One of Slattery's pals was the seedy Conforte, who might also benefit from Neal's legislation and lack familiarity with the ways of Carson City.

The irony had been pointed out to *Sun* columnist Paul Price, who had been waiting for a chance to pounce. The journalistic hatchet man had a scoop. By his count, only one of the twenty-two bills Neal had offered in his first term had survived." It was a law allowing the reinstatement of the civil rights of convicted felons, which under Price's practiced hand emerged as a gift from Neal to Mustang Ranch brothel owner Joe Conforte. The columnist's reasoning placed Conforte behind the scenes because Neal relied on the whoremonger's legislative point man Slattery.

Price was at his vicious best, declaring that of the many bills Neal served up, "exactly one passed. It happened to provide certain possible advantages for the ex-con and No. 1 panderer of Northern Nevada—Joe Conforte.... What would a state senator push out of his way to help this felon and trader in sex?...The matter will be explored later. It should be heartrending to let some people hang on the hook a few days."

The depiction was pure Price, who'd cut his teeth in the wild Los Angeles news racket and had served loyally as Benjamin Siegel's publicity man at the Flamingo before the infamous Bugsy was murdered in 1947. Price was not only known as a wickedly gifted deadline wordsmith, but one who was not above accepting gratuities in exchange for favorable coverage or none at all. Accepting payoffs wasn't considered a character flaw among Las Vegas journalists of his generation.

The brutal attempt at crushing a freshman legislator was not only heavy-handed, but bespoke of the power of the real hand behind the pen. Price wasn't above remaining silent on the subject of Conforte when it suited his interests or those of his friends, including defense lawyer and future federal judge Harry Claiborne. Most elected officials would have hunkered down, or sent a political ally to negotiate a truce.

Neal instead went directly to *Sun* publisher Hank Greenspun and demanded a retraction for the hit job.

Neal wasn't just apple-polishing the powerful and mercurial publisher. Greenspun had been an ally, but he was no altruist. In fact, Greenspun was a behind-the-scenes promoter of the very bill over which his bulldog had ripped into Neal. It was a moment that revealed not only Greenspun's association with mobbed-up Teamsters boss James Riddle Hoffa, but also Neal's skill at playing just enough hardball to deliver the message that he was no pushover.

"If Mr. Price had a question concerning my motivation, then he should have contacted me, for I most certainly would have given him an explanation. I would have told him that my motivation for introducing such a bill came from an ex-con in my district named Butler, and a meeting I had with you and James Hoffa on Feb. 22, 1973, relative to this matter."

Of course Greenspun remembered. And Price would never forget it.

The first session was full of lessons, some political and others philosophical. Neal many times considered how different his perception of the world was from his colleagues. As a Catholic, he was opposed to the death penalty and said so. But in tough-on-crime Nevada, that was considered political suicide.

When the Senate, in keeping with polite tradition, sought to acknowledge the reelection of the president, in this case a Richard Nixon mired in the Watergate scandal, Neal watched fellow Democrats fall in line out of a sense of historic protocol. The freshman from North Las Vegas declined. The vote was 19-to-1 to acknowledge the election outcome.

Like most elected officials, Neal followed the Watergate proceedings with interest. He became more personally connected when he learned that his old friend from his Louisiana voter registration days, attorney John Doar, was involved in drawing up the articles of impeachment. One of his researchers was a young lawyer named Hillary Rodham.

By the time Joe Neal's first legislative session ended, he'd gained a reputation and had already picked up a nickname from his old friend, attorney George Foley.

"He would say, 'Well, if it isn't old 19-to-1,'" Neal recalled, laughing.

Poetry, Prose, and Pay Toilets

NEAL ANIMATED THE expression made famous by former New York governor Mario Cuomo, who observed, "You campaign in poetry. You govern in prose." In the 1975 session of the Legislature, he did plenty of both. Just days into the proceedings, he once again stepped into the breach on behalf of the struggling Equal Rights Amendment. The studied senator Spike Wilson addressed the gathering and provided the amendment's legal details. Neal then infused a little fire and soul into the argument.

"This is an amendment that has been in labor for over 50 years, and the time has come for the State of Nevada to aid in giving it birth," he said. "There are those attempting to abort this amendment with the barren concept, and I say barren concept of states' rights, with fears of destroying the family, with the drafting of women, with the increase in homosexual marriages, and some have said it is too broad to accomplish any good."

Where other of the amendment's supporters expressed their opinions in understated tones, and some in whispers in the halls of the Legislature, the senator from North Las Vegas turned up the volume on what he perceived as the hypocrisy and chauvinism being displayed by his colleagues.

"I was talking to one of my colleagues this morning in the Senate lounge, and I heard another objection: that it is going to take too much money to enforce the law if passed." He then gave fellow senators a history lesson dating to Nevada's constitutional convention that put the states' rights issue in perspective. And, once again, he raised the plight of blacks and others who had long struggled for civil equality in a society controlled by white men. Then he finished with words from Langston Hughes's *Let America Be America Again*.

The poem is a trumpet blast and a reminder of the vast difference between the promise and potential of America and the reality for poor whites, Indians, blacks, and immigrants. It reads in part:

Oh let America be America again.

The land that never has been yet,

And yet must be.

The land where every man is free.

It was a stirring moment that, once again, reminded conservative legislators that despite a previous defeat Neal had no intention of slowing his assault on the status quo. In future remarks, Neal would once again speak up on the importance of creating a national health insurance plan that covered not just the elderly and those in abject poverty, but the vast working class that spent its income on food and shelter and had little left over for the luxury of seeing a doctor.

And he used a blunderbuss to attack a Senate resolution meant to restate the obvious, that Congress would refrain from enacting any law to "abridge the right to keep and bear arms." At the time, Congress was considering a ban on cheap so-called "Saturday night special" handguns that had flooded urban streets. Neal was no stranger to firearms; he'd worn one on his hip during his years in the Air Force. But he also saw a growing epidemic of handgun violence in the nation. He tried to remind his colleagues that the Second Amendment was written in a very different time.

"If we were living in the 1700s and had just gotten out from under the domination of England, I would assume that this would be appropriate," he said. "But I would like to remind you that when that provision was drawn into the Constitution, we had mere muskets, the old rods, balls of lead, which you had to stuff in order to get off a shot."

In the end, Neal's critics wrote off his remarks as those of a hopeless liberal content to shoot off his mouth in the face of the sacred Second Amendment.

When his colleagues were embarrassed by the press accounts of their attempt to hold some proceedings in secret, Neal seized the moment. During a hearing on the subject of broadening the Senate's standing rule on meeting closure, he cut the idea to the quick. "I think if you stripped all of the vernacular that we have heard here today, the basic question is the public's right to know," he said, scoring points with reporters present. "I would submit that that is a question that would take precedence over anything that we have discussed here thus far."

Then he pulled back the curtain on the social club to which he was only a member in name only.

"Let's not fool ourselves," Neal said. "There are groups that function here in this body together, of like minds, cliques, or whatever you want to call them. They can come together on things and decide when to close a meeting.... I don't think that they [meetings] should be closed because we are here for public business and if we cannot sit here and conduct the public business and enjoy the right of the public to know what we are doing, then I think that we should go out of business."

The measure returned to the shadows, and Neal had made his point. But he'd also further distanced himself from the club.

New Hampshire native Sam Foss was a librarian who enjoyed a modicum of celebrity as a poet of the common man in the late 1800s, but what fame he enjoyed had largely faded by the time of his death in 1911. In a legislative session filled with great potential for human progress but held back by conservative status quo politics on both sides of the aisle, Neal grew frustrated by the foot-dragging on almost any measure that would help Nevadans who needed it most. He conjured Foss's *The Calf Path* in hopes of pricking a few consciences with the poem's lesson about not choosing the crooked path simply because it is well-traveled.

> *For men are prone to go it blind*
> *Along the calf paths of the mind,*
> *And work away from sun to sun*
> *To do what other men have done.*

Uncharacteristically for a lawmaker already well known among his fellow senators for his fondness for the microphone, on that day Neal offered no additional commentary.

Neal's first-session acrimony with Governor O'Callaghan and his point man Chris Schaller had embarrassed the administration and certainly increased the profile of the freshman senator. The sparring was not without its purpose: O'Callaghan, a devout Catholic conscious of the needs of Nevada's poor, minorities, and mentally ill, had a rare opportunity to make substantive changes. But as ever there was a great temptation to speak too much and accomplish too little from the comfortable confines of the Governor's Mansion. Neal proposed privately to keep the governor on his toes.

The 1973 session was just weeks past sine die when Neal let it be known he was seriously considering running against O'Callaghan in the 1974 race. It was good for a laugh with the press, already arching its eyebrows at the outspoken Democrat, but it gave Neal an opportunity to remind the governor to keep his eye on the ball and on "people problems" of health care and rising food prices. O'Callaghan could almost be heard cursing Neal's insistence, but in time he'd grow to respect his antagonist and ally.

It's a sight that never fails to take the breath away from first-time visitors. To the west of Carson City, outside the chatter and chaos of the Legislature at 6,225-feet elevation, is deep-blue Lake Tahoe, North America's largest alpine lake. Sacred to the Washoe Indians and the second-deepest lake in the United States, Tahoe has been a thing of beauty and a prized possession for generations.

"Three months of camp life at Lake Tahoe," Twain enthused in *Roughing It,* "would restore an Egyptian mummy to his pristine vigor, and give him an appetite like an alligator. I do not mean the oldest and driest mummies, of course, but the fresher ones."

It has inspired important writers such as John Steinbeck and Bertrand Russell and been the subject of essays and poems by environmental spirits John Muir and Gary Snyder. "Like Mark Twain's impulsive trip to Nevada with his brother Orion more than sixty years before, Steinbeck's Tahoe odyssey not only altered his own life—it arguably altered the nature of American literature," Scott Lankford writes in *Tahoe Beneath the Surface.*

Protecting Lake Tahoe increased in importance during the rise of the modern ecology and conservation movements of the twentieth century. Appreciating its fragile environment became a topic of discussion between the governors of California and Nevada. Whether it was Pat Brown and Grant Sawyer, or Ronald Reagan and Paul Laxalt, important political friendships were forged across state lines with the lake's future as a common theme.

But by the 1970s, Tahoe had survived more than one generation of the abuse of its seemingly inexhaustible abundance. Its towering, old-growth giant trees were felled during the Comstock era, its shorelines invaded by settlers and swells seeking its priceless breezes and views. And above all, the snowmelt purity of its deep waters were by degrees being polluted. Algae were turning its pristine depths murkier with each passing year. Developers mocked the Zen poet Snyder's admonition: "The greatest respect we can pay to nature is not to trap it, but to acknowledge that it eludes us and that our own nature is also fluid, open, and conditional." Discarded, too, was Muir's insight: "Whenever we try to pick out anything by itself, we find it hitched to everything else in the universe."

Neal would appear an unlikely ally in the effort to preserve Lake Tahoe, but he spent the better part of a decade in a leadership role at a time some of his colleagues heard the call of the Nevada's power brokers over the call of the wild. In doing so he also found himself building an alliance with Governor O'Callaghan.

O'Callaghan's political pragmatism emerged on the important environmental issue of the quality of water at Lake Tahoe. The state Senate had to address the Tahoe regional compact, at the time a matter for the Natural Resources Committee, chaired by mid-decade by Neal. Interstate politics and in-state political pressures from developers, environmentalists, and the powerful hand of the casino industry layered the issue. Outdoorsman and conservationist O'Callaghan needed an ally. So he sent Schaller to arrange a meeting with Neal.

"O'Callaghan and I had been at odds, so I wanted a call from him," Neal recalled. "Instead, he sent Schaller. If anyone else had received a call from Schaller, they would have gone, but I wouldn't go. I'd call it a question of the 'separation of powers.'"

Then one day between hearings, Neal was walking in the hall outside the Senate chambers.

"Neal," a booming voice bellowed.

Neal turned and feigned surprise.

"How are you doing, Governor?"

O'Callaghan knew what was happening and played along.

"I've been asking you to come over to see me," the former Marine said.

"When do you want me to come over to see you?"

When he replied, Neal added, "Okay, I'll be there."

O'Callaghan played politics like Doyle Brunson with a poker hand. He brought Neal's former high school classmate Ida Crockett (later Gaines) as a reminder that he'd been doing his homework. O'Callaghan started the conversation about the precarious future of Lake Tahoe, and Neal immediately offered, "I don't have a problem with Lake Tahoe, and I will support Lake Tahoe."

Neal, too, had done his homework and was already conversant with the lake's water clarity and pollution challenges, the need to change how some businesses used it as a glorified sewerage system, and the difficult political challenges posed by the California Legislature on the matter.

"Because I wasn't from Northern Nevada, some people thought I wasn't supposed to know about Lake Tahoe," Neal said. "It's one of the two most pristine lakes in the world, but apparently I wasn't supposed to know that." Neal had a strong hand in renegotiating the compact, calling for limiting growth, and even took on a couple of developers who created their own faux citizens committee bent on investigating the committee that was revisiting the compact. Developers "didn't want anything to stop the building at Lake Tahoe," Neal said, and the casino bosses weren't used to being turned down, either. Along the way, Neal gained a strong working relationship with O'Callaghan and California state legislator (and future congressman) John Garamendi. Neal led a meeting of "the committee of the whole" at the Legislature that passed changes that protected the lake for years to come. With real bite in the Tahoe Regional Planning Agency, the lake at least had a chance. Of that pivotal time O'Callaghan would tell assembled lawmakers in 1977, "I hope the Legislature agrees that the time has arrived when we must halt further unrestricted development in the Lake Tahoe Basin. Otherwise, extensive growth will overwhelm the ability of government to insure (*sic*) the protection of this unique gift of nature."

While far from perfect, the new laws helped prevent an environmental calamity. O'Callaghan was pleased.

Nevada's Legislature had never been a bastion of openness. The public's business was most often done in private. Whether the power-brokers were from mining, banking, ranching, or gaming, much of the session was little more than theater performed for the entertainment and misdirection of the public and press.

"I was opposed to that. I thought that when we got elected, we came up there and were supposed to function in the open so people could see what the hell we were doing. We're not supposed to make any secret laws. I was opposed to the closed meeting—as they called it, executive session—which would be abused."

After some cudgeling by Neal, like-minded legislators added their voices to the side of keeping the Senate open, and supporters of the closed-door policy scattered.

Lobbyists had heavily scripted bills and prioritized policy at the Legislature. Their only challenge came in recruiting candidates capable of winning elections and willing to make those priorities their own.

"I had difficulty with that, and it made me more diligent when it came to reading the bills before they came to the floor," Neal said. "What I found as a result of that, those people who were trying to slick stuff through, pass something without the public knowing about it, they would be sitting in the committee that I was not on, contemplating how they were going to get a bill by me on the floor without me asking the question. One of the guys came and told me that, and I didn't believe him. He said, 'Joe, I just came from an interesting meeting.

'What kind of meeting is that?'

'They're in there talking about you.'

'What are they saying?'

'They're trying to figure out a way to get a bill through here without you asking questions about it.'"

It was a high compliment. But the sad truth was, many of his colleagues simply didn't read the bills that flowed before them.

"They depended upon the committee and their friends who brought something to the floor and figured if they had something they wanted, then it should be given to them. I'd go through those bills. If it took me until two or three o'clock in the morning to read them. And when I came to the floor for the eleven o'clock session, I knew I had questions about it. In the 1980s it got to the point where, particularly when a Republican was in charge, Ann O'Connell and a couple of the others would come to me and say, 'Joe, we've got these bills coming up today for a vote. Do you have any questions about them?' And I would tell them yes or no. They'd try to get them answered.

"Usually, you would find out the most simple things that could be answered and that should have been considered in committee."

Some treated Neal's questions as personal slights, Joe playing the legislative know-it-all by others. But many times they set the process off its usual course of thinly veiled control and cooperation with the state's lobbyists, who in many sessions authored more legislation than elected lawmakers.

"If they were running something there for somebody and you happen to pick up on it, you ask that question," he reflected. "And that's what I would do. Sometimes it became embarrassing to them. Because some of them would sit up and have to admit, 'We didn't consider that in committee.' The audience would know it was a simple question that should have been asked and answered in committee. Unless, of course, the legislators weren't interested in asking too many questions about the pet bills they walked through the process."

Neal made gains where he could, and during the 1975 session worked closely with conservative Democrat Mel Close, chairman of the Senate Judiciary Committee, to carve out a law that placed limits on how much a car dealer could benefit from vehicle repossession. It became known as the "collectible deficiency law" and essentially meant that if a repossessed vehicle was sold for more than was owed on it, the difference was owed to the deficient owner. Auto repossession wasn't on the radar in middle-class and more prosperous neighborhoods, but it was big in poor and minority areas.

At home in North Las Vegas, life at the Neal house fell into a familiar pattern. When father was away at the Legislature, Estelle Neal juggled the entire family and a job. When he came home on the weekends during the session, the living room was transformed into an office and meeting space that was sacrosanct. The kids remained on the lower part of the split-level tract home. With their father gone to Carson City for months at a time every other year, the Neal children relied on their mother for consistent support. Home life was centered on family first with a strong, disciplined emphasis on education. Joe and Estelle knew that it was only education, and the opportunities it created, that had given them the tools to rise in a society that didn't necessarily encourage their success.

Like all the Neal children, Dina Neal grew up in a political household and occasionally got tired of hearing the doorbell ring at all hours. The people at the door came from all walks of Las Vegas life. A legislator in a tailored suit one time, a homeless man looking to catch a break the next. When the doorbell rang, elected officials and total strangers were welcomed into the Neal living room.

"It was not until I was about sixteen that I started to be cognizant of the political life that I was somehow immersed in and needed to respect," Dina recalled years later. "It wasn't until I was 16 that my father's importance in the community started to come into focus. I recall my sister saying, 'Don't you know who he is?' I said, 'Yeah, but that doesn't mean that he has special privileges. You still have to be a normal person. To me he was just my dad, but to other people he was someone who might help them in their lives. And his attitude was, it's very important to be a common person. If you put yourself above everyone else, you are subordinating them. He believed you weren't supposed to treat people like you see some politicians treat people. They act like regular people are beneath them."

Nevada had long been known as a state bustling with hard-rock miners and desert-toughened cattle ranchers, and some of its political bosses made good use of that libertarian imagery, but in reality by the 1970s its population was increasingly concentrated in the Las Vegas and Reno metropolitan areas. Although Nevadans generally held strong, conservative views of the Second Amendment's right to keep and bear arms, the reality of gun violence in the city and police-involved shootings was difficult to deny.

So when yet another bromide on the importance of the Second Amendment was offered at the 1975 Legislature, Neal couldn't help himself. He was no gun-control fanatic, but he also understood the ramifications of the proliferation of firearms in the community—and its greater impact on minority neighborhoods.

"It was my position that the Second Amendment was drawn up at a time when we had muskets and did not have a standing army," he recalled. "You had to call out folks from their houses to defend the country. That was my concept of the Second Amendment and I guess it stems from the fact that when I was in college, I had courses in constitutional history and case law. If we were living in the 1740s, all the talk about the Second Amendment would have been appropriate. But not in the 1970s. Many legislators were members of the National Rifle Association, and most were in great fear of the NRA, which figured they had everything wired. So I could go in and say anything I wanted to. Their view was, go ahead and let him talk. So I would have my time and make my speech."

The greater challenge came when gun-rights zeal and tough-on-crime rhetoric inevitably encountered a question of fairness.

Through the years, the popularity of the Afro hairdo has ebbed and flowed with black fashion. Wearing one had never been a crime in Nevada, but the state Legislature did consider designating the large fork-like "cake cutter" commonly used to comb the hairstyle a "deadly weapon" following an altercation between black and white teenagers. The white had come away with a scrape across the face from one such comb. That was enough to send tough-on-crime legislators to their typewriters.

"That's how we came to be confronted with a bill at the Legislature to make carrying a cake cutter a felony," Neal said. "In those days, every black kid had one sticking out of his pocket, and under such a law they all could be arrested. It was the type of atmosphere that existed at that particular time, and of course I argued against it."

Neal found an ally in future Nevada governor Kenny C. Guinn, who was then superintendent of the Clark County School District. Guinn was no liberal, but he also understood that criminalizing a comb was a recipe for disaster.

"He made a statement to the fact that the kid would have fought with anything in his hand, a stick, a brick, whatever was available," Neal recalled. "It was a simple but profound statement that emboldened me to continue to fight against that particular aspect of the bill."

The bill eventually failed and faded as the session wore on, but it served as a reminder that in Nevada legislation tinged with racism and sexism was far from a thing of the past.

Neal had already gained a reputation as a busy orator on the floor of the Senate. He had almost as many opinions and questions as the law-making body had hours in the day. But he also had a purpose to remind his colleagues, who tended to hear the master's voice of the lobbyist and the special interest once they arrived in Carson City, that they also served constituents—some who were economically beleaguered.

That is how he wound up talking at such great length that not only the Republicans in the Senate but his fellow Democrats strained for relief. At one point in a talk about the virtues of public ownership of utilities, he brought ample statistics to help make his case. The numbers were, as longtime legislative watchdog and *Sun* columnist Bryn Armstrong called, "obviously the fruits of painstaking research," but Neal's colleagues had heard enough.

More than half of the Senate walked out on him. Senator Thomas "Spike" Wilson, a Democrat from Reno, who had been a staunch advocate of the ERA and an integral part of that uphill battle, had heard enough of Neal for one night and interrupted his colleague's speech by suggesting an absence of a quorum. Senators wandered out of the chamber and into the hall, and Neal kept talking about the advantages of leashing the state's powerful electricity monopoly.

"In effect special government privileges are offered to a private industry to help them out of a financial bind," Neal volleyed against a piece of legislation that would have made tax-free the interest paid on government-issued bonds used to build a power plant.

"It is my contention that if the federal and state governments are going to continue to subsidize private industries essential to the public good, it would be far better to simply have government own and operate these 'public' industries and, thus, be assured of giving the people something for their tax dollars. Rather than 'buying into' public utilities as we have with railroads and air transportation...it is time to realize that power generation and distribution is so vital to the public that we cannot stand by and hope that our government bailouts to the industry will eventually trickle down to the consumer."

Neal had done research that showed public ownership of the system in a co-op style would save consumers $30 per month, a dramatic statement in 1975.

But after Wilson's suggestion, the Senate's presiding official, Lieutenant Governor Bob Rose, another Democrat, ruled that Neal had lost the floor. Neal protested and resumed speaking after the interruption, but was ruled out of order by Rose. A vote was taken, and Neal lost, 18–1.

Neal reminded his colleagues of the rules, but they weren't listening. Legislative Counsel Perry Burnett was called in, and in a written opinion said Neal had been correct. His colleagues were in error. The senators used the wrist slap as an opportunity to chide Neal again for taking up too much time on the floor and forcing the cancellation and rescheduling of hearings.

Columnist Armstrong observed that the thrust of Neal's argument "was that the senators ought to be willing to listen to a proposition of much interest to consumers. A spectator noted that with all the poetry read on the Senate floor, and the time consumed in writing and adopting meaningless resolutions, Neal's subject was at least important enough to warrant a listen instead of what has been established as a violation of the Senate's own rules in silencing him."

The slight was duly noted by Neal, and didn't deter him in the least.

At the Neal home, the influence of both parents was evident. A lesson was never far from any conversation—even when the kids weren't in the mood for one more lecture. "We still laugh about it at Thanksgiving," Charisse Neal Washington said. "We used to watch out the window the other kids play outside during the summer. But we had these encyclopedias our parents bought. We had to read them from A to Z every year. By the time we were finished reading, it was too late to go outside. Believe me, education was instilled at an early age. We wanted to watch *The Flintstones* and *I Dream of Jeanie,* but by the time *The Flintstones* was coming on my dad was coming home from REECo. He'd come in and turn the channel to the news.

"One day I decided to challenge him and turn the channel back. He said, 'Do it if you want to,' and I did. He had his belt off and caught my behind so fast. It didn't hurt, but just the fact he caught me so quickly, I just fell down on the floor laughing. 'You can't get away from your daddy,' he said. We laughed and laughed about it. We had a lot of laughter.

"We didn't understand all the things he was going through, but the house was full of laughter and music. Ray Charles and Stevie Wonder would play, and we'd dance and have dance contests in the house. We'd see who could tell the funniest jokes.

"He loved to meet my teachers. At home I was like the clown, but I was quieter at school. During one of the meetings my teacher said, 'Charisse is the perfect child, so quiet.' My dad just laughed and said, 'Really, are you sure?' We had some good times. He was disciplined, but disciplined in a good way. Life is serious, but you can have fun with life, too."

Daughter Tania Neal Edwards remembered, "We would not ask him for school clothes. Or, back then, things like cassette tapes or albums. We knew not to ask him. We knew to ask our mom. Our dad was going to be a no. School supplies? The best backpack in school? He very much stressed education. He made us watch the news. We knew politics, what was going on in the world. If there was a program on Nixon and Watergate, we watched it. Dad would get excited and make us sit down in the den with him and watch it. He'd take us to the library after church. When the West Las Vegas Library displayed documents during Black History Month, we were there. He was very much pushing education. He was involved in it, more so than even my mom. He would go to our parent conferences, knew our teachers, knew the principal. It was kind of amazing considering he was so busy, but he made sure he was very much involved.

"He reminded us over and over that there's nothing you can't do," Edwards said. "He was your greatest cheerleader when it came to your education. He encouraged us whether we had to write a paper, had to give a speech, or ran for student council. Even if we really didn't want to do it, he encouraged us to try."

For Joe Neal Jr., youngest of the children and the only son, nothing seemed to get past his parents. Although Joe and Estelle were disciplinarians who stressed the importance of earning allowances, helping around the house and working toward goals, the early personal computer age created a dilemma for parents who also wanted their children to keep up with changing times. Joe Jr. had his eye on a computer model that cost $1,500.

"I remember wanting one and my dad and mother being torn because it would be giving me an opportunity to acquire education," he recalled. The computer would have to be earned, and fairness dictated it would have to wait.

Christmases were filled with joy, but not expensive gifts. Sharing was stressed, and a monetary limit was placed on gift giving: $50 per child, whether it was two presents or ten.

"You had to really think about what you wanted," Joe Jr. recalled. "There was a monetary limit no matter what age you were. The same for grades in school. It was never a capitalist household. It was always about fairness. And we only received money for As. Some people weren't getting paid at all. You wouldn't get money for a B no matter how hard you tried. It pushed us to work harder. They didn't slap money in our hands just for being alive. Allowances? That had to be negotiated. If we got allowances, we had to do chores."

Even an ice cream truck drive-by provided a teaching moment for Joe Neal. When the siren's song of summer approached, he would playfully put his salivating children through their paces: Explain why he should give them money for an ice cream. What had they done to deserve such a treat?

The kids would hurriedly state their case before the court of no appeal. After the transfer of coins, the race was on.

"As a child, by the time you explain it the truck is all the way down the street," Joe Jr. said. "He was teaching us always that nothing worth having comes for free."

For the elder Neal, reading the morning newspaper was an almost sacred ritual. He wanted his children to appreciate the experience and to value the knowledge at their fingertips. In fact, he insisted on it. Young Joe, for instance, read not only the comics page, but the front-page articles as well. Just to make sure he was paying attention, he was asked to recite the meaning of the story as he understood it. He was nine years old.

"'I want you to read this and explain to me what it means,'" the father would say. "And he would keep doing it until I got the concept,"

Joe Jr. said. "He wanted to get my mind thinking outside of the video games and trivial stuff that we were doing all the time."

Movies were also an opportunity to instruct while entertaining. Neal liked movies, but favored the political and social statements over cheap violence and light comedy. "When you get out of school, let's go to see a movie," the father would say. That meant *Amistad* or some other film that made a mind think and sparked a conversation.

The 1975 session would be known for many headlines and intrigues, the stalling of the ERA, and a few advances. But it would be well remembered for one issue above the rest. Call it the public's right to go.

It was the year the Legislature, arguably stretched to its progressive limits, saw fit to end the practice of pay toilets in publicly owned buildings. It was a tougher struggle than one might first imagine.

With the passage of time, the notion of pay toilets in public places seems almost laughable. Odder still is that there was a time it was an American standard. The use of pay toilets, by one credible account, started in the early 1900s at a time train travel increased through rural areas without much plumbing. The train stations were attractive and modernized, and locks were used to keep the local leakers from the loo. But that demanded that a train agent with a key be on hand to unlock the door for customers. American ingenuity being what it is, a solution was found in the form of a coin-operated lock. You might call it a pay-to-play system.

Over time, however, pay toilets became a steady profit center. By 1970, there were more than 50,000 in service in the United States. Although business owners and some government entities argued the practice was a constitutional right, the fact urinals were available without cost also made it a question of fairness. Across the country movements from Illinois to California started with a goal of ending the practice.

In Nevada, the political push came from diminutive assembly-woman Eileen "Queenie" Brookman, a Democrat from Las Vegas. Fond of wearing bright orange pantssuits and prints as a way of standing out in a crowd, she was a diehard progressive, an advocate of civil rights, Native American rights, and the ERA. She saw the issue not only as an attention grabber, but as an example of sexism masquerading as sanitation. And sexist laws were examples of the kind of discrimination the ERA sought to end.

She reminded her Assembly colleagues, "When you have to go, you have to go. And when you have to pay a dime, it's a crime."

Not surprisingly in Nevada, some of Brookman's conservative counterparts—and politicians on the Clark County Commission, for that matter—criticized the effort. They argued that the nominal charge was a necessary part of doing business and helped keep the system running smoothly. There was a chance the legislation would stall.

Representatives of the nation's two largest toilet door lock companies, Nik-O-Lok and American Coin Lock, argued that the pay function helped deter "drug addicts, homosexuals, muggers, and just plain hippies from haunting public restrooms."

Then Brookman went looking for an ally in the Senate, and Joe Neal stepped up. He would later laugh that he was always ready to lend a hand.

"Queenie, as we called her, Eileen Brookman, was such a decent person," Neal would recall many years after her 2004 death. "I knew Eileen before she went into the Legislature. She helped Flora Dungan to bring a lawsuit to end the state's old 'Rotten Borough' system back in 1964. Queenie was a real liberal. I visited her house back in the 1960s, and she was on the Economic Opportunity Board at one time and helped start a successful drug rehabilitation program. She was a Jewish lady who fought for liberal causes, and her husband, George Brookman, was a successful contractor with an office on D Street in the black community. George and an African-American guy were in construction together over there, and George also owned a motel downtown. They were very successful and very good friends with *Sun* publisher Hank Greenspun and O'Callaghan.

"She was a feisty kind of character who would pick up this issue and take it seriously. And she did."

There was plenty of opposition to the bill, but few of its critics appeared comfortable discussing the issue. And the press was watching. Senator Carl Dodge, a conservative from Fallon, in the middle of a twenty-three-year lawmaking career, argued that sanitation would be reduced if the pay function was removed. Like other critics of the bill, he was squeamish about possible unintended consequences of change and didn't see it as an issue of fairness.

"While I may agree that psychologically people may feel that there is a need for pay toilets, biologically I feel that we should have what this amendment proposes—that fifty percent of the toilets be open," Neal argued. "Because we are speaking of a biological situation here and sometimes the psychological cannot control you whenever you have to go." Without a clear path to the potty, "you are going to be embarrassed."

The passage of time has yellowed the issue somewhat, but in a state that relies on tourism it was a point of concern in 1975.

"When she came with that toilet bill, a lot of people laughed, but I thought it was a good thing," Neal recalled in 2015. "The Legislature, before I got there, had passed a damn bill legalizing pay toilets. Now think about it. If a person was not prone to naturally taking a piss, it would be different. But this was a situation where, if the urge hit you, you have to go somewhere. And the Legislature legalized pay toilets. The argument I attempted to make was one of fairness. It was the fact that they did not put a cap on the urinal, but the women had to go in and use the commode."

In Nevada, women had to pay a dime for the privilege men enjoyed for free. As usual, someone looking to make a profit had found a willing ear at the Legislature, and a law was passed. Revising it would take real effort despite the fact the pay toilets were used at McCarran International Airport. None of the Carson City brain trust thought twice about the message sent to the millions of tourists who had traveled from all parts of the nation to vacation in Las Vegas, only to be greeted by one-armed bandits and a lock on toilet stall doors.

"You'd better use the toilet while you're on the plane, because you'd have to pay to piss at the airport," Neal would recall years later.

Brookman was dedicated, but Neal was tough. When a previous attempt to ban public pay toilets failed in the Senate, Brookman declined to name the lawmaker who worked for its defeat. Neal was incensed and sent out a press release putting the senators who endorsed coin-op crappers. Although they crossed party lines, for some reason they were religious conservatives.

The vote wasn't close in 1975, and for once Nevada was riding with the tide of the nation. By 1980, thanks to efforts in many states, most pay toilets had been removed from public buildings.

On May 21, 1975, Governor O'Callaghan signed the pay toilet prohibition into law, and a sigh of relief was heard from Winnemucca to Searchlight. Newspapers from around the country carried the story and Brookman, flush with pride, became known as Nevada's pay toilet princess.

Her friend Joe Neal was proud to be her prince.

Showdowns, Putdowns, and Letdowns

WHEN HE WASN'T WORKING as a civil rights compliance officer at REECo or on legislation, Neal increasingly found himself
fielding constituent contacts. The needs of the community were broad
in scope and often included help in finding employment and job training. He also became a sounding board for citizen complaints about the
heavy-handedness of the Metropolitan Police Department's patrolling
Southern Nevada's poorest neighborhoods. Sheriff Ralph Lamb's officers were known to be particularly aggressive in predominantly black
areas, and Neal had fought for greater restrictions for police shooting
at fleeing felons because in minority communities they often confused
suspects with citizens. Governor O'Callaghan had signed a version
of the bill into law. Neal was also well remembered by the leaders of
the police department for appearing to equate the worth of a cop's
life with that of the ordinary citizen. In his community, he well knew,
the police presence was perceived very differently than it was in more
affluent neighborhoods.

Neal increasingly found himself in front of local judges arguing
over speeding citations and minor traffic infractions. He successfully
defended himself and privately noted the frequency with which he
found himself on police radar. Through the years he would be followed
by overzealous investigators and suspected by one particularly irre-
sponsible officer of conspiring to set fire to a church. From menacing
stops to threatening phone calls, he was well acquainted with the costs
of speaking out on public safety and more controversial issues. Some
cops and their friends in the media considered him a militant black,
an instigator. Whether they were concerted attempts to intimidate and

harass, or a matter of substantial coincidence, the negative interactions with police only seemed to redouble his activity.

Not long after the 1975 session ended, Neal's name reentered the headlines, this time as a double-deck banner in blue in the *Las Vegas Review-Journal*: "Nevada senator cited during arrest attempt." Newspaper readers couldn't be blamed for being alarmed at the alleged criminal activity involved. Normally, the top of the front page is reserved for the world's top story, and in June of that year there was no shortage of news. What egregious act was he suspected of committing?

Neal had received a ticket for allegedly "impeding traffic" after he'd refused to move his legally parked vehicle from the scene of a police call. Police had been sent to investigate a report of a man with a shotgun at a local Housing Authority apartment complex, and Neal was driving in his Ford Pinto with Senate member plates. No gun was found, but Neal refused to comply with the officer's demand that he move on.

"I told them I had a right to observe them in the performance of their duty," Neal told a reporter.

Legally parked across the street and more than fifty yards from the house, Neal suddenly became a focal point. "I pointed out there were other cars illegally parked in the area with persons in them," he said. "I assume they just wanted to cite me." He would recall in an interview with *Desert Companion* magazine in 2014 that, "I became a target. I was out of the civil rights movement in the South. When I was younger, I was willing to die for my beliefs. I was fresh from law school and knew the laws that governed this country. If a cop was abusing you, you had the right to match force with force. After I said it, cops gave me tickets all the time. If I felt the ticket was wrong, I'd challenge it in court. I got good at beating the tickets. In municipal court, I'd appeal to district court. In district court, the judge would knock it down to a parking violation. It became too costly for cops to ticket me and the court only gets forty dollars.... I didn't want to get hurt or to hurt anybody. But I'd seen cops have guys put their hands on the hoods of cars in the dead heat of summer. If the guys flinched, the cops would use that as justification to hit them with a billy club."

When Neal argued the citation in court, he reminded the judge that "impeding traffic" was a moving violation. The car wasn't moving, but was parked at the curb. Attorney Allan Bray, a former FBI man who had served on the federal task force that investigated the assassination of President John Kennedy, offered Neal free legal service. In the end, the judge dismissed the case.

It wasn't about Neal being picked on by the local cops, or about his ability to out-argue a beleaguered prosecutor. Such experiences weren't happening to his fellow colleagues in the Senate. Not because they were better drivers, or citizens, but because they lived in a different Nevada.

By 1977, time was running out on Nevada when it came to passing the Equal Rights Amendment. The makeup of the Senate was changing, and the arguments for the ERA were more vocal than ever. To that point in 1977, Nevada legislators had managed to pass on their opportunity to press for progress. The Silver State was one of just fifteen to fail to approve the ERA.

Of course, Congress had paid lip service to equal rights amendments since 1923. It wasn't until March 1972 that it adopted the resolution to amend the Constitution to include equal rights for women. With approval by thirty-eight states before 1979 (later extended to 1982), the Twenty-Seventh Amendment would become a reality. By 1979, thirty-five states had ratified the amendment. (Three states would later rescind their votes.)

The arguments for its passage were many, but it started with a legal system riddled with sexism and discrimination based on sex. A system of separate rights and responsibilities inevitably "leads to one group's dominance," proponents said. It's the rights of the individual, regardless of sex or sexual identity, that must prevail if equality is to be achieved. The fact sexual discrimination had continued was proof enough to many of the ERA's necessity. As a legislative briefing on the issue reasonably stated, "To supporters, the Equal Rights Amendment is both a symbolic goal and a practical instrument for change."

While its opponents often tried to write off the battle for the ERA as an attempt at crafting a grand metaphor for equal rights between the sexes, for its supporters the amendment far transcended symbolism.

In addition to the usual states' rights concerns, and their expressed fears that the amendment's passage would eliminate "rights and privileges" important to women and burden them with unwanted responsibilities and undo stresses on home and family, the ERA's opponents pointed to "legal tools" already in the Constitution and enacted by Congress. Among them: the Fifth and Fourteenth Amendments, the 1963 Equal Pay Act, the 1964 Civil Rights Act, and the 1972 Equal Employment Opportunity Act. All arguably helped balanced the scale, but in proponents' view left out something essential: a constitutional amendment.

If past performance meant anything, no Nevada handicapper would have given the Equal Rights Amendment the least chance of passing the Nevada Legislature in 1977. The ERA had found many allies in the Assembly beginning in 1973, but knew few friends in the Senate beyond Neal and a few progressives. It died in the Senate by a 16–4 vote in 1973, and improved only marginally, 15–5, in 1975. Of note that year was the change of heart of respected conservative Northern Nevada senator William Raggio. It was a decision that gave ERA supporters a glimmer of hope against a reality that the Senate was filled with religious conservatives who equated the amendment with the breakup of the family and gender confusion.

By 1977, in part because of the Democrats' post-Watergate surge, the election of Jimmy Carter to the presidency, and the unprecedented popularity of Governor O'Callaghan, the face of the Senate had begun to change. But legislators of the LDS faith, whose church was adamantly opposed to the ERA, held key committee positions.

"I think they must have had five Mormons there, some of them in key positions, and of course they were all opposed to the ERA," Neal would recall. "The church was opposed to it."

The showdown came on February 8, early in the fifty-ninth session after a long day of debate. Neal's view on the practical and symbolic importance of the amendment was well known, and he reminded his colleagues that he had voted his "conviction upon this particular issue" in two previous sessions. "I would further submit to you, Mr. President, that the reason I find my action of voting for this amendment to be a simple one, because as a black person in these United States, I know the value of having an amendment which you can appeal to when all statutory law seems to go against you. I can equate this amendment with the

Fourteenth Amendment of the Constitution in which time and time again black citizens of this State and nation have had to appeal to this basic constitutional principle of equal protection that is found in that amendment to gain their rights."

This time, Neal had allies, including Lieutenant Governor Bob Rose, acting in his capacity as president of the Senate. Rose, whose name often entered political conversations about future gubernatorial candidates, had succeeded future U.S. Senate majority leader Harry Reid.

Neal continued his discussion of the history of equal rights for minorities, something that had become almost boilerplate rhetoric and a long-playing record during his early tenure, but this time he had a surprise for the Senate's ERA naysayers.

For those opposed to the amendment, the game plan was tried and true: stretch out the process and delay the vote. With no consensus, and little negative political exposure, there may have been no vote at all.

But instead of waiting to the end of the hearing, Neal jolted the proceedings.

"If I am in order at this particular time, Mr. President, I would like to invoke Rule No. 30 when this question comes up for a vote and if I could be sustained by Senator (Wilbur) Faiss and Senator (William) Hernstadt on this issue, then we can move on. And thank you very much."

Rule 30 mandated a vote be taken if three members call for it. That gave those opposed to the ERA little time to persuade, and intimidate, others who secretly favored passage of the measure. Senators couldn't just leave the chamber to delay the process. From the rule: "Every Senator within the bar of the Senate shall vote 'aye' or 'no' or record himself as 'not voting,' unless excused by unanimous vote of the Senate."

Hernstadt, a successful television station owner and real estate developer, had been Neal's steadfast friend. Faiss, however, was an affable businessman and political neophyte, a soft-spoken fellow whose son, attorney Robert Faiss, was an integral member of the casino industry's effective lobbying force. But stand they did.

"The debate on the ERA went on for about an hour and a half to two hours, then it came to the vote," Neal said. "Lieutenant Governor Rose said, 'Rule 30 has been invoked, and each senator within the bar of the Senate has to vote yea or nay. Secretary, open the roll.'"

When the roll call vote was taken, there were ten votes for passage, eight no, and two abstentions. Rose placed the abstentions in the "No" column, making the procedural vote a tie. That, by law, then allowed him to step up and cast a tie-breaking vote. And he did.

For a shining moment, the cobwebbed and conservative Nevada Senate was showing that progress could be achieved with the right political footwork.

"He declared the house evenly divided—and boom!—he pushed that button, and the eleventh vote came on the screen," Neal recalled in a 2008 interview. "I'll never forget it."

Seated next to Neal, conservative Keith Ashworth kept his sense of humor by fiddling with the voting button. "Damn voting machine has gone haywire again," he said.

Neal responded, "No, the lieutenant governor just passed the ERA out of the Senate."

Some religious conservatives were about to have some serious explaining to do on Sunday. For his part, Jim Gibson, the respected Mormon elder who spent nearly a decade in the Assembly and served in the Senate from 1966 until his death in 1988, with eight years as majority leader, was staggered.

"A hush came over the Legislature, and everybody got quiet for what seemed like a full minute," Neal remembered. "All of a sudden, everybody in the gallery broke out clapping and applauding, and I saw Gibson had his head in his hands. I just got up and walked out of the Senate because it was over."

Over in the Senate, at least.

Afterward, Neal walked across the street to the Ormsby House. Floyd Lamb, a tough political battler, was returning to his room and caught Neal in the lobby. He walked up to Neal and said, "You did it to us, you rat, you!"

He was smiling as he said it. Lamb, a Mormon Democrat from a powerful Nevada political family that included Clark County sheriff Ralph Lamb and county commissioner Darwin Lamb, would eventually be convicted of accepting bribes in a federal sting operation. But the eldest son in the Lamb clan offered Neal a backhanded compliment that would remain with him the rest of his life.

"I like you, Joe," said a grinning Floyd Lamb, who was fond of cowboy boots and polyester suits. "You get knocked down, but you always get back up again."

Although he didn't initially realize it, that eventful evening had changed Neal's reputation. His many critics couldn't simply write him off as a loudmouth, or a socialist in sheep's clothing. "From that night on, I became the master of the rules of the Legislature," he would recall, laughing. "On that one little issue."

It was a proud moment for the sharecropper's son, and in interviews years afterward the incident provided insight into the fire that drove Neal to press through all attempts to alienate him and marginalize him. A "poor little black kid who graduated from Southern University—an all-black school" had beaten the Harvard, Stanford, and Naval Academy boys at their own game. He would say there was no better feeling.

"I think that in many instances, I got the better of them because my concentration was much greater than theirs on these particular issues," he said.

But there would be no chance to work the rules in the Assembly, which had passed the amendment in the previous session. The rush was on to move votes into the "No" column. Editorials published at the time capture some of the political ramifications of the Senate shuffle.

The *Las Vegas Review-Journal*, rarely in its history playing the role of progressive community leader, in February 1977 noted the obvious lack of recrimination against politicians who took a stand against the Equal Rights Amendment. Religiously conservative Democrats such as Senators Lamb, Gibson, and Ashworth might have infuriated the left end of the Nevada Democratic Party, but only pleased their Mormon constituencies when they tripped up progressive attempts to push the ERA through the Legislature. With Carter's popularity in Nevada slipping, and the extremely popular O'Callaghan a lame duck, powerful advocates for the constitutional change weren't plentiful.

The president clearly understood the importance of weighing in. Neal had been an important spokesman on the issue throughout the decade, and the Mailgram he received on February 3, 1977, as the Legislature was once again rumbling to life in Carson City, no doubt bolstered his spirits.

"I STRONGLY FAVOR THE PASSAGE OF THE ERA WHICH WOULD GUARANTEE BASIC HUMAN RIGHTS TO ALL AMERICANS, REGARDLESS OF THEIR SEX. MY ADMINISTRATION AND THE DEMOCRATIC PARTY HAVE TAKEN A FIRM AND UNEQUIVOCAL STAND ON THIS ISSUE, AND I WOULD HOPE THAT WHEN THE AMENDMENT COMES BEFORE YOU NEXT WEEK, YOU TAKE POSITIVE ACTION. THIS IS VERY IMPORTANT TO ME AND TO THE NATION."

Carter, who well understood the moral and political implications of the ERA, signed the missive. Women were a burgeoning and increasingly independent force in American politics, but his own voice was growing increasingly feint in Nevada political circles.

The *Review-Journal* noted as much and focused on Rose, one of the few officials openly backing the ERA, whose vote to push the amendment out of the Senate put members of the Assembly on the spot. Suddenly, they had to step up and let their constituents and their party leadership know where they stood. "Rose made some assemblymen, who didn't think the issue would ever surface in the Assembly, very unhappy," the editorial accurately observed. "Some of them didn't want to vote on it because it was so controversial.... Should some of those legislators fall as a result of revealing their positions they will naturally blame Rose and probably work against him. Then, of course, he will lose many Mormon votes when he runs for governor, which he is a cinch to do.... One has to admire his courage on this issue, but politically it will probably hurt him more than help him."

Sure enough, the Assembly faltered. The vote wasn't close, 24–15, and the dream of the passage of the ERA in Nevada collapsed. There was time for a reversal before the deadline, but there was no appetite to take on the state's conservative political forces, who were well capable of reaching across party lines to improve their position.

A year later an advisory question was placed on the ballot, but that made the issue even easier to demagogue with advertising meant to frighten families and raise the canard of same-sex restrooms. The vote opposing ratification was even more lopsided, 123,952 to 61,768.

As an Assembly Republican, Sue Wagner of Reno supported the ERA, but she was keenly aware of the concerted pushback being mounted by officials with the Catholic and Mormon churches, whose members pelted legislators with a letter-writing campaign unequaled in Nevada history. In her oral history, *Through the Glass Ceiling: A Life in Nevada Politics*, with Victoria Ford, Wagner noted that the outspoken "Senator Neal, I believe, said that he had received twenty to thirty thousand pieces of mail on this issue, during that particular time."

Wagner saw hope for the ERA at the Legislature fade when conservative religious and political organizations prevailed in not only pushing the question onto the 1978 ballot, but then knocking it out of the park statewide by a two-to-one-vote margin. She used the precinct results as part of her strategy to win election to the Senate from a Northern Nevada district that was generally in favor of progress—even if it was just an advisory question. At Gibson's funeral in 1988, Wagner was schooled in the behind-the-scenes efforts of church elders to defeat the ERA. She listened during one eulogy as the secret was revealed: a high-ranking LDS elder had flown to Las Vegas to implore an aging Gibson to run for reelection "in order to defeat this amendment," she recalled.

It was not news to Neal. Even if in the end Nevada's regressive machine had won, no one could say Joe Neal had failed to fight the good fight.

The Lake Tahoe compact between Nevada and California was one of the crowning achievements of O'Callaghan's eight years in office. But in the waning months of his tenure it became as clear as the lake's water that a movement had begun to loosen restrictions and allow more casino development. He looked to Neal for help, and the senator responded by sounding an alarm that further alienated him from his colleagues and even from the Senate Natural Resources Committee he chaired.

When casino insiders and their lawmaking friends attempted to isolate Neal earlier by locking him out of their legislative panel strategy session, he walked out when "it became apparent the panel was following every recommendation contained in a casino industry analysis" of the proposed compact legislation. The two sides were split on more than two dozen issues. Eventually, governors O'Callaghan and Jerry Brown of California carved out a compromise with help from Charles Warren, chairman of President Jimmy Carter's Council on Environmental Quality. The agreement was specifically designed to diminish the dominance of Nevada's gaming industry inside the Tahoe Regional Planning Agency. Although O'Callaghan would watch incoming Republican governor Robert List criticize the compromise and demand further changes, for once the environment at least temporarily won out over development interests at Lake Tahoe.

Nevadans overwhelmingly supported the bistate legislation to strengthen environmental protection of the lake, according to polls taken at the time. Those same surveys also noted that nearly half of the state's residents agreed the casino industry had too much influence on elected officials. O'Callaghan not only had the history on his side, but the vast majority of the people as well.

An attorney for Tahoe area casino owners vilified California's plan and predicted collapse if the gaming bosses weren't protected. "The State of California is not interested in negotiating anything with the State of Nevada," lawyer Gordon DePaoli said. "The goal of California, the League to Save Lake Tahoe, the Sierra Club, and others is to get gaming out of the Tahoe Basin, and they will stop at nothing to achieve that end."

Neal weighed into such breathless rhetoric with biological studies that made the casinos and the traffic they attracted substantially responsible for the environmental challenges the lake faced.

Meanwhile, the *Los Angeles Times* opined, "A committee of the Nevada legislature, under pressure from those who profit from the despoliation of the mile-high lake, has written a new agreement that would scuttle five years of bistate negotiations." The latest proposal "makes a mockery of the compact agreed on" by the governors. *The Times* called the casino influence "The Loch Tahoe Monster." In the *San Francisco Chronicle*, columnist Charles McCabe wrote often about the less-than-pristine politics and more than once singled out Neal as a clarion unafraid to go against Nevada's powerful special interests. After O'Callaghan's departure, Neal helped spread the word of the new effort to erode protections at the lake. McCabe credited Neal with saying "there is still pressure to continue the buildup at the lake, as Nevada state senator Joe Neal made clear after the league's report was issued. Neal said the survey results provided a means for Nevada legislators to 'see there are concerns outside the lake itself.'"

Where some saw business interests at work, Neal saw a puppet show. "The legislature doesn't always do what the people want," he told McCabe. "There is heavy lobbying and lots of dollars up at the lake, and we're going to feel that."

As usual with the Nevada Legislature, the potential conflicts weren't hard to find. State senator Ashworth served on the 1979 ad hoc committee while also serving as an executive with Del Webb Corporation, which owned the Sahara Tahoe at the lake. Neal was left off that committee despite serving as chairman of the Senate Natural Resources Committee. He didn't let the slight pass and emerged as a constant and formidable antagonist. Although the *Nevada State Journal* implored Neal to "back off" his effort to complicate the process, it admitted, "We can't blame Neal for a certain exasperation. The treatment of the revised compact by the ad hoc committee has been unique to say the least."

The committee's activity constituted a blatant end-around to the process and the public's right to know.

Neal's role in the issue wasn't lost on Michael Makley, author of *Saving Lake Tahoe: An Environmental History of a Natural Treasure.* Makley notes that Neal found himself siding with some California legislators against powerful Nevada casino operators. Neal was used to being targeted by gaming lobbyists, who were under particular pressure already because of California's effort to rein in their development at the lake. John Garamendi introduced what became known as the Warren Compromise in an effort to protect the lake despite competing interests. Makley wrote: "Las Vegas Democratic state senator Joe Neal, the chair of the Natural Resources Committee, was seen by many as a maverick in the legislature. He was a proponent of protecting the lake and said that, despite the public's view, legislation tightening environmental controls would be difficult to pass."

As a young member of the California Legislature representing El Dorado County, Garamendi made protecting the environment of Lake Tahoe a top priority at a time it was under unprecedented stress from housing developers and Nevada casino operators interested in building a resort corridor. The crush of visitors and new residents created traffic nightmares, increased air pollution, and imperiled the lake's famous water purity and clarity.

He found just three key allies on the Nevada legislative side, Neal notably among them.

"The three of them became the Tahoe patrons," Garamendi reflected four decades later. "We teamed up and began a two-and-a-half-year process of negotiating with the economic interests and the environmental interests to develop a method to protect Tahoe. It was a very difficult situation for the Nevada representatives because of the power of the casino industry and its interest in developing Lake Tahoe, he said "This was a Nevada issue, and it took incredible courage to withstand the political and economic pressures that were placed on these three leaders."

To Garamendi, nothing less than the fate of the lake was at stake.

"The bottom line is, Joe Neal, Joe Dini, and another senator from Nevada were absolutely critical in passing the revamped Tahoe Regional Planning Agency legislation and overcoming the objections of the casinos, all of which were in Nevada at that time," Garamendi said. "They stood tall, they stood courageously, and the result of that is they were able to get it done. Had they not been willing to take on the most powerful economic interests in the state, then as now, that is the casinos, Tahoe would have been destroyed. Many generations who now enjoy Tahoe and will enjoy it for years to come owe a very, very big thank you to the Nevada legislators.

Neal became such a lightning rod that Nevada's Tahoe contingent attempted to ostracize him from the process. Until the practice was exposed in the press, casino lobbyists and insider lawmakers kept a color-coded rating system for legislators based on their willingness to adhere to the party line. Green was a go, yellow a positive lean, and red was reserved for those who posed real problems. There was one red label. It was reserved for Neal, who put his supposed colleagues on the spot by identifying the system and making sure the press discovered it.

Since the late 1960s Neal had been leveraging his role as a civil rights compliance officer at REECo to help frame a way of introducing trained minority workers into local trade unions. As chairman of the Administrative Committee of the Greater Las Vegas Plan, as it came to be known, gains were made within several labor organizations, which took advantage of apprentice training programs and slowly began allowing blacks and Hispanics into their ranks. (Ironically, the reluctance to integrate in later years substantially damaged several union locals in trades that became flooded with nonunion undocumented immigrants. Some unions had traded short-term security for long-term strength and paid a high price.)

Its success and legacy were mixed, but the Greater Las Vegas Plan was among the boldest attempts to open the doors of opportunity for a generation of Southern Nevada construction workers of color. Neal had played an integral role in drafting and designing the cooperative agreement between the building trades, contractors, and key members of the community.

"Affirmative action" might have been scoffed at in private, but Neal tried to make sure it was taken seriously in public. He knew that the only way to change the status quo on the Westside and in other poor neighborhoods was to train a new generation of workers for good-paying jobs. He attempted to win over skeptics and assuage contractor concerns by offering seminars "on 'Equal Opportunity/Affirmative Action' designed to meet your needs," as one circular optimistically put it. There was little interest in his one-man effort.

Training unskilled workers was only part of the challenge. Contractors and union bosses, many of whom weren't shy about expressing their biases and had never hired a minority employee, were reluctant to participate and only did so out of a fear of sanction or the reward of a government set-aside. The trouble came from the bottom up and the top down: federal dollars for training programs were never abundant, and by the late 1970s were woefully inadequate. By August 1977, Neal was forced to announce the Greater Las Vegas Plan, which had been created in 1971 and had managed to balance the interests of eleven local construction unions, 250 general and specialty contractors, and representatives of the minority community, was wilting on the vine. It received less than $40,000 annually to monitor and support the training programs, and Neal was accused of putting undue pressure on contractors to participate.

"The only year the Plan received sufficient funding to perform properly the functions set forth in the Agreement was in 1973," he said. "...As a result of the Plan's achievements during that period, it received national acclaim as one of the two best hometown plans in the nation." No less a union expert than nationally syndicated columnist Victor Riesel took time to laud Neal's efforts for high compliance with many larger cities, Portland, Oregon; Providence, Rhode Island; and Trenton, New Jersey among them, bringing up the rear.

Neal didn't give up. Using his status in the state Senate, he implored the Office of Federal Contract Compliance Programs to aid the Southern Nevada strategy by providing enough funding to oversee the local unions. He sought not only increased funding, but also strengthened regulatory review. For the most part, he would be disappointed with the federal response, but undeterred in the goals of the hometown plan strategy: improving job training and employment opportunity for minorities and women.

Ever the proverbial saddle burr for police and local prosecutors, Neal only made them more irritated after it became clear he wasn't a candidate for intimidation. From his perspective, the district attorney's office and police department didn't reflect the demographics of the community, and that held the threat of less justice for minorities.

But how to make the case? For starters he tapped Frank Dunbaugh, his ally from the U.S. Department of Justice, who by 1977 had risen to deputy assistant attorney general, in an effort to compel action on minority hiring practices in professions that received any source of federal funding. In Southern Nevada, that once again meant taking on the Metropolitan Police Department, the District Attorney's Office, and the Clark County Fire Department, predominantly white male fraternities. The fire department had a tradition of being led by chiefs who had conservative religious affiliations and fought the hiring of minorities and women. But this time Neal focused on the police and district attorney's use of funds provided by the federal Law Enforcement Assistance Administration. As usual, he led with statistics and noted just twenty-three blacks were employed at the 1,100-member Metro, with only fourteen officers among more than 700 in the department.

"Presently, the District Attorney's office does not have any black attorneys on its staff and appears unwilling to hire any, even though black attorneys have applied for work with this office," he wrote. "It would seem to me that the LEAA, by the continued giving of funds to these organizations, is participating in racially exclusionary practices."

In a county in which twelve percent of the population was black, but fewer than three percent of police officers were persons of color, the disparity was striking. Neal was clear about his intentions. "I am sure that the Justice Department is not aware that government money is being used to perpetuate the situation which is exemplified by these statistics," he wrote.

With increased contacts in Washington, Neal championed the causes and careers of friends and political allies. He wrote glowing recommendations on behalf of O'Callaghan administration special assistant Harriet Trudell, who was up for a position as director of Women's Affairs for the Democratic National Committee. He not only penned a missive to the DNC chairman, but added a letter to President Carter as well.

A trip to Memphis, Tennessee in 1978 came as a welcome surprise for Neal after spending most of the decade toiling at the Nevada Legislature and scrapping for small gains in Southern Nevada's poorest neighborhoods. He represented the state at the Democratic National Conference hosted by Democratic National Committee Chairman John C. White, with an appearance by President Carter. Neal couldn't be blamed for feeling like he'd finally arrived, even if the stay was a brief one, in a place of national political prominence. His trip to Memphis surely recalled a previous trip he'd made to Atlanta as a teenager back in the days he owned a single shirt.

"I have never attended nor read about such a conference which was so national in scope and at the same time made our national government touchable," he wrote the president on December 15 in a letter of thanks. "As I look back over the three days I spent in Memphis, I have come to the conclusion that Jimmy Carter should not have any opposition from the Democratic Party in 1980."

Carter, as history would note, had some trouble from his own party that year, thanks to a primary challenge by Senator Edward Kennedy that he fended off far more easily than many political experts expected. But there was a political steamroller headed Carter's way being driven by Ronald Reagan. Neal related to Carter as a Southern Christian gentleman even though the former Georgia governor's ideology was more conservative than Kennedy's.

When members of the local branch of the Southern Christian Leadership Conference protested the lack of minority hiring on construction jobs in minority communities at the Las Vegas Convention Center, it received a thorough browbeating from Neal's ink-stained nemesis, *Las Vegas Sun* columnist Price. Ever on the side of the establishment, Price rose to the defense of the offended majority whenever Neal or his allies in the local black community and national civil rights movement pressed for changing the status quo of glorified Jim Crow. The goading Price called out the SCLC chapter leadership as "a group dedicated to improving the lot of the black minority.... It doesn't seem concerned with other minorities, Chicanos, Puerto Ricans, Indians and Asian Americans.... [T]he conference's cause might have more validity if the horizon was broadened.... The Las Vegas Convention and Visitors Authority is under fire, presumably because it doesn't hire enough blacks, doesn't advertise in black magazines and doesn't bow to misapplied strength."

Price then telegraphed a plan by the city attorney to possibly apply a felony coercion statute against local reverends who warned of possible civil unrest if hiring improvements weren't forthcoming. It was the kind of poison pen Neal was used to, but observers may have been left to wonder whether Price would have taken on members of the clergy in any other community for speaking out on behalf of their economically beleaguered congregants. For Price and much of the Southern Nevada establishment, whatever black gains that had been made during the heart of the civil rights movement ought to have been more than enough progress for one oppressed minority.

There was, in fact, a determined push to effectively remind Las Vegas blacks of their place in local society. The Clark County Commission, long a stronghold of religiously conservative elected officials, made no secret of its intention to have Registrar of Voters Stan Colton redraw district maps. Neal responded by going to whatever members of the press who would listen and told the commissioners, "We will protest this either in the commission or on the streets."

Meanwhile, on those streets, black business owners were experiencing what they called harassment from county licensing personnel and Metro police. One of the places targeted by investigators was Woody's Place, a bar on H Street owned by former assemblyman and County Commission contender Woodrow Wilson. Wilson had helped start the Westside's first neighborhood credit union and the black chamber of commerce, but nearly two dozen officers with police dogs overran his bar. Patrons were forced to lie on the floor while their purses and wallets were examined. Some were made to remove their shoes and socks in an apparent search for contraband. The cops peppered their speech with calls of "nigger" and "boy."

In a press conference announcing the possibility of a counterprotest and the potential for a riot, Neal was joined by Dr. James McMillan, who said the officers "mishandled one black who was attempting to respond to their inhuman treatment, and when he was subdued, they went back into the establishment and forced everyone to lie on the floor. Then the officers alleged someone had said there was cocaine in the club, but they never identified the suspect nor confiscated any cocaine." It may have been the only bar and nightclub in Las Vegas in that era where a thorough search wouldn't have produced cocaine.

The police under Sheriff Lamb had set up roadblocks along streets leading into the black community and were stopping white motorists attempting to enter the area, supposedly to deter drug sales. The effect was devastating for a variety of struggling Westside businesses, and did nothing to improve relations between the community and the police.

Despite painful setbacks, those seeking social justice in Southern Nevada had seen substantive political gains through the heart of the 1970s. But late in the decade those benefiting from the old status quo enjoyed their share of victories, too. The reapportionment that had carved out state and local districts that enabling poorly funded blacks and other minorities to gain elected office was in the process of being overturned on what critics alleged were constitutional concerns.

But at least a few political observers, who had watched LDS candidates benefit from previous gerrymandering, were wise to the mechanics at work. A *Las Vegas Sun* editorial headline chided, "Voting Districts Created to Serve Only Incumbents." "Gerrymandering protects incumbents. Nowhere is it more obvious than in Clark County, where county commission districts have been redrawn to splinter the voting effectiveness of the predominately black West Las Vegas area.... The enclaves of voting power remain predictably untouched. The 'ins are intent on remaining in office. The result is partisan and self-serving. It does a disservice to each of Clark County's registered voters.

"Our elected representatives at every level of government must be those closest to our problems, who understand our daily frustrations and speak clearly enough for those who elected them to office to get results. By their latest efforts our county commissioners have shown they don't trust the voters. Without that trust, they no longer serve the people—only themselves."

As ever in Nevada, identifying the problem was the easy part. Neal knew compelling change was the real challenge.

The Measure of the Law, Tested by Fire

WHEN A LAS VEGAS police officer shot and killed a purse-snatching suspect, one who supposedly had wielded a butcher knife that wasn't found at the scene, Joe Neal spoke up. Las Vegas had a long history of questionable officer-involved shootings involving blacks, and Neal had familiarized himself with each one.

He wasn't shy about calling print and television reporters to fill them in on developments in the official investigation and his own independent inquiry. Some saw him as a grandstanding politician, but he was undeniably a "great quote."

While white society in Southern Nevada and most newspaper editors wrote off such shootings as yet another "Westside misdemeanor," Neal demanded to be heard. While it was good for his profile among his constituents, he was sometimes written off as a "militant" and even "mau-mauing" community activist.

After a grand jury called the shooting death "justifiable homicide," the at-large community failed to respond. The press reported the available facts and moved on. Neal was left with a decision to either stand silent or respond to another in a long line of suspicious police shootings.

He did more than call the media. He also phoned the Federal Bureau of Investigation and demanded a meeting. The result was a promise to investigate the fatal incident. Although the federal inquiry didn't change the outcome of the grand jury decision, it put Clark County sheriff John McCarthy on notice that the department's policies, procedures, and performance weren't above scrutiny.

Neal wasn't above pushing buttons and inflaming passions. At a meeting of black community leaders at the Second Baptist Church, he intimated that a police shooting of a white suspect might have been an effort to quiet the rising discontent emanating from the Westside. "Wouldn't it be a shame to find out that this shooting was just a way for police to equalize the killing of a black man," he said.

Ned Day, a pugnacious *Valley Times* columnist and a confidant of the sheriff, wrote a backhanded appreciation of Neal's ability to get under the skin of the establishment and move the top cop, then considered one of the most powerful political positions in Nevada, to not only take the bait but also to emerge with a new department shooting policy. (Although in reality it made few changes.) It was clearly a political victory for Neal, but he'd receive little credit from the establishment press. Day accused the state senator of "mau-mauing Sheriff John McCarthy. A hulking and never-more-black Joe Neal demanded answers and action.... He thundered to his audience that mass Strip demonstrations may be necessary if Sheriff McCarthy refuses to make 'significant changes' in the official policy governing use of firearms by officers. Neal's weeklong tirade had reached a fever pitch. It was time to march, to hit the bricks, time to menace Whitey's pocketbook."

What neither the press nor the public appeared to fully understand was the personal and political risk Neal took on when he challenged the sheriff of Clark County. The department had a notorious history of setting up and singling out its critics.

Neal positively goaded the community's law-enforcement leader when he told a reporter, "McCarthy stated and repeated that officers need to exhaust all reasonable alternatives before shooting someone. Of course, there's a difference between written policy and execution of policy. We'll be watching."

Aside from the racially charged rhetoric that was in common use in the press of the era, the column published July 20, 1979, was headlined "Sen. Neal Masters the Art of Mau Mau." Day hit on a point that those who followed Neal's legislative career knew well: "Whatever success Neal enjoys as a legislator, according to one fellow lawmaker, stems not from his demagogic speech-making and posturing, but rather from his keen knowledge of parliamentary procedure."

Neal was accustomed to being damned with faint praise. But he also saw a growing trend in Southern Nevada policing when it came to shooting incidents involving unarmed or fleeing black men. He would spend the remainder of his public career speaking out time and again after a coroner's inquest ruled such questionable fatal shootings justified. Metro's deadly-shooting record eventually led to an investigation by the Department of Justice and numerous procedural changes. The changes would come after nearly three decades and many more questionable shootings.

Neal indeed had been accused of demagoguery as the sixty-first session of the Legislature tuned up in Carson City in 1981, and he cleverly raised the same issue with fellow senator Mel Close, a partner in one of Nevada's most powerful law firms. Each session, Close or one of his colleagues took time out to celebrate the Second Amendment and offer resolutions and hosannas in its name. Neal, in turn, would respond with an essay on the founding fathers' view of the right to keep and bear arms in an era of the long rifle and musket ball. But by 1979, with cheap handguns flooding the inner city, Close suggested the state's Constitution be amended to effectively encourage citizens to "strap on a gun if you so desire" in the name of "security and defense."

The trouble with further colorizing the Nevada Constitution: the Second Amendment already existed. And if there was already a Second Amendment in the U.S. Constitution, that certainly superseded anything in the Nevada Constitution. After bantering with Close, Neal offered, "Let me just ask you just a very general question as to why we need to put this in the Constitution?"

Close was a seasoned attorney, but expressed unfounded fears that "that there have been some statements by different groups to the effect that weapons should not be allowed to be owned by citizens of the United States. Some countries do preclude that right." Then he quavered, and his nonsensical argument collapsed entirely. "I presume that the introducers of this resolution would avoid that question from coming before the State Legislature," he said.

"Believe it or not," Neal recalled, laughing to an interviewer in 2008, "the toughest issue that I couldn't get on that I wanted to get on was getting rid of the Highway Patrol's radar gun. I used to drive back and forth and a couple of times I got caught speeding with the radar gun. I wanted to get rid of the radar gun. I had a good argument! Good argument! I brought the bill to the Senate a number of times, but I never could get it passed. We got it passed one time because Senator Lamb got a ticket, and he passed it out of the Senate, but then they killed it in the Assembly."

Neal went so far as to request, and receive, a radar gun from the highway patrol to use in a show-and-tell with his colleagues.

"It was clear that the rest of the senators did not understand the radar gun because I picked it up and was showing it around, and they were ducking under their desks. If they felt that way, why not get rid of it?"

His fellow lawmakers had no reason to fear. No one had ever accused the Nevada Legislature of moving too quickly on anything.

But Neal, half in jest, made a point of reminding his colleagues that the state was endorsing the use of a tool capable of clocking "a tree going eighty-five miles an hour." Changes were later made that helped ensure the speed gun could be properly calibrated and, for instance, used while a patrol car was moving. Neal failed to change the law, but his effort helped change the status quo.

In time, similar efforts would take on greater gravity when he helped lead a group of citizens and elected officials calling for a police review board following repeated incidents of officer-involved shootings of unarmed black men.

The morning of Friday, November 21, 1980, began like any other in tourism-driven Las Vegas. Graveyard-shift workers ended their nights, and an army of day-shift employees arrived for their jobs dealing cards, serving meals and cocktails, and cleaning rooms at Strip casino-hotels. Las Vegas, the remarkable factory town, was humming as Thanksgiving week approached.

Just after seven a.m. at Kirk Kerkorian's behemoth MGM Grand Hotel and Casino, heralded as the largest hotel in the world, day-shift employees were preparing to open the Deli, one of several restaurants clustered at the southern end of the hotel. As the *Las Vegas Sun* reported, a maintenance supervisor heard the crackling sounds of fire coming from the ground-floor kitchen and smelled smoke near a waitress station. He rushed to notify guards. At about the same time, a waitress saw flames near an electronic keno board in the restaurant. Smoke immediately began billowing from the restaurant. A chef's attempt to knock down the growing flame failed.

In less than a minute, the $106 million MGM Grand was on fire. In under an hour, "the news had circled the globe." Toxic black smoke filled the hotel and its stairwells, and a forensic examination after the fact measured the speed of the fire's spread at seventeen feet per second. By the time the fire was finally extinguished and the terrible carnage assessed, eighty-four people were dead with hundreds more injured. Las Vegas had suffered an unprecedented black eye when it was discovered the gargantuan hotel had been built without a fire-safety sprinkler system of the type that easily might have extinguished or at least contained the fire.

Joe Neal was driving on the freeway that day and saw the smoke. He knew something had to be done, but like most Southern Nevadans he was reduced to praying and waiting on the sidelines. Las Vegas hotels, once oversized motor courts with a country-club style, began going vertical in the mid-1950s. And at the time the MGM was the largest and most audacious architectural statement yet. Built in 1973, before state law mandated fire sprinklers, the MGM was twenty-six stories tall and featured a 60,000-square-foot casino and 2,100 rooms and suites. On that fateful November morning, the hotel was ninety-nine percent occupied.

In the aftermath, ugly facts about the cause of the fire and the construction cost cutting that invited tragedy spread almost as fast as the fire.

During the building process, Clark County Fire Department inspectors recommended sprinklers, and MGM's own consultant Orvin Engineering concurred. But company chairman and Kerkorian inner circle member Fred Benninger demurred. He had a budget to maintain, and the $192,000 expense to outfit the hotel with standard fire-safety sprinklers was too costly. Aided by a Clark County building inspector's friendly interpretation of the fire codes to exempt sprinklers in the casino and the nearby Deli, Benninger applied for an exemption—and county building inspectors signed off on the shortcut.

The blaze was eventually attributed to an improperly installed electrical system that overheated, but when the public learned that MGM officials had lavished the property with marble flooring while cutting back on fire-safety sprinklers, people were understandably appalled. Forced to make real changes in the face of death and disaster and accusations of running, as the *Arizona Republic* opined, "a town without heart…a town without pity…a town without shame," casino bosses found themselves in a well-deserved bind.

Although a special prosecutor eventually would be assigned to the fire investigation, no criminal charges ever were filed against Benninger or anyone else associated with the company or its deadly decisions. (Kerkorian instructed underlings to settle claims as soon as possible. It was a decision that helped preserve MGM's brand and value, but led to a lengthy litigation with the resort's insurer.) Under heavy media scrutiny, the gaming industry wasn't yet off the hook.

In Nevada, fire-safety legislative issues fell under the purview of the Human Resources Committee, which Neal chaired. If he couldn't rush up and help put out the flames, he would soon discover a way to stand up and help make certain such preventable tragedies never occurred again.

And unlike other instances in which the gaming industry was challenged at the Legislature, this time it was in no position to spin the argument. MGM Grand had little choice but to install a state-of-the-art fire-safety system. And a plan floated in Carson City called for fire-safety mandates. Fire codes would be toughened, at least on paper, but there would be no expensive retrofitting of systems in all hotels. Neal would have none of it. He quickly studied the issue and found an ally in State Fire Marshal Tom Huddleston. He drew up legislation with professional input and asked his friend and fellow senator Bill Hernstadt to sign on as a cosponsor. Hernstadt was happy to comply. Other legislators were far more timid in dealing with the powerful casino industry.

"At the time, we had a rule that required an introduced bill to be kept in the desk overnight," Neal recalled. "They didn't want to send bills right to the committee. They wanted it to sit up there, and let people look at it. I don't know why. I always thought it was because the legislation I had started to introduce in the Senate could have made it, but they wanted to put it up in the desk and let it stay overnight."

Then tragedy struck again. An arson fire started in the Hilton on February 10, 1981, sent smoke skyward and negative news around the world about another Las Vegas casino. In the end, eight people lost their lives and many more were injured.

"On that same night, they had the Hilton fire, and more people got killed," Neal said. "I was able to get only one person to sign on to that retrofit bill, and that was Bill Hernstadt. Bill Hernstadt signed onto that bill, and we pushed that through."

Neal found an energetic ally in Huddleston, "who realized, more than I did, the effect of this piece of legislation. My concern was on the MGM fire, but he saw the wider applications of that. Actually, it turned out that we retrofitted the whole state!"

It was no sure thing. At one point in the struggle, Huddleston admitted to a UPI reporter, "No matter how unpopular it is, it's still something that has to be accomplished. We don't want to lose people."

The bill draft emerged in the Senate on February 11 with the Hilton fire in the headlines. The effort to soften the legislation began almost immediately.

Even with all that there was political maneuvering first to shape the legislation, then to attempt to soften its terms, and at last to ensure that certain political leaders, embattled governor Robert List not least, receive abundant credit for its creation. The MGM officials, whether out of a pang of conscience, a sense of duty, or just plain good public relations, announced during the debate that it would unilaterally install a "fire-safety system employing the latest technology to monitor, detect, and react instantly to fire danger anywhere in the hotel," the *Sun* reported. And UPI's Myram Borders noted, "Sprinklers, smoke detectors, and speakers will be located in every room. A ventilation-purging system will be capable of exchanging all the air inside the hotel complex within ten minutes."

As difficult as it might be to believe in the wake of two major fatal fires in a matter of months in Las Vegas, there was yet no shortage of critics of the legislation. That some lawmakers would balk at mandating fire-safety improvements in the casino-hotel businesses that were essential to Nevada's economic health might seem difficult to believe. However, such was the lapdog fealty the gaming bosses had ingrained in some legislators, while others simply suffered from the libertarian ethos that for government to mandate anything was automatically bad. In its comprehensive report on the fire and its aftermath, the *Sun* offered, "Some Nevada legislators still joined in the chorus of protests over the necessity of retrofitting fire-safety equipment in existing buildings. One, state senator Lawrence Jacobsen of Minden, claimed it would hurt Nevada's tourist-based economy." And Jacobsen was not alone.

In one of few instances in which credit was given where due, *The Day the MGM Grand Hotel Burned* (by *Las Vegas Sun* staff) acknowledged, "On the other hand, two other Nevada senators, William Hernstadt of Las Vegas and Joe Neal of North Las Vegas, introduced a bill for hotel owners in Las Vegas, Reno, and elsewhere to equip their buildings 'with an approved system of sprinklers for protection from fire.'"

Buildings fifty feet or taller and intended to hold at least 150 people were mandated to add fire-safety sprinklers. Churches were exempted—even Neal knew when not to press his luck.

"We didn't deal with churches," Neal said. "So that bill was pushed out of my committee and sent to the Assembly."

That is where more politics awaited. List was feeling heat of his own. Having been embroiled in a scandal at the outset of his tenure that involved his alleged acceptance of complimentary rooms at the mobbed-up Stardust hotel during his tenure as state attorney general, then dealing with economic struggles worsened by a national downturn, the Republican governor desperately needed positive press. He'd been deeply moved during a tour of the MGM not long after the fire had been extinguished and in time would gather a commission led by banker and future governor Kenny Guinn to study the issue. (The commission's findings and recommendations, to little surprise, landed on the conservative side of the ledger.) With the public still on edge and the state's tourist-driven economy at stake, it was an issue the gaming industry couldn't simply market its way out of with discounts and paparazzi press accounts. List sent his administration's bill to the Assembly.

"He wanted to get credit for it," Neal recalled. "But he sent it to the wrong committee, which was chaired by a friend of mine—a guy named Jack Jeffrey."

Jeffrey was a Clark County Democrat and a proud member of the machine who already had nearly a decade of legislative experience. He served until 1990 with stints as majority leader. With List's bill in hand, Jeffrey came to Neal's office and asked the senator about his next move. They could make hay out of the opposition's bill, even try to bury it. Instead, Neal said, "Take all the good things out of the governor's bill, amend them into mine, send it back up to us, and we'll pass it. And that's what we did."

For once in a great long time, Nevada found itself a national leader in a positive category: commercial fire safety. It found itself in a progressive column. It only took the deaths of ninety-two people to do it.

Neal crowed that "that became the best fire law in the world dealing with high-rise structures. There's no legislature in the world that did what we had done with that piece of legislation by retrofitting all of the high-rises in the whole state."

The law not only changed Nevada for the better, but it helped lead to improvements in fire-safety and retrofitting laws in California and across the nation. "Today, fire codes throughout the country are much stricter because of the MGM Grand tragedy," a 1990 report in the *Los Angeles Times* concluded. "In 1980, many high-rises were not equipped with smoke detectors—much less sprinkler systems. The year after the disaster, both the Nevada and California legislatures beefed up state fire ordinances."

Hernstadt was not long for the Legislature. Fire Marshal Huddleston left the state and became an executive consultant on safety issues. Perhaps appreciating that the credit for the retrofit law would likely go to the person with the highest elected office, Governor List, Huddleston wrote Neal a letter of congratulations that even decades later still made the retired legislative warhorse proud. The letter "said that the state owes me a debt for what I had done. This bill will save lives, and it will reduce insurance premiums. He said that because of my bill, this state and its industry are safer as a result, and their premiums would go down in terms of their insurance costs."

Not that the passage of the retrofit bill left the Nevada Resort Association in any mood to send Neal a bouquet. In the short term, it would cost millions.

The MGM fire generated almost 1,400 lawsuits, and more than $200 million—about twice the cost of construction of the resort—was paid out in settlements.

"Tragedies happen in any life, whether it's a car accident or a fire. The fact that we spent $5 million on life safety now makes this one of the safest hotels in the world and people know it," an emotionally detached Benninger said.

Of the statute that emerged, special commission chairman Guinn offered, "It's not a perfect law, but it's a start. We've set a foundation for the state to grow on." Years later, others who studied the fire's aftermath were more optimistic. One reporter concluded, "Every structure in the state was required to comply—no exemptions, no grandfathering. Resorts, schools and universities grumbled at the expense but understood the necessity."

More than 35 years after the historic legislation, Neal remained notably proud of the accomplishment: "The most famous piece of legislation that I was associated with came after the MGM fire in 1981. That was the Retrofit Law. I pushed it through the Legislature mainly because I was chairman of the Human Resources Committee, which took care of all fire legislation.... The hotels didn't like it too much."

The gaming industry wasn't just going to accept its responsibility and pony up the price of improving fire safety. Not when there was another angle to work.

"Instead of them actually paying for the retrofitting," Neal said, "they got revenue bonds, which meant the whole nation paid for it."

By the 1979 session, conservative Jim Gibson was still stinging from the embarrassment Neal had helped cause him in the ERA vote. He pushed to change a rule of order, making it more difficult for the Neal-Rose maneuver to succeed. Neal, becoming one of the more experienced members of his caucus, couldn't reasonably be denied a committee chairmanship. He had been given the Natural Resources Committee position, and the vice chairmanship of the Human Resources Committee. Gibson made sure his fellow religious and political conservatives maintained their control of key committees. The state's so-called citizen Legislature had long fit comfortably in the pocket of the state's powerful business interests. So when Neal and Senator Hernstadt defied the status quo and pushed for transparency in internal legislative proceedings, including releasing the recordings of meetings that hadn't taken place in public view, some of their colleagues vilified them. The Legislative Counsel Bureau sealed lawmakers' travel and expense vouchers from public view. Citizens were also not allowed to know what elected officials were making use of the State Highway Department's airplane, which was regularly available to Senate leaders Raggio and Gibson.

At the Legislature, the easiest way to impress voters and reporters is to propose a law that increases the sentence for a crime. The offense can be great or small. In fact, the offense itself is secondary to the political importance of making the punishment more draconian. So it was with Nevada's drunken-driving law.

Improvements were needed in the law, and eventually the legal limit of alcohol impairment would be reduced to .08. For his part, Neal had no problem with getting tough on those who drive drunk. His beef was with the inconsistency with which such laws were enforced in Nevada. Although alcohol consumption was conspicuous and crossed social, economic, and racial lines, the local drunk tanks were full of brown and black offenders.

And so when the Assembly passed a bill calling for two days of jail time for first-time offenders, Neal noted the social and racial disparities—and was immediately pummeled for being soft on crime. He managed to gather support from three of his Senate colleagues, who opposed the bill for their own personal reasons, and set about to slow the legislation. Drawing on his knowledge of parliamentary procedure, he sought a delay by requesting a written interpretation of the rules. Newspaper editorial pages snorted their disapproval.

"Lowering the limits and adding mandatory jail time sounds fine, but it would have had a disproportionate impact on the district I represented," he said. "In a mostly black district, knowing that those jail cells weren't full of white folks, I was very much concerned about the people it would impact. Getting arrested and being forced to go to jail had a greater impact on the lives and livelihoods of the poor. They would often lose their jobs as a result of a mistake. It definitely had a greater impact on the poor and minorities. It's the way the system worked."

But who was going to speak up and say that? Not even the Legislature's handful of self-styled progressive white politicians could speak up using such life experience.

On May 13, 1983, Neal took to the floor of the Senate and reminded his fellow members that their glasses were only half full on the issue.

"I know most of us realize that driving and drinking is a problem, not only in this state, but throughout the country," he began. "And I believe that it is a problem, because drinking is a part of the American culture. In fact, it is deeply imbedded in the American culture, as exemplified each evening when we cross the street when we go to Jack's Bar. Yet, when we see these particular issues, something seems to happen to the legislative mind when it attempts to address this problem. That is, we seek means by which to penalize those who drink and get into trouble by doing so."

Not satisfied to offer a bill simply increasing the penalties for a DUI conviction, its authors chose to add a provision calling for a first-time offender to be clothed in "distinctive garb" to designate their guilt. It reminded Neal of the photos of Jews under Nazi rule, and Nevada being Nevada he suspected not everyone convicted would be outfitted similarly.

"Those 'distinctive garbs' are not going to be worn by the wealthy," he said. "They are not going to be worn by the powerful. And I doubt whether or not they are going to be worn by any of the lawyers in this state. It is going to be those individuals who find themselves lacking in political power, who find themselves lacking in money to purchase the expertise to beat these types of cases. Those are the individuals who you are going to be finding on the streets of this state, picking up cans, paper, and what-have-you. These will be the people that the judges will make an example out of."

Then there were the partying tourists to consider, he said. Could they reasonably be expected to return to the state to wear a scarlet letter and comb the roadsides in official shame?

"What is going to happen to the State of Nevada when the word gets out that some tourist, because he did not have enough money to hire the expertise of a Senator Wilson, or a Senator Raggio to beat this type of law, and he finds himself walking the streets in 'distinctive garb.' Do you think he is going to come back to the State of Nevada? I would venture to say that he will not."

Neal offered reasoned alternatives that in those days were far-fetched: an education campaign about the dangers of drinking and driving, a change in the way alcohol is advertised, and the placement of breathalyzers in bars to help patrons better understand the effects their drinking was having on their blood alcohol levels.

"But we have not done this," he said. "We have faltered under the onslaught of emotionalism to rush to get a bill out to please some of our constituents. I think that we could do more."

The Senate revised the bill, and a more effective measure was passed without making offenders dress in "distinctive garb."

By the early 1980s, Neal's zeal on popular and unpopular issues alike generated an interest in politics from a new generation on the Westside and beyond. Morse "Moose" Arberry was a homegrown political talent who understood that the door to the opportunity to enter elected office had been opened in large part with Neal's help. He would remain a loyal friend through twenty-four years in the Assembly.

"I met Senator Neal back in the day when I'd come home from school, and everyone knew him as the senator from the community," Arberry said in a 2017 interview. "I grew up in the community, and everyone knew him. When I decided to run for office, I walked the district door to door, and the first words I always heard were, 'Are you running against Senator Neal?' I would quickly say, 'No, I'm running for the Assembly seat.' He was just that well liked and well respected in the community. He knew the district better than anyone. He was consistently in touch with the people who put him in office. They were the union workers and the people who worked for the casinos. They had to have a voice. Somebody needed to carry it to Carson City. They felt very comfortable with him carrying water for them.

At the Legislature, Arberry soon realized that Neal's contacts stretched far beyond Carson City.

"When I was blessed to be elected and able to serve as an assemblyman, I learned that Joe was well known outside the local community," Arberry said. "His Senate district included rural areas, and at the Legislature many of the rural boys told me about him. He knew the people in the rural areas, not only in the urban area he represented. He wanted to hear their plight. For him, it was about Nevada. This was not just his home, but he represented the working-class people and their ideas.

"Not only was he my senator, but I was blessed because he was a mentor to me. He knew that *Mason's Manual* very well. He taught me the ins and outs of working in the Legislature. When I became chair of a committee, I spent many days in his office trying to learn from him. I could never learn everything he knew, but he was a source of information, and he was well-respected by other senators."

Neal also provided an opportunity for Gwendolyn Chapman when he hired her as his secretary and assistant in 1995. An African American, she appreciated the opportunity and was challenged by the work—but it took time to get used to Neal's imposing style. "When I started I was kind of intimidated by him," she recalled in an interview. "He was a large man with a big voice. After probably a month or two, I realized he was really just a big teddy bear, that's how I felt about him."

Those who misunderstood Neal when the Senate was in session also entertained Chapman. "He would be quiet and lean back in his chair and they would think he's sleeping in the committee, and all of a sudden he'd rise up and ask a question that would throw everyone off. It was, like, oh, he wasn't sleeping."

And he was always up for a good legal fight—especially against the liveliest intellect from the opposition party.

"He knew the law right down to the tip of a needle," she recalled. "Although Senator Raggio was an attorney and Senator Neal was not, Senator Neal knew the law in every detail. There were times I think Raggio knew he was fighting a losing battle. Joe would fight him tooth and nail."

Between hearings, Raggio would sometimes laugh with Arberry about enduring yet another broadside from the apparently tireless Neal.

"Senator Raggio (as chairman of Senate Finance) and I became pretty close after I became chair of Assembly Ways and Means," Arberry said. "Bill and I would talk often, and sometimes he'd say, 'Moose, I'm having some guests come in today. Could you ask Senator Neal not to beat up on me today?' We would just laugh."

Raggio, so often on the receiving end of a Neal diatribe, was only half joking.

Joe Neal's mother, Josephine Neal.

Estelle at the time of her college graduation.

Neal working with Equal Rights Commissioner Bob Bailey (right) in the 1960s.

Neal in a suit during his unsuccessful first run for office in 1964.

Neal after his enlistment in the U.S. Air Force

Neal, right, on duty at Indian Springs Air Force Base.

Estelle and Joe on their wedding day.

Neal arrives for the 1973 session of the Nevada Legislature as the first African-American to serve in the Senate.

Neal arguing a point of order with Senator Mike Malone looking on.

Neal made scores of headlines and often read from them to prove his point.

Neal giving a fiery speech in support of Culinary Union workers.

Neal speaking in support of Culinary Union workers outside the MGM Grand in Las Vegas.

Neal in the White House with President Clinton

Neal circa 1979

Campaign photo of Neal during his run for Governor

In the mid-1980s at Southern Nevada's Nellis Air Force Base, military veteran Neal was happy to take a ride—in the backseat—of an F-16 jet fighter.

When Neal was named President Pro-Tempore of the Nevada State Senate, his family accompanied him to Carson City for the occasion. With wife Estelle at his side, and Joseph, grandson James, Cherisse with grandson John, Withania, Tania, and Dina.

Neal with UNLV President Carol C. Harter on the occasion of him being honored as a Distinguished Nevadan.

With seniority came a (slightly) better office.

Neal with Nevada newspaper editor Jack McCloskey.

Joseph M. Neal STEAM Academy was dedicated to Neal in 1991.

Joe with granddaughter Alexandra Neal and Assemblywoman Dina Neal.

Neal leads a Democratic Party welcome for the Clinton-Gore ticket that includes from left to right former Gov. Grant Sawyer, Senator Richard Bryan, Congressman James Bilbray, Attorney General Frankie Sue Del Papa, and Senator Harry Reid.

Neal makes a point in the senate chamber. Neal for Governor

Fighting Apartheid in the Silver State

Y EARS BEFORE THE anti-apartheid movement made headlines in Las Vegas, it had a humble headquarters at Saint James the Apostle Catholic Church on H Street in the heart of the Westside. Franciscan Father Louis Vitale was better known as an antinuclear proliferation activist who wasn't afraid to stand up, march to the gates of the Nevada Test Site, and be arrested for his beliefs.

Vitale found what some might consider an unlikely ally in his congregation: Neal, whose work as an equal employment opportunity compliance officer at REECo regularly took him through the gates of the test site with a Q clearance. The priest was well aware of Neal's work loyalties, but was more focused on seeing his face in church during Saint James's musical Sunday services. The church played an active role in feeding and clothing the poor in some of the Las Vegas Valley's most impoverished neighborhoods.

The two found a kindred connection in the battle to raise the apartheid issue in a community with its own ugly history of segregation.

During those informational meetings, Nevadans Against Apartheid was born.

"I had worked at the test site for many years, and during much of that time Father Louie was at our parish," Neal recalled. "I used to see him go out and march. He never asked me questions about the test site. I guess he understood that I had to work and I needed the job.

"Saint James had become a missionary parish. We had many of our meetings there. I got to know Father Louie and the Franciscans, who had taken vows of poverty. It was the first time I realized that all priests didn't take a vow of poverty."

In the United States, the attempt to ban trade with South Africa with a goal of ending apartheid was first introduced in 1972 by U.S. Senator William Roth of Delaware and several fellow Republicans. The pressure continued through the four years of the Carter administration, but languished under President Ronald Reagan, a cold warrior who saw South Africa as a strategic ally in the fight against the spread of Communism. Carter managed to raise America's collective consciousness on an issue that mirrored our nation's own ugly civil rights history. But it took a vote of Congress—and an override of Reagan's veto, led by a fellow Republican, Senator Richard Lugar of Indiana—in 1986 to pass the Comprehensive Anti-Apartheid Act (CAAA) into law. It exposed Reagan's political tone deafness on civil rights issues as never before, and at last moved the United States away from its Cold War–era support of South Africa. Reagan had mistakenly valued South Africa's strategic importance above its institutionally repressive racial policies and nightmarish human rights record.

Nevada's U.S. Senators Paul Laxalt and Mayer Jacob "Chic" Hecht, both loyal political allies of Reagan, voted against the act and the congressional override.

At the Nevada Legislature, Neal had weighed in on the issue for several sessions by the time the politics reached the state's backyard. His criticism of South Africa hadn't gone unnoticed. From his Louisiana childhood, he'd experienced the pain of living in a society separated by race and economic class. Although daily life was only marginally different when he arrived in 1950s Southern Nevada, the ensuing years had brought dramatic legal progress, if often modest appreciable gains, for blacks in Las Vegas. His own story was a metaphor for the promise of the possible and the frustrations of the probable in the place sneeringly known as "the Mississippi of the West."

So no one had to tell Neal that change took time, respect was hard fought, and patience was a necessity as well as a virtue.

But when the Las Vegas City Commission saw fit to squire Frank Land, a representative of South Africa's apartheid government, around Las Vegas in the name of economic development and polite politics, Neal was beside himself with anger. It wasn't the 1950s or '6os. It was the 1980s, and he believed the disrespect being shown the black community was inexcusable.

Neal helped fire up the local branch of the NAACP, which had not lacked for good intentions, but was seen by some as too patient with local social traditions. Neal often found himself stepping out front on controversial issues. When an eighty-member delegation of South Africans allied with its apartheid government received red-carpet treatment in Southern Nevada, Neal was apoplectic.

At least one Clark County commissioner, Thalia Dondero, was contrite. She was no racist, but she hadn't realized that joining the Las Vegas Chamber of Commerce president and a real estate executive in officially greeting a representative of the apartheid government would be seen as an insensitive slight on the local African-American population. "I'm very sorry I didn't," she told a reporter. "I was looking at the tourists with dollar signs in my eyes. I really didn't mean to offend anyone. I have considered myself a friend of the black community."

For his part, Land was a skilled spokesman who presented the Afrikaner view of South African history in a soft light that bespoke of more fatherly benevolence than institutional racism. During his Las Vegas tour, he met with cordial members of the City Commission and dined with influential Southern Nevadans who were politically connected in South Africa. Although he couched the trip as a routine diplomatic excursion through the West from the consulate's Southern California office, it was clear he was spreading a message riddled with historical revisionism. He was hesitant to answer questions on apartheid and politely attempted to move the conversation toward South Africa's bustling economy and its gold mining kinship with Nevada.

"If you look at South Africa beyond the headlines, which seem to stress the racial issues, you'll find that seen internationally South Africa is really a very stable country," he told a Las Vegas newspaper. "In fact, the overall stability is such that we are regarded as a better investment risk today than other countries like Great Britain, Portugal, Spain, and Italy."

Nationwide upheaval was downplayed into a mere "potential for conflict." Apartheid, a major issue? On the contrary, "There is a peaceful change taking place in South Africa against a background of economic stability and military strength. We have fewer incidents than

Britain has with its Irish problems. South African leaders planned to distance themselves from apartheid in time, but it's not simply an issue of skin color, but a matter of cultural differences, languages, and ways of life. Historically we have not had much integration with ethnic groups. It is not a policy goal. What we are seeking to do is to provide protection for each group and the opportunity to protect their identity."

The veteran diplomat found willing hosts in Las Vegas. Their disconnect from the undeniable changes taking place in South Africa, and America's role in that human rights battle that so mirrored our nation's own civil rights struggle, was entirely lost on them. Poverty in the United States was nearing a fifteen-year high. African Americans were incarcerated at staggering rates. Shootings of unarmed blacks by Las Vegas police went unpunished.

And the South African diplomat was receiving first-cabin treatment—and not a murmur of protest—in Southern Nevada. Neal was incensed. He was a chorus of one, but he roared in the press, to which he'd become such a reliable source of outrage on issues that discomforted so many other political leaders.

Decrying what ought to be have been perceived as an obvious insult to the black community, Neal charged, "It would not be in the best interests of Nevada or any other state to promote trade with South Africa because of their racist policies."

Neal responded in the press where he could, then took to his typewriter and blasted the local elected officials for their insensitivity. He squared up on City Commissioner Al Levy when the politician and real estate broker saw fit to escort representatives of South Africa's government on a goodwill business mission to Southern Nevada. He later admitted he was harder on Levy, a Jew whom he believed ought to have been more sensitive to the plight of his fellow man, than he might have been on others.

Neal conjured images of placating promulgators of the Holocaust and the violence of the virulently anti-Zionist Palestine Liberation Organization in his November 12, 1981, broadside.

"I will not sit idle and allow you to impoverish the dignity of my people or my ancestral relations by such a despicable act as giving the keys to the city to a racist government such as South Africa just because

it was your 'job,'" he wrote. "...If you cannot bring yourself to render
the keys to the city to the PLO, or declare Adolph Eichmann an innocent man, then I certainly think that you owe the black community of
Las Vegas an apology for doing such to the representatives of the South
African government!"

He signed the column, "Respectfully yours."

As usual, what Neal derisively called the "white press" quoted the
outraged senator from North Las Vegas, but failed to take a stand with
him. The timidity was palpable. Only *Las Vegas Sun* columnist Judy
Carlos appeared willing to weigh in with a measure of the scorn Neal
had leveled at Levy. She reported that another elected official—a fellow
state senator—who had read Neal's incendiary remarks was livid. Not
over Levy's fealty to the representatives of a tyrannical government,
but over Neal's rude stridence.

"This other state senator allegedly said, 'Joe Neal is not going to tell
me what party I can go to.'

"Well, maybe Joe won't, but I will. It will be a cold day on the veldt
before you come to mine, Bobo. City Commissioner Al Levy, who
hosted the cocktail party, seemed downright confused over the issue,
and said our town's leading lights were only showing their good manners by toasting the development of free trade. That's all, a real polite
guy who sure knows how to sell a house in a sandstorm.

"The official South African line is that we shouldn't let mere politics get in the way of a beautiful friendship. There, with one swift,
adolescent wink and a wave of semantics, we are supposed to dismiss
our traditions and our constitution in the name of the almighty buck."

Neal saved the Carlos column clipping for the next 36 years as a
reminder of the time someone in the mainstream press joined him
without equivocation. He later traveled to New York to testify before
the United Nations subcommittee on apartheid. "I remember quot-
ing Martin Luther King in 'Letter From Birmingham Jail.' He said,
'Injustice anywhere is a threat to justice everywhere.'"

The meetings at the UN were informative, but essentially uneventful until an explosion was heard in the building during a subcommittee hearing on apartheid. Parts of the building were evacuated, but it
turned out to be a problem in an exercise room.

The real intrigue occurred when Neal returned home and discovered a Georgia congressman had been so infuriated at the gathering that he'd collected the names of every attendee and put them on the public record.

"I thought that was unusual," Neal said. "When I researched the congressman, I discovered he was one of the guys who was supportive of South Africa. He wanted the public to know who was appearing at the conference so that action could be taken against them."

At the Nevada Legislature, the South African government had no overt defenders, but the lawmakers always managed to find a way to vote down attempts at divestiture; "They always voted against the state's pension fund from investing in South Africa. And that's what the whole situation was about."

People had their reasons to vote against divestiture, some of them economic. The issue was complex, but Neal perceived it in clear and simple terms. He recalled in an interview, "What I saw was white people protecting other white people, and business being business."

The issue tore even some progressive Las Vegans. One local business couple with a long history of supporting civil rights in Southern Nevada spoke glowingly of South African investment. At the time, they were pursuing an interest in a casino there. Others argued that the South African government was a bulwark against the spread of Communism across the continent.

Neal generated so much negative publicity that the South African consulate general came to Las Vegas from Los Angeles to attempt to get a meeting with the outspoken legislator.

"He came here because I had raised so much hell and gotten so much press," Neal recalled. "He was staying at the MGM at the time not long before the fire. He said he wanted to meet with me, and I agreed. He wanted to meet in his room, and I declined. I figured he would be recording me and trying to get me to say something he could take out of context, and I told him I would meet him in a loud place downstairs."

"Mr. Neal, I want you to understand that South Africa is not New Jersey," he said. "It is not part of the United States. It is very different."

Neal quietly seethed at the thought that the supposedly civilized fellow sitting across the table was saying that blacks in South Africa were somehow incapable of self-governance.

"He tried to convince me that what I was saying was wrong, and they had a right to do what they were doing," Neal recalled. "I wouldn't buy that." Neal had already been in contact with Dumisali Kumalo, the former journalist who had essentially been run out of South Africa and had devoted his life to ending apartheid.

At the 1983 session of the Legislature, in his role as a member of the Government Affairs Committee, Neal authored Senate Bill 266, a facsimile of unsuccessful legislation he'd proposed in 1981. The new bill sought to ban the investment of Nevada's public funds into South African business. What seemed like the right thing to do in 1981 was an even more obvious choice in 1983. At least in other states. In Nevada, where Neal was the lone African American in the state Senate, the language of change was complicated by its own racial history and the call was much tougher. So Neal enlisted the help of exiled black South African journalist Kumalo, who addressed the effectiveness of anti-investment laws in a well-timed press conference.

"We're not talking about morality, we're talking about money," Kumalo said. "When you talk money, it hurts.... It's unfair to try and portray that corporations are in the business of saving blacks. South Africa is going to blow up. Where is the prudence in investing in racism?"

At the hearing, Neal was opposed by Will Keating, the head of Nevada's Public Employee's Retirement System (PERS), and John Sande, the state's leading oil industry lobbyist. In the short term, divestment would damage the PERS bustling returns. Keating laughably postulated that it would be a challenge to track the South African investments. Sande argued that because American oil companies engaged in fair hiring practices, his clients could be excluded.

"Our state monies should not to go any government to enable it to maintain a system which rejects individuals based solely on the color of their skin," Neal said. "Our money should not go to any government which uses violence to maintain a system of apartheid, a system which would be illegal under our Constitution."

Neal then reminded his uncomfortable colleagues, most of whom had never experienced second-class citizenship, that the Legislature had only recently paused to reflect on the Holocaust.

"It was a recognition," he said later, "in my judgment, that this cruel loss of life under a system which required the extinction of a people should never happen again. It is happening again, and this state is a contributor."

Away from the Legislature Kumalo and Neal kindled a lasting alliance. Kumalo addressed policy makers in twenty-six states, twenty-four counties, and more than ninety cities in an effort to have officials take economic action against apartheid. He became the projects director for The Africa Fund and in 1999 was named South Africa's ambassador to the United Nations after he "worked tirelessly to educate the American people about the injustices of apartheid and helped mobilize effective public support for the struggle for freedom."

Neal was proud to call Kumalo a friend and would long remember the first time he escorted him through the Westside.

"He said it reminded him of the ghettos of Soweto," Neal said.

Death and Life in the '80s

THE 1980S BROUGHT a conservative revolution to Washington and a resurgence of political austerity in Nevada. Ronald Reagan's resounding victory over President Jimmy Carter sent a message that reverberated from the halls of Congress to the streets of the Las Vegas Westside. Appreciable gains for blacks and other minorities would be harder to come by.

As ever, Joe Neal remained a singular voice at the Nevada Legislature on the seemingly impossible battle to abolish the state's death penalty law, which he'd consistently argued was biased toward minorities. He found allies, if little momentum, but also noted the increasing lack of patience with such unpopular causes. "I don't have to state what my position is on this particular issue," he said during the floor discussion of Senate Bill 392, another attempt to abolish the death penalty offered during the 1981 session, "but I can say to you that I was not the one to request this bill to be drawn. It was given to me for introduction, and I thought that the bill does have merit, since we are talking about a life or death issue. If we are going to play the game in this Legislature that we are going to cut matters off before they are heard, then let's open it up. Let's everybody play that game.... It has been my experience in this legislative body that such an issue of this nature does not require a considerable amount of time to deal with and dispose of it. So I'm very concerned now, that if we bring something before this body, it's going to be sidetracked in this particular manner. I guess we can equate this issue with that of the ERA which came before this body, that we would make motions that we not consider it, when there is a great need and a great concern in this state to have such a matter be heard."

Neal increased his awareness and support for a repeal of the state's capital punishment statute after the U.S. Supreme Court's 1972 decision in *Furman v. Georgia*, a 5–4 vote that held that the arbitrary and inconsistent imposition of the death penalty violated the Eighth and Fourteenth Amendments and constituted cruel and unusual punishment. It created, in effect, a moratorium on capital punishment cases while courts and state justice systems worked to bring their statutes into constitutional alignment. Within four years, thirty-seven states had enacted new death penalty laws with increased standards and safeguards in place that, at least in theory, would reduce the racial and economic bias defendants traditionally faced when they entered a courtroom in capital murder cases.

Neal only realized later that, with his first statement on the Senate floor, he had entered a marathon that would find few Nevadans cheering for him. "You couldn't just have talked about it one time," he recalled many years later. "The issue was too important. So I just kept going and going and going."

Whether calmly or with great umbrage, Neal would continue to demand to be heard on this issue throughout his career. Time and again he would raise the question of fairness on the issues of the application of the death penalty, the sentence of life imprisonment, parole and probation, and the restoration of civil rights for convicted felons.

At times his frustrations were undeniable. When the bodies of black children began turning up in Atlanta, the apparent victims of a sadistic serial killer later identified as Wayne Williams, Neal again took to the Senate floor. He recounted memories of the 1950s Nevada he'd been introduced to and reminded his colleagues there was still plenty of racism in the state and, indeed, in the state capital.

"I know that even in Carson City, since I've been coming up here, I have experienced some of the racial problems," he said on March 11, 1981. "In fact, in Enrico's one night, a couple of white men came in and called us a 'couple of niggers.' I've received letters addressing me in the same way."

He revealed another part of his personality that day.

"Of course," he said, "I'm not the type of individual who subscribes totally to the Martin Luther King philosophy of nonviolence, so they were under a great risk of doing that. I would not attack anyone just for the calling of a name, but if there is any indication of any physical contact, I'm ready and very capable of handling myself in such a situation."

It wasn't a simple display of braggadocio. Neal's commentary echoed the frustrations of many blacks in a decade in which much of the nation had signaled a willingness to retreat from hard-won social and civil rights gains.

His efforts at abolition resoundingly rejected, a session later he was arguing against the method of administering the death penalty by lethal injection. "The arguments for such a bill as lethal injection are very interesting," he said. "We hear and read of such things as it would eliminate the carnival atmosphere surrounding the scene of execution, and that it is a humane way to die. I find the latter to be a very strange argument because it is, after all, a human being who is being put to death.... I find these arguments a cowardly way to shield ourselves from the awful spectacle of death. We do not want to hear or see a human being fight for life as the gas or electric current begins to consume the life process. We look for ways to hide the gory details as the victim leaves the land of the living and enters the kingdom of death. We would much rather not be reminded of one's struggle for life which sometimes signifies itself by the wrenching and quivering of the body, the bulging of the eyes, saliva dripping from the corners of the mouth—as the body fights to live.

"I would say that the scene of lethal injection is far more palatable to the people as represented by these nine reputable citizens in this bill than the popping of the eyes from the hangman's noose, or one who is being shot to death."

His colleagues had heard his arguments against the death penalty for a decade and, to a great degree, had written them off as politically impractical or rejected them on personal philosophical grounds. After ten years, Neal hadn't budged an inch.

"We have entered into a dangerous period when the blindfold is taken from the eyes of justice and more of a concern is given to who committed the crime than the crime being committed. Yes, it is a dangerous period when the color of one's skin can dictate whether or not he can receive life in prison, or lethal injection. It is a dangerous period when our economic status is far more likely to dictate that we receive death by lethal injection. And I want to point out this because of the fact that we have something like on the order of seventeen or eighteen people on death row in the State of Nevada. Not a single one of those individuals is wealthy. Not a single one of those individuals is a politician. They don't have the power to defend themselves against the rule of law that we are attempting to improve upon.... Yes, we are in a dangerous period when we begin to think of alternative means of execution in terms of being less expensive. We are in a dangerous period when the execution of a human being becomes symbolic of putting a dog to sleep."

While many of Neal's efforts often fell short, or were written off by the lawmaking establishment, in time the energetic voices of a new generation of legislators continued the call for change.

"I was functioning on the basis of what was happening to the people I represented at the time," he recalled in 2016. "I tried to be their voice in the Legislature in terms of policymaking. When it came to restoring the rights of ex-felons, the idea came to me from a fellow named Butler who was a shoeshine man. I went to him for a shoeshine one day, and he said, 'You should do something about those ex-felons. They can't even get a job.' So I introduced a bill calling for the restoration of their civil rights. It eventually passed—with a ten-year waiting period.

"But in time, Bob Barengo and Chris Giunchigliani and some others fought successfully to reduce the waiting period to six months. And then Chris got it whacked out altogether. So that worked out pretty good in the long run, but it took two decades."

As the Reagan era wore on, conservative legislators became even more zealous in their tough-on-crime positions. During the 1985 session, a time in which the Republican-majority Assembly floated a bill attempting to limit time for death penalty appeals, Neal found himself with an unlikely but welcome ally in Republican Senate Majority Leader Bill Raggio. As the Washoe County district attorney, Raggio had carved a legend for himself by burning the Mustang Ranch brothel and sending its whoremaster Joe Conforte out of business and into hiding.

Neal began his opposition by calling out the bill's laughable time limits, a mere five months to mount an appeal.

"When we deal with the question of putting someone to death, we do it in the name of the people of the State of Nevada," he said. "By doing so, I think that each individual, no matter how heinous the crime that he or she may have committed, should have the time that is necessary within the judicial system to appeal that sentence. We should not put the court in a straitjacket in deciding this type of issue. That is what this bill does."

Then it was Raggio's turn. He was a strong proponent of the death penalty and had prosecuted a dozen capital murder cases that resulted in the ultimate punishment, but he also knew the rule of law and the separation of powers, and he believed it was "invading the judicial province.... I believe this is something the court itself should adopt by rule," Raggio said. "I would certainly suggest that there are better ways to bring this to the attention of the court than to pass a statute which on its face appears to be a violation of the state's constitution."

Legislative observers would have been within their rights to be startled by the unlikely alliance. But by decade's end, Neal was once again imploring his colleagues to use their best judgment against cutting off avenues of death penalty appeal after an Assembly resolution urged Congress to expedite federal review.

"We seem to be asking, with this resolution, that that right, under the Constitution of the United States, be denied," he said. "It seems to be that we would be saying…that the State of Nevada would have the ultimate decision by rendering the sentence of death under its laws. And, that there should not be any review of that decision.

"The decision of death is final. Once it takes place, there is no recourse whatsoever, even though the facts uncovered later may prove that the individual is innocent. I find that we are in very strange company in this area that relates to the death penalty. We find ourselves in the company of the Soviet Union, China, South Africa, and Iran. All of these countries exercise the death penalty. We, in this country, would be appalled if we saw someone hanging by their thumbs. We would say that would be cruel and unusual punishment. Yet, we are willing to see an individual hanged by their neck in carrying out the death sentence. We would be appalled to hear of or see a man having 150 volts applied to his testicles, yet we would applaud 250 volts being sent through a person's body."

He also advocated for improving abortion rights for Nevada women, arguing that the push to outlaw and effectively criminalize the medical procedure would hurt the poor most. An attempt from the Assembly side to revise and restrict requirements for consent and notice in abortion cases drew particular ire. At best, making it tougher for residents to obtain an abortion would result in an "increased number of Nevadans, particularly those who have the money to catch a plane, to drive, to take the day off, to go to the clinics in California, Tahoe City, Sacramento, Los Angeles; and those individuals who find themselves not able to come to their fathers and mothers and address these particular questions as to whether or not they are pregnant will find themselves going into the backrooms with crude instruments, or coat hangers, and things of that sort which induce an abortion."

The bill had momentum, and he was once again in the minority, but Neal kept hammering his conservative colleagues, raising the issue of the influence of the Moral Majority and the violation of the physician Hippocratic Oath.

On the issue of abortion Neal found a formidable foe in Ruth McGroarty, a devout Catholic who lobbied with passion to ban the medical procedure or at least make it much more difficult to obtain. Neal appreciated her effort although he disagreed with her views, and one day in the halls of the Legislature he stopped her and asked, "Why are you pushing this? As soon as these kids are born, society doesn't want to do anything for them. And many of them wind up in jail, some even on death row. And the church never takes a position on that."

McGroarty agreed with her adversary, but that didn't prevent her from battling onward and, later, opening Life Line, an abortion alternative center for pregnant teens and indigent mothers.

"In the Reagan era, you saw a lot of changes taking place, and a lot of setbacks in terms of civil rights progress," Neal remembered. "I saw that as far as I was concerned not a lot of good was going to happen under him."

The conservative revolution's influence was felt in Nevada, when in 1982 the understated Chic Hecht knocked off four-term powerhouse

Howard Cannon in the U.S. Senate race. Democrat Cannon, the state's senior senator, found himself under political assault with a primary challenger and FBI investigation in connection with Teamsters Union corruption. The weight of the ongoing battles wore on Cannon, never much of a dynamic campaigner, and he was shoved into retirement.

Neal had worked on Cannon's campaigns since the 1960s. Before Cannon left office, he performed a career-saving favor for Neal, who had been approached by two business-minded chemical engineers to head an investment in a Nigerian oil field. With the potential profit of a nickel a barrel, Neal would share in a vast fortune. All he had to do was front the paperwork, lease a tanker, and use political contacts to make the right connections in Africa and Louisiana. Millions of barrels were potentially in play.

The deal seemed too good to be true, and Neal contacted Cannon in his U.S. Senate office for assistance with the contacts. "I did not know that the oil company involved was fronting for the CIA, which had gone in and changed the government there," Neal said. After he extricated himself from a potential scandal, "Cannon and I had a big laugh about it."

Neal would have to keep his day job at REECo, after all.

Cannon was a friend and fellow Democrat, but on other occasions Republican senator Paul Laxalt sought Neal's company. During a trip to Washington for a conference, Laxalt contacted him and sought a private meeting. Laxalt, best known as a close friend of Reagan's and briefly a top choice for vice president, had known Neal as an acquaintance since the 1960s. Laxalt had won important votes in the Westside in 1966 by supporting then-Republican Woodrow Wilson's Assembly candidacy. But Laxalt was no leader of the state's civil rights movement, and indeed had held hands with Howard Hughes in the secretive effort to defeat fair housing legislation in the late 1960s.

Laxalt greeted Neal warmly at the Washington Hilton, and the two talked about Nevada politics. After a few minutes Laxalt moved to his real reason for the chat. He asked Neal to accompany him to a function at the hotel. He was a bit starstruck by Washington and the whole scene, and got up to the door of the event before realizing it was no place for Nevada's only black Democrat in the state Senate. He looked inside and smiled. It was a well-dressed affair with women in pearls, and the room had few persons of color.

"Thank you for meeting with me, but I'm not going in there," Neal said.

"Why not, Joe?" Laxalt asked.

"That's not my crowd," he said.

Neal's allies were often few, and some powerful enemies sometimes chided him as a one-note politician. But as the years passed, at the state Legislature some of those who watched Neal were moved to acknowledge, and even appreciate, his influence on other lawmakers and the lawmaking process itself. There were some surprising victories left to score.

Causes, Crotchets & Column Inches

SINCE HIS LOUISIANA boyhood Joe Neal had always been a voracious newspaper reader. The habit, gained early out of a fascination with current events and a lack of a structured library in his Louisiana childhood, paid big dividends as he elbowed his way into politics and tried to change the system. Knowledge has always been power, but in the age before the internet the only way for most to remain current was to pore over pages of daily newsprint. And so Neal read the *Las Vegas Review-Journal*, *Las Vegas Sun*, *The Valley Times* of North Las Vegas, and the *Las Vegas Sentinel-Voice* black community weekly. When the Legislature was in session, he added the *Carson Appeal* and *Reno Evening Gazette* and *Nevada State Journal* newspapers to his routine. Over the years he found himself quoted frequently, occasionally smeared by columnists and editorial writers, and even complimented on occasion.

But as the 1980s dawned Neal also found himself taking the power of the fourth estate into his own hands. He started writing a column for the feisty *Sentinel-Voice*, a shoestring operation that spent decades working to keep the black community informed in tumultuous times. He struck a serious tone, and wasn't shy about taking up local causes or afraid to throw rocks at the institutions of the day.

Stuffing a newspaper with the windy proclamations of politicians was nothing new. The canned musings of elected officials, often written by uncredited underlings, have long been a staple of Nevada's smaller newspapers. Publishers saw it as a way to fill column inches on the cheap and make friends in elected office. Politicians generally saw it as a way to communicate with the common folk. But where others submitted windy rhetoric on politically safe issues that often appeared more advertisement than editorial, Neal dug hard into local and national topics with trademark candor.

One of his early causes was a defense of the Reverend Albert Dunn, a black minister who in 1981 was in the midst of appealing a 1980 federal conspiracy conviction by an all-white jury in a counterfeiting case. During the trial, two of the defendants testified that Dunn had nothing to do with their plan to print money. Under a grant of immunity, a cooperating witness testified on behalf of the government.

In Neal's assessment, Dunn had been railroaded with the sneering assistance of U.S. District Judge Harry Claiborne, whose animosity toward the defendant was clear. (Claiborne would himself eventually be convicted of income tax evasion in 1986. He would go down in history as the first sitting federal judge since 1936 to be impeached and removed from the bench.) Dunn, according to published reports, had loaned a hot plate to a man who was part of a ring that attempted to print the funny money. Dunn's proximity to the men made him an easy throw-in defendant for U.S. Secret Service investigators and the U.S. Attorney's Office.

Dunn sought post-conviction relief from the U.S. Ninth Circuit Court of Appeals, which ruled in his favor and wrote, "The principal issue in this appeal from a conviction of conspiracy to counterfeit United States Currency is whether certain marginally prejudicial irregularities, when combined with an extremely thin case for the prosecution, require a new trial.

"The only evidence connecting Albert Dunn with the conspiracy was the testimony of one of the counterfeiters who was caught in the act of manufacturing money and who was granted immunity for testifying against Dunn. All of the so-called corroborating evidence of Dunn's cooperation in the venture was consistent with his innocence." The court was "left with profound uneasiness about the proof of guilt of this defendant."

The only "journalist" to come to his defense was Joe Neal, who offered, "It has been said that what powerful people cannot control, they will try to destroy. We are now witnessing the destructive forces of the establishment being marshaled against Albert Dunn. But so far, Dunn has proven to be indestructible." Neal took time to attend Dunn's trial before a berating Claiborne, who sentenced the reverend to three years in prison for the conspiracy conviction.

After taking apart the prosecution point by point and revealing the Ninth Circuit's opinion, Neal concluded, "In light of the foregoing statements by the court, you would think the United States Attorney's Office would not attempt to prosecute the Rev. Dunn again. Well, you are wrong. Dunn is scheduled for retrial."

Lifelong educator Claude Perkins made history in 1978 by becoming the first black superintendent in the history of the Clark County School District, which was rapidly becoming the fastest-growing public school systems in the country. It was an important choice in a district plagued by foot-dragging on integration and bussing and accusations of pigeonholing students in poor neighborhoods with inferior facilities. Perkins was a breakthrough candidate and by all appearances was more than qualified for a position, whose recent predecessors included future Nevada governor Kenny Guinn.

But when the school board terminated Perkins's contract, Neal believed the decision reeked of politics and conservative religious influences. He rose to Perkins's defense in his capacity as both a state senator and prominent leader of the black community, and in the pages of his "People, Places and Politics" column in the *Sentinel-Voice*.

"We were aware the board had in mind getting a local person, but what we did not know was how it would be done," he wrote. "Now, we know."

The school board, under political pressure, had drummed up a technical reason for forcing out Perkins, and Neal bristled.

"It seems to use that the school board would have knowledge of this when, in an impromptu manner, they forced Dr. Claude Perkins to resign his position. We believe this to be the case. How else were they able to remove a superintendent who had done an excellent job, other than the board just wanted another person, probably white, to be their superintendent?"

He minced no words, accusing powers inside the Church of Jesus Christ of Latter-day Saints of playing politics with the public school system with its real estate expansion near some campuses. He wrote, "We are aware that the Mormon Church has acquired land near all the high schools for the purpose of building religious centers, designed to allow for 'release time' for their students to attend religious services."

It was far from the only time Neal would take on Nevada's political-religious monolith. But he was in a fighting mood, and added members of the mainstream press to his list of sparring partners.

"There has been a lot written as to the reasons why Perkins was forced to resign his position as Superintendent of Schools. The white press has been almost universal in its opinion that Perkins's resignation was not racist. Somehow, it is difficult to get black people to accept this opinion. We know that it is a basic tenet in the moral majority philosophy that 'blacks have gone too far.' It is this philosophy that has perpetuated the concept of 'reverse discrimination.'

"White America, as James Baldwin tells us, seems unwilling to accept a person of color in a decision-making role. The reason for this, he says, is that 'whites do not want to be judged by people of color.' While I can understand that Dr. Perkins's reasoning for stating that what happened to him was not racial but political, I'm also aware that racial politics can be practiced, too. Blacks usually do not need racial discrimination explained to them. They can feel it.

"The moral majority School Board should understand that black people will demand and get the proper education for their children. They will not tolerate their kids being kicked out of school because of some untested reason, and they will not accept anything less than an equal education.

"The moral majority school board must realize that 'whites as a group do not have any intrinsic values that black people should need or want.' The only thing they have at the moment that blacks should want is power and no one stays powerful forever."

The Perkins issue particularly disturbed Neal, in part because he believed the presence of a black superintendent at the top of the state's largest school district could only help improve learning conditions on the ground in poor and minority neighborhoods. In a community starving for even the slightest sign of positive change, Perkins's appointment was a beacon, a real reason for optimism.

Clearly exasperated by the coverage and lack of support in the daily press for Perkins, Neal went on the attack. He labeled the reports in the local dailies the incomplete work of the sensationalist "white press," which was clearly meant to barb reporters relying on the same old establishment education sources to attempt to get them to balance their portraits of Perkins. Neal clearly benefitted politically from fearlessly defending Perkins to the exclusion of mentioning even one of the education administrator's shortcomings.

"There is no question in my mind that a free press is needed in our modern society," he wrote. "In order for the press to remain free, it has to be responsible. Responsibility begins before the printed word is put on paper.

"I have used the phrase 'white press' many times in this column and it is not my intention to have this phrase interpreted in a negative or racial connotation, but more or less as a state of mind which is often without the frame of reference to properly speak to the minds and motivations of blacks in responsible positions."

The fiscal and foreign policies of the Reagan administration provided regular fodder for his terse commentaries, in which he pulled apart the conservative agenda that was sweeping the nation. It surprised no one who knew him that he'd come down hard against politicians who preached about the need for small government while kneeling at the altar of big business. "Mr. Reagan has implanted in many minds the thought that 'big government' is the cause of 'big business' and 'big oil' not being able to develop a strong economy," he wrote. "In my judgment, this is a vain attempt to shroud the lack of social responsibility on the part of 'big business' and 'big oil,' to hide their illegal acts and allow them to escape accountability for this.

"It took the prodding of 'big business' by 'big government' to begin the elimination of racism and sexism from the (Titanium Metals and Basic Magnesium) plants. It took the prodding of 'big business' by 'big government' to eliminate the abuse of child labor and to increase safety in the plants and on the jobs.

"So long as there are 'big business' and 'big oil,' we need 'big government.'"

As a black elected official writing in a minority community weekly newspaper, he wasn't likely to reach a wide audience with his progressive rhetoric. But in Southern Nevada, whose conservative nature has always run in stark contrast to its libertine reputation, Neal's opinions and arguments were some of the only liberal rhetoric being written in local columns.

Neal spent many years attempting to raise the consciousness of his fellow Nevadans on the subject of South Africa's white apartheid government. Long before the movement to oust the ruling white minority government from power seemed possible, he was reminding his constituents and neighbors of the evil injustice masquerading as a government. He was largely written off by white Southern Nevadans, who, in addition to largely being unconcerned about racial issues generally, were even less interested in the affairs of a country thousands of miles from their own backyard.

But not all of his topics were so weighty and divisive. Neal found time to offer commentary on matters such as football and the appearance of Sammy Davis Jr. at the annual NAACP Freedom Fund Banquet.

At that fundraiser, Davis recalled his early days performing for all-white audiences and sleeping in a room in the all-black Westside. Davis, who had generated ample controversy in the black community when he embraced President Richard Nixon at the White House, told the crowd how important it was to not to forget one's roots. "If you do, there is some brother out there who will remind you."

In column after column, that brother was often Joe Neal.

In mid-September 1981, Neal took a long drive through Nevada and expressed his affection for the state that had treated blacks with such indifference and disdain. Instead of the vitriol and righteous indignation that had become his trademark, he showed a softer side.

"One cannot travel within this state without being acutely aware of how insignificant human beings are when looked at in relationship to the natural forces which have caused mountains to appear. Human beings become dwarfed in their presence. But yet, this quiet repose of nature seems essential to the lives of many in our state as it generates the very essence of life."

He reminded readers of the importance of protecting Lake Tahoe and the state's precious water resources. He didn't brag that he'd played a key role in rewriting the Tahoe water quality policy and had fought to protect the shoreline of the sub-alpine gem from overdevelopment.

A more sensitive side of Neal briefly emerged. The majesty of the snowcapped Sierra Nevada and the grand scale of the Great Basin carved out a rugged beauty that had to be seen to be believed. He'd spent decades mostly at odds with the pinched racial dustbowl of Southern Nevada, but he knew an awesome sight when he saw one.

"After almost thirty years of living in this state," he wrote, "I'm beginning to like the place."

A Day for Dr. King, Years in the Making

THROUGHOUT HIS LONG legislative career, Joe Neal used his bully pulpit to call for death penalty and prison reforms, national health care, women's rights, increased funding for public education and libraries, better environmental protection for Lake Tahoe, greater commercial fire safety, and higher taxes on the gaming industry. Along the way, he never stopped reminding his colleagues of the many contributions African Americans have made to U.S. history and the need for a national holiday commemorating the life and legacy of Dr. Martin Luther King Jr. With the advantage of time, such a request seems self-evident, almost embarrassingly so. King's call for peaceful protest for civil rights for all was clarion and echoed far beyond America's shores.

But the groundswell of support for a deserved recognition of the man whose name is mentioned often with those of Gandhi and Lincoln was a long time coming. It was in a spirit of respectful commemoration on April 4, 1985, that Neal gave a testimonial to his fellow senators as they prepared to leave Carson City for a holiday weekend:

"We are getting ready in a few moments to adjourn the session so that many of us can go and engage in the Easter festivities which begin this weekend. With that in mind, I wish to remind the senators that on this day 17 years ago, Martin Luther King was assassinated. He was a man of nonviolence, but yet he was stricken down by a violent act. Those of you who have been reading the papers are aware of the situation of the white supremacy group that was arrested not too long ago who had as their goals and objectives the overthrow of the government by violence.

"Martin Luther King's philosophy simply was that if you see an unjust law, then you should challenge that unjust law through a nonviolent act. In so doing, you must also be willing to pay the consequences of that challenge; that is to go to jail, which in essence reconfirmed the law. That was simply his philosophy and one in which many of us have tried to spread throughout the nation by asking those legislatures, some twenty-five of them, who have adopted the law honoring the birthday of Martin Luther King. It was not that we honor such a man, but he had become symbolic of a principle within this country that many of us should aspire to. I know that some of the senators have raised some questions as to whether or not this would be appropriate. As I have been told, that the only birthdays that we have had were George Washington and the birthday of Jesus Christ. Even the birthdays of those famous individuals are ones in which we represent, aspire to, acknowledge as being symbolic of their times and what they represent. If we took them separately and tried to find fault with each of those individuals, we probably could....

"So it is this symbolism that a person like Martin Luther King died for. He spoke against degradation and the many problems that black people have had since that Dutch ship appeared off the coast of Jamestown in 1619 and sold twenty black people into slavery. It is symbolic of the fight and points up over 400 years of unrequited love that black people have shown this country but yet cannot, as of this day and even in the State of Nevada, have such a measure passed to honor this symbolism that this gentleman represents. Even though this state, which prides itself on coming into the Union is opposed to...slavery." Hence Nevada's official slogan of Battle Born.

"I ask my colleagues today, as you go home for the Easter break, to think about these things. Think about what it means. Think about the change that such an action can bring. It is better to be nonviolent in a situation than to be violent. It is better to send a signal to those who ascribe to the principle of white supremacy and who want to go out and take over the government through armed rebellion. It is better to send a signal by creating a day in memory of Martin Luther King who represented nonviolent actions to unjust actions."

Little more than a month later, Neal was back on the floor of the

Senate imploring his colleagues to see the King birthday commemoration in the light of history. And history, he said, would not be kind to the small-minded. Neal had maintained his sense of humor through many years of snubs, disappointments, and excuses from the Legislature's Democratic leadership and Nevada's political bosses. The state's motto could easily have been "Profit Over Progress." Neal was not deterred.

But on May 14, 1985, his patience appeared exhausted. The Legislature, once again, was fiddling with joining a majority of states in officially recognizing the King birthday for respect. It was, once again, being blocked by delay and inaction despite marginal fiscal cost to the state. Although Neal acknowledged he believed he had many friends in the chamber, he called them out for their insensitivity.

"I know that it is difficult for many of you to vote upon a measure that would honor a black person in this country," he said. "Over twenty-five states have done that. They did it because the representation of black people in this country has meant something....

"It is painful that in 1985 that I find it necessary to have inserted into the journal words that speak about my representation in this country and my unending quest to see that the Declaration of Independence applies to me also."

He then launched into a liturgical-style reading of black contributions to history, reeling off the struggle of slaves and the bravery of the duty-called. The names poured forth from Neal: from mess hall worker Dorie Miller at Pearl Harbor to the legion of volunteers who fought during the Civil War; opera singers Marian Anderson and Leontyne Price, heavyweight champions Joe Louis and Floyd Patterson, Nevada pioneers Ben Palmer and Lorenzo Barton. On he went until legislators from every corner of Nevada were reminded that blacks had been part of the state's history from the start.

Reading from a prepared text, Neal offered, "My history is not of one that has just come upon the scene a few years ago. It has been ingrained in this country ever since you sought to have a country. So when I asked for a holiday, it is not because it is a representative of the man whose name would carry that particular holiday because we need some points of reference.

"Who among you would give your life for a cause? Who among you would try to establish a principle of justice and say to the nation as a whole that you can turn the other cheek when you have been stricken by violence? I don't think that many of you can do that. Who among you can say that if you have an unjust law on the books, you are supposed to challenge that law? Even though in challenging that law, you must be willing to pay the consequences even to go to jail and therefore reconfirm that law. That was the philosophy of Martin Luther King and that is the idea that this holiday speaks to.

"Let me tell you about some of your actions here today and what it represents. I could become the butt of that action because you have people going around the country today who call themselves the Aryan race, which means they believe in white supremacy. They go out and kill people. I could be killed today as a state senator just because I was a state senator. Your action breeds that type of activity when you do not recognize the fact or even consider the fact that black people have a right and they have a place in this country. I know that some of you have said that you don't believe that Martin should have a holiday. Martin gave his life because of the things he believed in. Martin could have said to some twenty million black people, 'Don't march. Get some guns and go out and fight.' He could have said that, but no, he did not say that because he was a much stronger person....We listened to a person who said, 'No, that is not the right way even though you have been beaten, slaughtered, or killed because of your color, because of your race and because of who you are. You must not resort to violence.' That is Martin Luther King.

"So what I am saying to you today is raising the issue because some of you who are my friends do not understand. I want to tell you how I feel and about how black people feel about the action that was taken here today." Neal's remarks were met with quiet support from his Senate allies and silence from the rest. He'd once again called for a shift in the status quo.

Las Vegas had promoted itself for decades as an entertainment capital, but in late April 1964 it was briefly the focal point of the civil rights movement with the arrival of Dr. Martin Luther King Jr. In his own way, King was as big an attraction as any of the Strip's celebrated crooners. He'd been named *Time*'s "Man of the Year" in January and played an important public role in promoting President Lyndon B. Johnson's "War on Poverty" program. The two speeches he gave on April 26 would be long remembered by those fortunate enough to be in attendance.

King came at the request of Las Vegas NAACP leader and civil rights activist Reverend Marion Bennett and received high-roller treatment at the Sands at a time working-class blacks still received glares and worse in some local casinos. The gambling bosses still dragged their feet when it came to hiring blacks, and some flatly refused to integrate their workforces under a cry that it was bad for business. In those days, the Clark County School District was still largely segregated, and blacks suffered greatly from a lack of affordable housing, business vitality, and institutional lending in their own community.

But, at least for one day, the power of King's influence and celebrity eclipsed all that. With a full escort from the Clark County Sheriff's Office, King addressed a spirited rally of approximately 1,200 locals at the Las Vegas Convention Center and later gave a speech to the NAACP's sold-out annual "Freedom Fund Banquet." With tickets going for ten dollars apiece, the banquet featured Governor Grant Sawyer and Mayor Oran Gragson in attendance. Many whites attended and the local NAACP chapter membership increased in the wake of King's call to "learn to live together as brothers or we will perish together as fools."

Like many other Westside residents and those in the community at large, Neal heeded King's wise words, but he also understood that wishing it so would not generate the dramatic change Southern Nevada required if it was ever to achieve a semblance of racial equality. And less than four years later, after a heartbreaking April 4 evening in Memphis, the push for a holiday honoring the slain civil rights leader would begin. It would come to symbolize the greater struggle African Americans faced as the 1960s faded into the history books.

In Washington, Michigan representative John Conyers and his New York colleague Shirley Chisholm began a push for a King holiday that would take more than a decade to gain traction. They offered legislation year after year and watched it get rejected for one reason or another. In Las Vegas, the local chapter of the NAACP, with its mixed-race membership, pressed for more public respect for King's memory. Attorney Charles Kellar and Las Vegas Democratic Party and civil rights activist Jan Smith were among the members of the committee bent on honoring King's legacy and memory even as racial tensions simmered and boiled throughout the greater Las Vegas Valley.

There would be civil unrest, riots in local high schools, and calls for peace in the martyred King's name. The call echoed beyond the Westside, but by the time the Legislature convened in January every other year, Nevada's myriad other maladies and legislative priorities drowned out the argument for a King holiday.

Neal's biennial call for a King holiday and a celebration of African-American historical contributions came like clockwork each session. Year after year he made the case for its inclusion, and he called forth historical anecdotes of the contribution of blacks to Nevada and the nation at large. And each year, for one reason or another or no stated reason at all, his voice echoed through the building and died away.

With the 1982 election to the governor's office of his friend and fellow Democrat Richard Bryan, Neal and like-minded legislative allies gained an advocate for the King holiday.

"Last week, Martin Luther King Jr.'s memory was honored at services throughout the nation," Bryan said in his inaugural address in January 1983. "Dr. King's faith in the American system and belief in nonviolence as a means for bringing about change continue to serve as inspirations to us all. It is only fitting and proper we recognize his legacy. I am proposing that Nevada join the other states which have made his birthday a holiday."

It was a memorable moment for Neal more than three decades later.

"Richard Bryan called me into his office just before he went to give his State of the State," Neal recalled. "He said he wanted me to know he was putting this into his address. He was going to ask the Legislature to approve the holiday. Prior to that time, the issue would be brought up in the Assembly and it would pass, knowing of course that it would go to the Senate and it would not pass. (Assemblyman) Gene Collins and some others were pushing it and making a big thing of it that I couldn't get it passed in the Senate. Collins tried to make some hay out of it and ran against me and got his butt kicked. But when Governor Bryan, whom I'd gotten elected with [to the state Senate] in 1972, offered that language in his speech, it was an important moment."

Although Bryan was a popular governor, his call for action seemed to lose traction once the Legislature began grinding bills. Efforts in ensuing years also fell short by the design of the majority. Key state senators from both sides of the aisle made it clear from their lack of passion that the King holiday was a nonstarter. Some echoed long-held sentiments that King had kept company with the Communist Party. Others simply wrote him off as not important enough to the general public to warrant such a high honor.

Everyone knew where Neal stood, and Bryan once again reminded lawmakers and members of the judiciary in the State of the State address of the importance of King's "dream of equal opportunity for all Americans." The governor called for $10 million from the budget to be devoted to state job training office to help unemployed Nevadans reenter the job market.

Neal considered the fact the governor raised the issue in the State of the State address a kind of success in itself, but as ever in Nevada, the wheels of progress turned slowly. Motivated state legislatures found ways to circumvent a slow-moving Congress by passing their own holidays, as Illinois did in 1973. A decade later, Congress officially recognized King's birthday. Bowing to rising pressure from civil rights organizations, some of which assembled and marched in Washington, D.C., a compromise moved the day of recognition to the third Monday in January. In 1983, President Ronald Reagan signed into law the bill making King's birthday a federal holiday.

Other states were extremely reluctant to accept the change, including Nevada. Some Southern states insisted on also offering holidays honoring Confederate generals, and Arizona governor Evan Mecham's first act in office in 1987 was to rescind the holiday—a stunt that generated a boycott and cost the state millions and its Super Bowl site. New Hampshire failed to mention King's name until 1999, instead calling the holiday "Civil Rights Day."

Bryan, easily one of Nevada's most popular governors, found a steadfast ally in Neal on many issues—even those that appeared to be long shots for success. When Bryan's hospital reform legislation initially got a cold reception, Neal stepped up in support of it. "I only had one commitment, and Joe Neal was the only guy I had. If he was with you, he was unshakeable," Bryan said.

"This guy was no political weather vane. When it was popular, he was there, and when it was unpopular he was the same guy. He didn't blow with the wind. I grew to respect him."

After years of standing up on behalf of a holiday for Dr. King, Neal was gratified by his friend and political ally Bryan using his executive status as Nevada's governor to declare a holiday in Nevada for the slain civil rights leader at a time other Western states, neighboring Arizona and Utah among them, were still waffling. Bryan came down to West Las Vegas and signed his order at Nucleus Plaza, which only a few years later would burn during the civil unrest related to the acquittal of Los Angeles Police Department officers involved in the beating of black motorist Rodney King. But in 1983, as Bryan remembered, "Joe Neal was there and very proud, and I gave him a pen to commemorate the signing."

It wasn't until 1991 that the Senate, with Republican Bill Raggio sitting as majority leader, finally ratified the King holiday into being. By then, after speaking many thousands of words about the importance of the King holiday and of African American history generally, Neal's colleagues finally appeared to see the light—or at least recognize the absurdity of their recalcitrance. And for a rare change, Neal wasn't the only one speaking up on behalf of the fallen civil rights leader. Suddenly—almost a decade after Bryan's call for action—the Nevada Senate was motivated to celebrate King's legacy.

The greatest change, it appeared, had come over Raggio, the Reno native who by 1991 was generally recognized as the most powerful man in the Legislature. Raggio's early life experience with the South was burned in his memory. In the military in 1944, he trained at Ruston in northern Louisiana and later attended Louisiana Tech University.

In what was for Nevada's King holiday law something of a victory lap, in 1993, Raggio listened to yet another impassioned remembrance of the civil rights leader and, when his turn came, weighed in as never before. Neal's warning about being vigilant and not resting had clearly emotionally moved him on a relatively minor laurel. "This calls to mind, with this resolution, that we have not gone further," he said. "Even though Joe Neal can stand here in the Senate, how did he get here? Is that progress? It could or could not be. As long as we, as people, begin to draw those circles to keep others out based upon an idea and understanding, not about humanity, but on the skin color and texture of our hair, then we have not gone very far in dealing with the dreams of Martin Luther King. But there is still hope that we, as a people, can achieve that dream."

Raggio, so often Neal's formidable foe, was moved to recollection. He privately would admit that, because he was Italian, he was sometimes considered more "colored" than white in the Louisiana he first experienced in the military.

"As events occurred, I was later to reflect upon the irony of the fact the parish where I first observed racism was the parish known as Lincoln Parish," Raggio said on the floor of the Senate. "I had not been out of the State of Nevada excepting to cross over into California at that time.

"...My orders were cut, and I proceeded by train to northern Louisiana. I can assure you that I was shocked by what I saw there. The first thing I noticed were signs, at the railway station, indicating 'color' on restrooms, water fountains, and all other public facilities. This was completely foreign to me and not to be understood. Other things followed as I went into my indoctrination into this concept. People were asked to get off the street. Blacks would leave the street when a white would travel on the sidewalk. I can tell you it was a situation that left an impression on me that was to last a lifetime. I vowed, after leaving the service, that I would never be part of that process. It was demeaning, humiliating, and embarrassing to me. Over the years, on a personal note, I tried to instill that understanding and feeling into my own family and with those in which I came in contact.

"When I arrived at this Senate, in 1973, I first met a young man dark of skin, and was introduced to Senator Neal. I guess when I met him, I thought back to that experience because that attitude was still prevalent in Nevada at that time as it was throughout the country. Not to enlarge upon the very important remarks made by Senator Neal, it has now been two decades since that meeting. We were both privileged to live at the time Reverend Martin Luther King made his memorable address, 'I Have a Dream,' and over the course of that time, we were privileged to watch history unfold. We've had great men in our times of all color. Certainly Dr. Martin Luther King's name is on that list.... He sent a clear message to the effect that all men are created equal. Toward that end, we have committed ourselves in this Legislature to that ideal and that concept. I'm particularly pleased that it was this Senate, and I might add if I may that it was during the time that the Senate had a Republican majority, that we were able to finally enact the law that set forth a holiday honoring Dr. King in this state."

For once in a very long time, Joe Neal let the defense rest.

King: "We are simply seeking to bring into full realization the American dream...a dream of equality of opportunity, of privilege and property widely distributed; a dream of a land where men no longer argue that the color of a man's skin determines the content of his character; the dream of a land where every man will respect the dignity and worth of human personality—this is the dream."

Having attended Louisiana Tech, Raggio had his own experience with the South. Although he had clashed often with Neal, they had found common ground.

Standing on Shaky Ground

IN THE LATE 1970S, thanks to the political activism of Neal, Dr. James McMillan, Assemblyman Lonie Chaney, and others, blacks had made significant strides in public office. It was neither a civil rights accident nor the enlightened self-interest of the majority community that produced this result. It was through good old-fashioned redistricting. That led to representatives at nearly every level of government in previously all-white boards, commissions, and legislative bodies.

Some clearly saw the strides being made by black politicians as threatening the status quo and began to question the constitutionality of drawing a district that gave rise to a black official representing a largely black constituency. In 1977, a bill moved through the Nevada Legislature that enabled the Clark County Commission to redraw election districts. Within months it had drafted two district maps, both of which greatly diminished the possibility of a black candidate being elected to the commission. McMillan, Chaney, Neal, and former commissioner Aaron Williams, whose brief political career had been written by the redistricting that occurred early in the decade, attempted to be heard on the issue. They were sometimes referred to in the press as "a dissident group of blacks" and were countered by the rhetoric of Commissioner David Canter, who offered, "Would this map gerrymander or subvert the black community? The answer is no. No intentional effort to subvert one ethnic or religious community is at work here." Canter stressed that open housing laws, on the books in Nevada just a few years and only reluctantly adhered to in many sections of Southern Nevada, where real estate red-lining was common, had successfully enabled blacks to move into "integrated neighborhoods."

It might not have been the intention of commissioners, but that was the effect of their decision: to greatly diminish the likelihood that a black candidate in 1970s Southern Nevada would be elected to the commission.

George Franklin's lawsuit in 1975 led to a court decision declaring the old districts unconstitutional. A native of Jarbidge, Nevada, Franklin read for the Nevada bar without graduating law school and served as district attorney and in several other local government capacities in a long and controversial career in which he also wrote a firebrand political column. His redistricting battle once again landed him on the front page. The court's decision forced commissioners to run countywide in 1976 that year, and George "Sam" Bowler took advantage of an opportunity to oust the lightly funded Williams.

And the battle was on.

A signature recall of Bowler began. Bowler, who was white and a graduate of Brigham Young University, benefited from the commission's redrawing of the districts to include a higher percentage of nonblacks. He defeated both the incumbent, Williams, the first black ever elected to the commission in the primary, and Franklin in the general election of 1976.

Williams had been elected after the new district had been redrawn for the predominantly minority community. In a twist that defined Southern Nevada's race-charged politics, Williams was ousted from office after the district line was redrawn in the name of fairness to nonblacks.

In an interview, Bowler couldn't quite understand what all the shouting was about: "Whether the handful of 'black leaders' really represent the wishes of the people is yet to be determined. And I have yet to hear from any one of them on what specifically I haven't done to represent the voters."

Bowler had beaten Franklin at the polls, but he took him on during the redistricting fight. Franklin's legal hammering had led to a court ruling a previous district map was unconstitutional, which in turn led to the commission receiving relief from the Legislature.

Neal didn't hesitate to accuse Mormon political leaders of moving to marginalize black participation in the process. "We're in a political fight for survival," he told hundreds of churchgoers at a rally on H Street. "The Mormons have taken over that government. If Mormons can serve Mormons, black folks can serve black folks."

Although followers of the Mormon faith made up approximately seven percent of the population in Southern Nevada, they comprised a majority of membership on the County Commission and filled positions of leadership throughout county government and in law enforcement, fire services, and the justice system. Neal was one of very few elected officials to point out what seemed obvious to many. He also decried the commission's meeting in secret as a sign of underhanded tactics.

As angry but more politic, McMillan threatened, "We will find candidates to run against them. Not just blacks, either. We have a lot of white supporters."

For his part, Bowler was feeling picked on after being accused of largely ignoring the needs of the minority community. But when he was compelled to admit he hadn't toured the Westside in at least a year, he bristled, "I haven't been to Laughlin this year, either.... I have been everyone's representative. I have to be responsive to everyone's problems. I've spent more time over there during the ten years I've been in this town than a lot of people ever will."

His own words betrayed his marginalizing view of the black community. Although Bowler was being targeted, he reflected the sensibility of most of his fellow commissioners. When Neal, McMillan, and others raised the traditional threat—to picket the Strip, disrupt the casino-resort mechanism, and generate adverse publicity for Las Vegas—they were pelted with the sort of protectionist responses residents of the minority community wouldn't dream of ever receiving from their elected leaders.

"There are pockets of blacks all over town," Commissioner Jack Petitti chided, obfuscating the issue and apparently failing to appreciate that his views might be considered offensive. "We can't lump them all together in one district."

"No matter what district they're in," Commissioner Bob Broadbent said, deflecting, "they'll still be a minority of the population."

"I thought the whole purpose was integration," Commissioner Thalia Dondero said, adding inaccurately and naively, "We don't create ghettos. We don't create ethnic districts."

In fact, the Westside had been created to separate blacks from whites. Racial red-lining was an open secret in much of the real estate community.

For Commissioner Manny Cortez, who had worked on the Strip and like his fellow public servants received a large portion of his campaign contributions from the casino bosses, "Picketing and demonstrations on the Strip aren't going to serve any useful purpose. In fact, it would set the black movement back."

What he declined to admit was the fact that redrawing the commission districts had already led to the ouster after one term of Williams. Williams blamed his loss in part on his light skin color, McMillan would recall years later, noting "he was too light to be black and to represent black folks." Bowler, whose qualifications for the office were far outweighed by his public profile as a radio and TV newsman, survived the attempted ouster, only to lose a re-election bid in 1980.

One of the more outspoken voices belonged to black Reverend Albert Dunn, who called on Governor Mike O'Callaghan to step in and compel Bowler's resignation. He also said he would help organize a Strip protest. Dunn would later be targeted in the counterfeiting conspiracy that brought Neal charging to his defense.

The efforts from the grassroots level to the front door of the Governor's Mansion fell short. After defeating a first redistricting attempt on a technicality, the coalition of black community leaders watched as the commission passed another map that essentially ignored their concerns and protected the two commissioners—Bowler and Petitti—whose districts included substantial percentages of black residents.

"You white folks know you're wrong," Dunn remarked. "We have to have more than eloquence. We have to have some power. You have planed us into a ghetto."

Even businessman Bob Bailey, who was known more for his friendships in the majority community than his outspoken criticism of it, declined to remain silent. "The greatest revolutions were brought about by a lack of representation," he told a reporter.

Another minister observed, "This map is telling the people across the nation that we are going backward instead of forward."

Neal must have been struck with a sense of déjà vu. He'd heard similar reasoning just a few years before when he pushed across political party lines to change the districting lines to at last favor residents of the Westside, including himself.

The ground Neal and others worked so hard to gain moved uneasily beneath their feet.

"The justice that flows from this commission is designed to protect the district in which each commissioner lives—to satisfy his own selfish needs," Neal said. Black voting strength, never a threat to the majority, would be "minimized and diluted" by the decision.

Franklin would write in his firebrand "By George!" column in the *Las Vegas Sun*, "…the plan they did elect will prevent any black from being elected this time around. The Westside is not included in any of the three districts up for grabs this election year, and then after the election maybe they might re-district and thereby protect another incumbent. Damn it, why didn't they have the guts to just once district by principle instead of personalities?"

In the same commentary, Franklin took a moment to describe his occasional ally, Neal: "Joe Neal is not the most popular elected official in Clark County among white voters, and they didn't have to worry about his opposition—now that at least six of them will be safe and secure in their mainly white district. For goodness sake, Joe Neal is so controversial he doesn't even like 'By George!'"

Franklin noted correctly that the commission's decision would prove "pure futility because the plan is not in compliance with the law, and will be set aside in court." He would know. He'd litigated the previous districting plan, and it could be argued he started the controversy four years earlier. At the end of his newspaper column, in an uncommon example of self-disclosure, Franklin wrote, "I have fought certain blacks more than any man in public office, but not because they were black, and I hope that someday we will all become colorblind."

But Neal, McMillan, and their allies weren't through fighting. They took to the neighborhoods and promoted the candidacy of former assemblyman Woodrow Wilson, whose political connections were well established. He was first elected to the state Assembly as a Republican, and became a favorite of Governor O'Callaghan after switching parties. He'd not only started the first credit union on the Westside, but he also served as its first Boy Scoutmaster, a position that familiarized him with many members of the Mormon community. At the time he defeated Bowler in 1980, he was a member of the Nevada Equal Rights Commission.

The victory made a statement that the black community, when so motivated, was capable of overcoming the restraints of Southern Nevada's traditional conservative political structure. Wilson would leave office in disgrace after being convicted in 1984 of accepting a bribe to change his vote on a zoning matter. Operation Yobo, too, tripped him up.

But the willingness of Neal, McMillan, and others to clench their fists and rally their constituencies had paid off in an apparent lesson learned. For the powerbrokers on the Clark County Commission and behind it, it became much more tenable to include a member of color on the dais than to continue to stack the lineup. In the years to come, Dr. William Pearson, Yvonne Atkinson Gates, Lynette Boggs McDonald, and Lawrence Weekly would win office without the walls of county government crumbling.

Open Doors and Open Books

PERHAPS IT WAS INEVITABLE Joe Neal would one day find himself joining the fight for the right of Nevadans to have reasonable access to public libraries. In his Louisiana boyhood, he'd been banned from even setting foot in the local library, which was for whites only.

"We had a library in Tallulah, but we were forbidden to go there," he remembered. He had graduated from high school in 1954, but it would be several more years before blacks were permitted into the library.

Nor was it surprising that Neal's early years were essentially book-starved. There were none in his home. Most of the available reading material was limited to *Jet* and *Ebony* magazines, and weathered copies of the *Pittsburgh Courier* that the principal at Thomastown High School made available. Worn school readers featuring pale-faced characters named Dick and Jane, he would recall with a laugh, "had no relationship to my life. Them going on vacation and all that stuff was something I simply couldn't relate to."

In the Air Force Neal was introduced to a variety of reading material, most of it in the form of manuals, but it was at Holloman Air Force base in New Mexico that he first learned of the existence of classical literature from a fellow airman named Herschel. A young man of German-Jewish heritage, Herschel seemed to spend every extra dollar he earned on books. In his private time, when other airmen were off base, Herschel would read the works of Shakespeare into a tape recorder so that he could learn the plays. One day he left the door to his room open, and Neal overheard him.

"He used to read all the classics into the tape recorder," Neal recalled decades later. "I never saw him spend money on civilian clothes. He bought books instead. I'd listen to him read, and it was the first time I'd ever heard of the classics. I didn't know what they were, but I'd learn. Sometimes Herschel would have me over to read certain parts of the Shakespearean plays. He read the letters his parents wrote him in German and went on to a successful career in the intelligence community."

Neal also remembered how he struggled with his college composition and was forced to take remedial courses because of his lack of early reading. The first book of literature he read at Southern University was Henry Fielding's *Tom Jones*. His military experience had helped forge the discipline he needed to stick with his studies when he was struggling. "If I had gone to Southern right out of high school, I would not have made it," he said. "I would not have graduated. I needed to go through the military first, and as a result I was able to go right through Southern."

He had a lot of catching up to do and spent the ensuing years with a thirst for learning not easily quenched. "One of the things I learned at Southern that has stuck with me to this day and I have tried to pass along to my children, is that education is information, and information is education. You must read and educate yourself."

But to do so, citizens must have access. It's something Jean Ford and other legislators also understood. And she was willing to fight for it.

Ford was a wife, mother, and homemaker in 1962 when she arrived in Southern Nevada with her husband and children from Oklahoma. She soon fell in love with her adopted state and became a community activist during a time of great challenge and change. Elected to the state Assembly in 1972 as a Republican, she served four years and returned to Carson City after being elected as a Democrat to the state Senate in 1978. She fought for the Equal Rights Amendment throughout the decade and, when it faltered, battled to eliminate sexist laws.

When it came to appreciating the power of education and information to change lives, Ford and Neal were kindred spirits. Ford had a hand in creating the Clark County Library, and at the Legislature was motivated to improve the state's scattered and tattered public library system.

And she needed help. A public bond issue had faltered, and Ford turned to the Legislature.

"She introduced the bill to create libraries in rural areas, and it didn't go anywhere," Neal recalled. "I liked Jean. She was a very dedicated woman who believed in people. She wanted them to have access to information. I said to her, 'Jean, why don't you let me take that bill?' And she agreed. We worked on it and pushed it through and wound up getting $20 million for those libraries."

Neal's appearance at a library convention became front-page news in the *Elko Free Press* in October 1979. He understood well the importance of libraries to rural and inner-city residents. In a pre-internet age, libraries were capable of opening worlds and closing great distances and were, he told fellow members of the Nevada Library Association, an "integral part of the democratic system of government." He reminded his colleagues in Elko that Nevada's public library system was suffering from malnutrition and part of an ongoing class struggle.

"It will be the average citizen, on whom the success of democracy depends, who will be shortchanged. In the absence of libraries, the well-to-do, the elite, and the intellectuals will have information anyway," Neal said, offering two essential ingredients to the maintenance of the system. "The first is that it be accessible, and the second is that it be free."

Unlike some of his Carson City colleagues, Neal was more than willing to fight to expand the state's library system—especially in fast-growing Southern Nevada. He found an energetic ally in Clark County library director Charles Hunsberger. Their relationship was friendly and mutually beneficial.

As Human Resources Committee chairman, Neal helped Hunsberger gain the legal authority to handle the tax revenue designed for library development. All the expansion plans in the world were not good if Clark County bureaucrats kept sidetracking their goals. The law was changed again when the balance of power in the Senate shifted a few years later, but by then Hunsberger had nearly completed the largest public library expansion in state history. But none of it would be possible, Neal assured Hunsberger, if the Westside didn't receive a much-needed new library.

Neal's demand of Hunsberger wasn't entirely altruistic. It was, in fact, seasoned with politics. In addition to the obvious need, Neal also realized the addition would mean that longtime community activist Ruby Duncan would be hard-pressed to argue for the necessity of the small lending library at D and Jackson streets that she managed with a grant in association with the Operation Life outreach. In her oral history, Duncan recalled bringing 250 women and children to the library board meeting to persuade its members into choosing her group over one led by civil rights activist and club owner Bob Bailey. She pressed her son, attorney David Phillips, into an unsuccessful run for Neal's Senate seat. In opposing the new library construction, she enlisted assistance from members of the clergy on the Westside, persons with clout among their parishioners. Locals saw through the political squabbling, and soon enough they were the proud recipients of a sparkling new library with a theater near Doolittle Park. It was immediately popular and soon featured a handsome section on African American history.

Despite Duncan's protests, the library was almost impossible not to like.

"It turned out to be a very good thing for the community," Neal said. "Ruby was trying to play politics running her son against me. And, of course, I kind of got the impression that she was tied into some people on the Strip. The hotels did not contribute to my campaign in the primary. At the time, Richard Bunker was the head of the Nevada Resort Association. I never counted on their contributions, but they got around to sending a check after the primary. When the lead wasn't in doubt, I think they wanted to make sure they had money on the winner. Ruby got some of the preachers on her side during the library issue, but people saw that her criticism didn't make any sense. Preachers opposed to a new library? What the hell? We were able to overcome that."

The higher hurdle was twisting Hunsberger's arm when it came to placing a library so close to the new downtown library near Cashman Field Center. In time, he got the message, and the Westside got its accommodation. Hunsberger's own legacy would be sullied in the *Las Vegas Review-Journal* after he was accused of wasting library funds on the creation of glorified community centers.

Neal's success enabled him to travel to Washington, D.C. to participate in a national gathering on public libraries. His knowledge of parliamentary procedure served him well as chairman of the rules committee. He managed to navigate the proceedings amid a crush of PhDs and library science specialists. A veteran of the chaos of the Nevada Legislature, he found sorting the issues and bylaws of the library rules committee a relative breeze by comparison. He noticed, but wasn't surprised, to find himself one of two black faces in a crowd of hundreds. In less than four hours, all opposition was quelled and the bylaws were amended.

"I remember one woman librarian from the state of Mississippi came up to me afterward and said, 'I sure wish you lived in my state,'" Neal recalled.

Some of his legislative opponents in Nevada may have desired the same thing.

Back in Nevada in his capacity as chairman of the Human Resources Committee, Neal made sure that every public library received a complete, regularly updated copy of the Nevada Revised Statutes. He also helped set the stage for a major expansion of libraries in Clark County by forwarding enabling language that diverted dollars previously controlled by the County Commission to the library board of trustees.

On the floor of the Senate, Neal occasionally waxed nostalgic about those early days in Mound. In a 1997 speech, he recalled his childhood in segregated Louisiana, where the public library was as forbidden for him to set foot in as the Governor's Mansion.

"Since I have been in the Senate, I have always supported libraries and been very much a part of having the library system expand throughout the state," he said. "The reason for my interest is because there was a part of my life when I could not attend the library. The doors were locked to me.... Libraries are very important for a constitutional democracy. It is also important because it is the only unit within our system that can truly be classified as a 'poor man's' university. It is so because there is no tuition paid to enter a library to read the books. You read, use references, check out books and return them on time. If the books are not returned on time, the library can charge you for the time it takes to return the books. This is a very good system.

"Those of you who are familiar with World War II and the rise of the Third Reich and Hitler will remember that the first thing Hitler did when he conquered a city was to burn the libraries. He burned them to the ground because by denying citizens knowledge and understanding about themselves and others, those citizens would always be conquered."

Neal was sometimes criticized for his lengthy oratory, but he was especially effective when speaking from the heart and from personal experiences. Looking back, the library expansion issue became one of the proudest moments of his legislative career. In a 2008 interview, Neal recalled, "One of my great supporters in that was a lady who had moved up from the Assembly—Jean Ford. She was very heavy into libraries, so we got together and passed that bond issue. When Jean left the Senate, I went on and further developed that in terms of the local people here in Clark County, giving them the authority to go ahead and build libraries. That's why you see a lot of these big libraries around the county here. Then we followed that up by making sure that all the bills that we passed within the Legislature or the ordinances passed within the county—if it's local, county, or city—would be put in the libraries within that area. All of the laws that we pass now go to those libraries throughout the state. That was not being done, yet we charged our citizens with knowing the law. But they did not have access to the law, so we gave them access."

Of the many awards he collected during his long legislative career, Neal would reflect that the "Distinguished Service to Libraries" honor he received in 1993 from the Las Vegas–Clark County Library District was among his most prized.

Radioactive Politics

I N THE FINAL DECADE of his legislative career, Joe Neal experienced not only the intrigue and tumult of changing times in Las Vegas, but also a sense of déjà vu. From the late 1980s into the new century, Las Vegas became known as one of America's fastest-growing communities. The business and housing markets boomed along with the population explosion, and on paper times were especially good.

But Southern Nevada generally, and its evolving minority population specifically, continued to sputter in a second-class status. Whether the economic indicators were rising or falling, banks remained extremely reluctant to open branches on the Westside. It wasn't difficult to find anecdotal evidence of red-lining by some real estate agents, who steered blacks who qualified for homes in better neighborhoods into areas more traditionally African-American. Trade unions that had been so reluctant to open their books to minorities now found they were increasingly being outflanked by skilled immigrant labor, much of it from Mexico and some of it undocumented.

Police shootings of unarmed black men continued to occur despite some movement by the department to improve relations with the community. As Neal saw it, blacks were too often the recipients of harsher sentences than others convicted of crime. (This played out in a high-profile way when the office of Nevada's federal public defender Franny Forsman successfully sued over the uneven sentencing of those convicted in crack cocaine and powder cocaine cases.)

For Neal, his rise in 1989 to the top of the Senate was a long time in coming. Just fifteen years earlier, more than one Senate leader had called him "that black guy." Now he was among the lawmaking body's most senior members. It didn't make everyone comfortable.

In fact, he not only had to face the loyal opposition, which had kept the Democrats in the minority for much of his three-decade tenure, but he also found himself on the outside of various cliques within his own party. Early on, it was Jim Gibson, Floyd Lamb, and the LDS-heavy leadership. By the late 1980s, there were new faces and power players. And few found Neal particularly willing to be a team player for policies that most often had the effect of protecting big gaming and mining interests.

Through that field he'd amassed enough seniority and respect to be named assistant minority leader by a retiring Gibson and was in line to hold the minority leader mantle before running into a campaign by fellow Democrat Jack Vergiels, a favorite of party leaders. With help from Dina Titus, who cast a crucial vote, Neal was named minority leader in the 1987 session, and that logically meant that he'd become majority leader if the Democrats took back the Senate.

But as the campaign season wore on it became clearer that Democratic leaders had other ideas. Word spread that future governor Bob Miller favored Vergiels, and casino industry insiders were adamant that Neal's appointment was a nonstarter. In Nevada, few politicians in history had been willing to buck the casino bosses when they were motivated. They almost always got what they wanted. And they wanted anyone but Joe Neal.

A meeting was called at Herb Tobman's Mr. T's Cafe on Industrial Road in Las Vegas. In the small world of Las Vegas politics, Tobman was also the former casino operator who had welcomed Ruby Duncan and her allies during the historic welfare mothers' march more than a decade earlier. Senate Democrats converged on the diminutive diner. Neal felt blindsided, but quickly caught on that he was on the menu. The discussion, as Neal recalled many years later, remained passionate but professional. Multiple votes were taken before Vergiels mustered the five needed. Ever in command of the applicable parliamentary procedure, Neal reminded his colleagues that under Rule 15 the senators weren't allowed to change leadership until after the upcoming election.

"I raised so much hell about it they tried a compromise," Neal recalled. Vergiels told Neal he'd appoint him president pro tempore of the

Senate. Neal shrugged and reminded him that it wasn't an appointed position, but one voted on by the entire legislative body. After what some in attendance described as some hurt feelings and bitter words on Neal's part, the process moved forward.

Longtime legislator Chris Giunchigliani said Neal was "hurt and sad" after being passed over for the leadership role. "Neal had a well-earned reputation as a progressive and iconoclast," Giunchigliani recalled. "New lawmakers often tapped his institutional knowledge and keen understanding of the rules of legislative procedure. Some on the Democratic side of the aisle considered him a mentor and influence no matter the political issue." Giunchigliani had first encountered Neal in 1981 when she sat on the Clark County Teachers Association's politics board. "He had a presence. He was such a wonderful orator. With that deep voice, he could capture and captivate you from the get-go. He was glib, he was funny, and so smart." Although she felt there was inherent racism at the Legislature, she thought that for Neal "it was never about whether he was an African American. He was just Joe Neal, a voice for a lot of people who were underdogs. He was an outspoken black man, and that made some people uncomfortable. They can call it whatever they want to, but it was there, just as you see sexism to this day whenever a strong woman speaks up."

Several lawmakers interviewed echoed a similar theme: while it was possible Neal's race might have played some role, his strong opinions and stances—especially those involving the state's moneyed casino interests—were a far larger factor. "He called them on the carpet," one legislator said. Added another, "The Democrats needed someone with better relationships with the other side. . . . People respected Joe, but he could be bombastic and uncompromising."

"I worked with Jack Vergiels a long time, and I walked door to door with him," Giunchigliani said. "I don't feel Jack was racist, but I do think that there was probably some of that from some of the caucus members. It's that inherent piece of, 'Do we really want that person to be our spokesperson?' It was sad. It was a sad day."

News articles were written that captured an element of the bigger story. Neal would become president pro tempore, which *Las Vegas Review-Journal* legislative reporter Ed Vogel later reminded him put him in line, directly behind Lieutenant Governor Sue Wagner in succession, should Governor Miller be out of state or incapacitated. A few weeks into the session, just such a scenario occurred. Miller was away on a personal matter in California. Wagner was also out of state. That, the excited reporter shouted, put Neal in charge of Nevada. For his part, Neal just laughed and had fun with the prospect of being the acting governor. Miller made clear to an interviewer that he was just about to return to Nevada.

Neal's "reign" was brief, but he kept his sense of humor. It would come in handy when the Legislature entertained increasing its pension from twenty-five dollars for each year served to one hundred dollars for each year. Some of the Legislature's elder statesmen were interested in securing a reasonable stipend in retirement. Northern Nevada Democrat Don Mello introduced the bill, which moved swiftly through the process just below the press radar. But it surfaced when former Nevada governor-turned-*Las Vegas Sun* editor and columnist Mike O'Callaghan had a field day peppering the hides of any lawmaker audacious enough to stand up for the bill. O'Callaghan quickly labeled it a "300 percent pension increase," and reporters at both ends of the state largely followed suit. It became a radioactive issue for many legislators, and Nevada political reporter Jon Ralston still recalls how some of the savviest minds in the Democratic Party failed to appreciate how vulnerable the vote made most of its lawmakers.

Senate Democrats would be swept from the majority after a single term. Governor Miller tried to help stanch the political bleeding by vetoing the bill, but the political damage was done.

Neal, however, was spared the wrath of the voting public. His seat was as secure as ever, and in fact the following election marked the only time in his career that he received no opposition at all. "I was in midterm, I couldn't retire," Neal recalled. "There was a good argument against the increase. By law you could not increase your salary while you are in session. I liked the idea. I thought it would be a good incentive for poor folks to run. It would make it worthwhile to serve a long term. And it wasn't a lot of money, but it sure sounded terrible when it was labeled a '300 percent increase.'"

The creation of a high-level nuclear waste repository at Yucca

Mountain less than 100 miles from Las Vegas became political, with Republicans generally supporting the idea and most Democrats, after a fashion, opposing it. For his part, the outspoken Neal had long experience with the Nevada Test Site, contaminated for all time by atomic testing, and knew it as a major employer for Las Vegas. If the test site was a cherished job creator despite its well-known radioactivity, how could a reasonably safe and secure radioactive waste dump be so bad? In Nevada, the subject itself was politically radioactive. Any Democrat who dared to peek behind the stagecraft's curtain was sure to be spurned as a traitor.

The so-called "Screw Nevada Bill " ramrodded through Congress narrowed the number of possible sites until the Silver State was targeted. That set off a fierce battle to oppose it led by U.S. Senators Richard Bryan and Harry Reid. A few of many issues: the lack of fairness of the selection process, the scientific safety of the project, the nebulous and impossible-to-ascertain financial gains due the state. Reid was the famous son of a humble hard-rock miner from Searchlight, and in principle wasn't opposed to benefiting from drilling a large hole in the ground. To be fair, gold and nuclear waste have slightly different effects. But once the die was cast and the political sides chosen, in Nevada, Yucca Mountain was a hill to die for. And the Legislature had previously made its feelings known in the form of tersely worded arguments that made up for in rhetoric what they lacked in the weight of law. In Nevada, even a resolution calling for a tax on the nuclear waste should it ever come to the state was considered a treasonous act of submission by some Democrats and *Sun* publisher Hank Greenspun. As legend had it, Greenspun had ridden hard against nuclear testing as a favor to the paranoid billionaire Howard Hughes, whose under-the-table donations to presidential candidates Richard Nixon and Hubert Humphrey in 1968 had been based in part on expecting the winner to stop the bombs.

On June 28, 1989, Neal climbed that hill and declared a view different from that held by powerful members of his own party. He followed Republican Majority Leader Bill Raggio in opposition to an Assembly bill calling for a prohibition on any storage of high-level nuclear waste in the state.

"I've noticed that in 1987 we passed out Senate Joint Resolution No. 21," he said on the Senate floor. "That resolution attempted to place a tax upon this facility if it should happen to come to the State of Nevada. Of course, that resolution still resides in the Taxation Committee and has not moved on its second leg this session, which would have permitted it to go before the people of this state.

"I do know there are some, in political office in this state, who feel the great need to have this particular bill. I don't know whether or not it would mean that the governor would call out the National Guard and station them on every artery that leads into the State in order to stop this waste from being transported into the state…but it certainly tells me that if we have any type of truck on the highways that run interstate, we have a problem with trying to stop that waste.

"Certainly it has been said we do not have any authority to say where this waste would even be located because we have been told time and time again that it will be located on federal land and not that land which is owned by the citizens of the State of Nevada…And, if it is so it will be placed there…for the simple reason that the State of Nevada cannot predict the federal laws of this country. We tried it once, during the Civil War, and it didn't work. Nevada, by passing this legislation, will find it is not going to work now…

"I wonder what would happen to the highway patrolmen who would try to stop this because certainly they would have to become involved in trying to enforce the police powers of this State…Another alternative would be to call out the National Guard. I don't think that even the people of this state would want to have that image of lawmen trying to protect the highways leading into this state in order to cut off transportation of this waste.

"The state has obtained quite a few million dollars to conduct research. But, what about the money that could be gotten for the infrastructure, for the roads, to build that additional bridge over the Colorado River? What about that money? No one has proven, to the satisfaction of this nation, that nuclear waste, as described in this bill, would be harmful to the state of Nevada if it is placed at the Yucca Mountain site…I have worked in association with high-level nuclear waste for over twenty-five years. I do not fear it. I know the harm that can be done if you get too close to it and don't use protection, but we have been told, and many of us have seen, the experimentation that has been done at the area called Climax under the Nevada Test Site. Many of us took that tour and looked at those facilities."

Failing to toe the party line made him an easy target for the *Las Vegas Sun*, which crusaded editorially against Yucca Mountain with Greenspun and O'Callaghan tag-teaming all enemies real and suspected.

"After Mike left the governorship, I used to pick on him to no end about the Yucca Mountain nuclear waste dump," Neal recalled. "I would tease him because Greenspun was so opposed to it. It was such hypocrisy in a state that had celebrated the Nevada Test Site for a generation with its exploding atomic weapons and radiation leaks."

At the Legislature, Neal settled into his room at the Ormsby House in Carson City. Greenspun was on the hunt for him for failing to fall in line with the antinuclear waste mantra emanating from the *Sun*. He called Neal repeatedly in an attempt to bully him. Neal declined to return the calls.

Until one morning at two a.m.

"He answered the phone at his house. I said, 'This is Joe Neal. You asked me to call you when I got in. I'm just getting in. What can I help you with?'"

A cranky Greenspun replied, "Tomorrow, the headline in the *Sun* will read 'Neal Nukes Southern Nevada.'"

"And he wasn't lying," Neal said, laughing at the memory many years later. "That's what it said.

"I understood more than some people about what went on at the test site. I had had a Q clearance when I was in the Air Force. I was stationed at the test site. I was very much familiar with what was going on up there, with the plans and the bombs. So when Yucca was suggested, I thought, 'We've been busting bombs up there since 1952. They're not going to be building any goddamn hotels up there. Where else are they going to put it? What place is better than this one? It's already contaminated, and no one lives near it. It made sense to me. It also promised to employ working people."

But making sense was not always on the minds of Yucca's critics, who sought to stop the nuclear waste repository plan in part because of the dangers of transporting high-level nuclear waste across country and in part because the project was getting rammed down the throats of Nevadans with almost no appreciable fiscal upside.

By the 1993 session, Neal's rhetoric had evolved from skepticism to advocacy for the Yucca Mountain project, a decision that further distanced him from many of his Democratic Party colleagues and made him an easy target for *Sun* editorialists and headline writers.

In a long speech, during which he waxed nostalgic about his time at the test site from 1956 as a military policeman to recent years as a representative of REECo, Neal further established himself as a friend of the increasingly controversial, multibillion-dollar repository.

"We happen to live in a state which has a record of dealing with radioactivity since the 1940s," he said. "I have observed, since approximately 1956, the activity that this state has permitted to happen. When we had aboveground testing, people used to stand and look at the display. At that particular time, it was the public policy of our country to engage in this kind of activity. It was also public policy that was established thereafter, that nuclear energy would be utilized for the purpose of electricity in nuclear reactors throughout this country. And, we began to build those reactors. I think that the people who are now telling us that we should fear this energy rather than manage it are wrong. The Nevada Test Site has been there since 1945. Through the years, they have generated the expertise necessary to deal with nuclear wastes and other types of wastes.

"To have such statements placed on record and to try to influence people of this community that this state cannot handle this kind of energy is wrong. They can handle it. You have no greater workforce, no greater experience anywhere else in the country for dealing with this particular problem than you have at the Nevada Test Site."

Having made his pitch for Nevada and against states such as New Mexico, easily Nevada's coequal when it came to making atomic history, Neal continued to establish himself as a tireless spokesman for the project. In this regard, much to the chagrin of Bryan, Reid, and Miller, he was unfailingly consistent. If Neal was conflicted by his long employment tenure associated with the vitality of the test site and things nuclear, he was refreshingly upfront about it.

"Another thing, for those of you who live in Las Vegas, we have had atomic weapons within eighteen miles of us for years. No one told you about that, but our present and past elected officials have concentrated on Yucca Mountain and not said a word about what is happening within an eighteen-mile radius of the City of Las Vegas [Note: at Nellis Air Force Base.] Let's wake up, try to look at the facts, and deal with them. Nevada is being placed in an awful position. We are presently being placed in the position to make a decision, for the nation, in the handling of nuclear waste by-products. Where we go with that decision will determine, in the long run, what will happen to that material....

"I take the position that Yucca Mountain is the right and proper place for this particular waste to be stored."

With that, Neal clearly established a position that put him in diametric opposition to Nevada's Democratic Party platform. He had become, in effect, politically radioactive.

Nearly two decades later, Neal still maintained his stance. "I looked at it from the standpoint that if we're going to have a problem it's going to be with the transportation," Neal argued. "But if you're going to allow the fission rods to accumulate outside of the various areas where you had the nuclear reactors, that was going to be a problem, too. You had to find some means to transport it safely. I had some experience in dealing with some of that stuff. And I looked at these guys and said, 'You're going to have to do something with this waste.' You either have to stop producing electricity or something, but as long as you've got it and are utilizing it, you have to find a way to store the waste safely."

18 The Death of Charles Bush

WHEN NEAL WASN'T BUSY trying to buck the tide at the Legislature, he was home trying to make up for lost time with his family. He took particular interest in ensuring his only son, Joe Neal Jr., understood what was at stake for a young black male. Whether at school or on the street, there wasn't much room for error.

Neal Jr. recalls politics being more noisy than interesting in his youngest memories. He eventually learned that his father was one of the important noisemakers as a second grader at George E. Harris Elementary, a public school to which he was bussed as part of an integration program his father had debated and discussed with then-superintendent and future Nevada governor Kenny Guinn. That was when he first realized his father "was different than other dads in the neighborhood." One of few black children at the school, his last name was identified with the firebrand state senator who had stood up for increased funding for public education.

Young Joe didn't appreciate the political nuances and was surprised when the teacher asked him if his father would be willing to speak to the class. "I was probably seven years old. I'm thinking, 'Why would you guys want him to speak to the class.' At the time we were discussing government and civics. My teacher was almost giddy about the opportunity for him to come speak once she realized who my father was. I of course thought it was strange. But I thought that if she's this excited, he must be some kind of big deal. I didn't know the gravity until later. I have family from Louisiana, but I didn't really learn the dynamics of the South until I was older. He kind of kept a lot of it away from me. A lot of the racism on the Westside was not as overt. You might not be called names, but you wouldn't have the same opportunities to achieve things."

A couple of years later, young Joe and his sisters traveled to Carson City to see the Legislature and meet Governor Bob Miller, the son of a Las Vegas casino man and former lieutenant governor, who would go on to serve a decade in the state's highest office. "It was a big deal," Joe Jr. recalled. "It wasn't cheap to bring five kids up to the top of the state. Education is such a big deal to my parents that they would not ever pull us out of school unless it was something they deemed super important. At the Legislature, when I saw the respect and admiration he received, it made me proud. I began to see him in a different light. Republicans didn't like him necessarily, but they respected him. They were going to agree to disagree.

"We ended up at the Governor's Mansion. Bob Miller's kids had a den set up in the basement, and it was full of games. It was like an arcade...they had an air hockey table. I remember seeing that and seeing how my dad wasn't impressed. Those things stick with you. I still get emotional thinking about it. As an adult, I have a five-year-old now. I get choked up when my wife and I are raising her, I have a base to use. I am reminded not to be impressed by outward things. Material things are nice, but my dad was never on that road."

During his teenage years in 1990s Las Vegas, young Joe was reminded time and again by his father that as a young black man he had to take extra care in public. There would be little time to hang out with friends who weren't known to his parents. Although it was only occasionally discussed, the line was clearly drawn. The wrong friends would trip him up, and the authorities wouldn't be forgiving. He would be judged by the least of his friends and the slightest of his teenage indiscretions. "I began to understand that, no matter what position in government my dad held, I started to look like what they considered to be a suspect. By the time I was sixteen, a couple of my classmates had been shot to death."

Joe Neal called out racial injustice wherever he saw it both as a citizen activist and elected legislator. He spoke up so often, and with such pointed clarity, that he was sometimes written off as a man seemingly in a constant state of outrage. In truth, even as Nevada's social strata evolved with the times, there was much for him to be angry about, and much that other Nevadans should have been angry about. The case of Charles Bush, an unarmed black casino employee choked to death in July 1990 while in police custody during a highly questionable confrontation in his apartment, became a turning point for Neal and for the Las Vegas community.

When Bush's girlfriend was stopped on suspicion of soliciting prostitution, a charge never proven, three police detectives questioned her. She led them to the apartment she shared with Bush, who was asleep and unclothed when police retrieved a key from the woman's purse and let themselves into the room at the Paradise Inn hotel near the Las Vegas Strip. When the plainclothes detectives went to take Bush into custody despite the lack of a warrant and questionable probable cause, a struggle ensued. Bush died, a coroner's report later determined, from the effects of a chokehold.

Three officers, including a longtime pal of Sheriff John Moran named Gerald Amerson, were put on paid leave during the investigation. But eyebrows raised even in jaded Las Vegas when district attorney Rex Bell declined to prosecute the case. Neal was among a small group of civil rights leaders to express their outrage at the injustice, and this time their voices were beginning to echo outside insular Southern Nevada.

Neal well knew the little-hidden history of racism inside the police department. For decades it had few black officers and a deserved reputation for failing to promote qualified candidates for sergeant and higher ranks. When top brass repeatedly passed over former Basic High School star athlete Larry Bolden, his then-attorney Harry Reid filed a discrimination suit. When Bolden prevailed, the department slowly began to change with the times.

Bush's death made many suspect a lot more change was needed.

"The community of Las Vegas was somewhat up in arms over this incident and expressed their disdain over the fact that the district attorney refused to prosecute the case," Neal recalled in 1991. "Some of us decided to ask the state attorney general to do so."

The state attorney general's office, at the time led by Republican Brian McKay but soon to be run by Democrat Frankie Sue Del Papa, took over the investigation and determined charges were warranted under a little-used state law, "felony oppression of individual rights," and involuntary manslaughter charges. Both McKay and Del Papa had ambitions for higher office. Neal had monitored developments in the case from the start. It was hardly the first time an unarmed black man had been killed in a struggle with police, who often wrote in reports that a suspect made a "furtive move" to appear to endanger the officer. The investigation eventually wound up on the desk of experienced and studious chief deputy attorney general John Redlein.

The fact that charges against the cops were referred at all was an unprecedented act in Nevada, where traditionally the police violated the rights of minorities with impunity. A few members of the press focused a critical eye on the incident and the investigation—a big change from only a few years earlier, when such police-connected scribes as Paul Price and Don Digilio might have struck a pro-cop perspective filled with purple prose about the dangers of the mean streets of Las Vegas.

Bush was no flesh peddler. He was a former University of Nevada, Reno basketball player who worked as a casino floorman and had been with the same company, Holiday Inn, for more than seventeen years.

The trouble for the prosecution was clear. Save for the possible observations of a suspected prostitute, there were no independent witnesses to the altercation. A jury failed to reach a verdict with eleven of the twelve empaneled voting to acquit the cops. Amerson, who Metro brass privately admitted was an incompetent who had no business actively working cases, was fired from the department.

By the end of February 1991, with the Legislature back in session, Neal received word that Del Papa's office had decided not to retry the Bush case. Neal had the attorney general's press release read into the Senate record—dragging the injustice into the official light of the Legislature. Where the state's top prosecutor determined the case would not be retried for legal and practical reasons, Neal felt no compunction to drop the matter and go quietly. Not this time.

Some of his colleagues no doubt winced. There went Neal again, making things uncomfortable for everyone.

"That case, if I might remind you, involved a young lady that was allegedly picked up on charges of prostitution," he began. "Her purse was searched, during which a key was found to a room situated in the

Paradise Inn, a hotel in Las Vegas. The officers proceeded to go to that room, opened the door, looked in and saw a black gentleman lying on the bed, naked and asleep. By some means, the officers awakened the man and a struggle ensued. During the course of this struggle, the man, Charles Bush, was choked to death.

"No crime had been committed, neither by the lady nor the gentleman. The man was located in the place of his residence, found asleep and awakened to a death struggle with an officer utilizing the 'chokehold.'"

Neal then turned his attention to the procession of legal sins, including a decision by the Clark County district attorney not to prosecute the officers involved.

"Given the fact that there was no search warrant involved in this case, no crime had been committed. It was believed by many that these officers entered this room illegally; on a mere pretense because sometimes they make an arrest for prostitution, there were children left alone. However, once they opened the door to the room and find there were no children in the room, the room is dark and the only person they see is an adult asleep, one has to ask the question, 'Why enter the room?' The attorney general has taken the position that because there was a hung jury in this case, one brave soul who decided that the rights of individuals to be secured in their homes is a right that we should all be concerned about, the case need not be considered any further."

As Neal's anger stirred, he raised further questions about the moral obligation to continue to pursue justice in the case despite the lopsided hung jury verdict.

"What this does, as far as the black community is concerned, is it takes us back to the era of the late fifties and the sixties when we could not depend upon the state laws to protect our civil rights. We had to depend upon the federal government to hear the cases in the federal courts in order to protect our civil rights. Some of those who are supposed to ensure those rights, who hold the offices for protecting those rights, for some political end or whatever, decide that those rights are not important. I tell you today, ladies and gentlemen of the Senate, it is sad when you see a case in which the rights of an individual were so blatantly violated as were the rights of Charles Bush and the attorney general says I wash my hands of the matter and the perpetrators can go free."

Neal wasn't finished painting the scene for his colleagues.

"[Bush] went out one night to visit a friend, had a few drinks, asked his friend to drive him home, drove to his house and went to sleep only to be awakened by...policemen who had entered his house illegally and then killed him. Do you tell me that this is not sufficient cause for the attorney general of this state to prosecute this case to the full extent of the law?...Somehow, it seems that the rights of Charles Bush are less than the rights of the majority. That is the wrong attitude to take."

"I know that some of you say that you get tired of Joe Neal making some of these statements. I get tired of making these statements, too, and I get tired of problems that cause me to have to make these statements. When are we going to learn that the law is supposed to apply to everyone equally?"

Although the criminal case failed to result in a conviction, the civil case was settled in 1991 with $1.1 million going to the victim's estate in what one Las Vegas columnist called "the Charles Bush Memorial Cure." It didn't clean a chronic and festering infection in the police department when it came to taking the lives of unarmed black men, but for a change the deceased was portrayed as a victim.

Led by Neal, the spotlight on the Bush case eventually forced changes in Metro's controversial "lateral-vascular neck restraint," or chokehold, policy. It was a policy halted by Los Angeles police after similar incidents in the late 1980s.

The shock of the Bush chokehold death eventually faded, but the Southern Nevada community would soon once again be reminded of just how close it was to Southern California.

Smoke, and Fire, and Rodney King

As THE 1990S UNFOLDED, booming Las Vegas once again emerged as a darling of business publications and real estate developers. A glance at the headlines told the highly confident story of Southern Nevada's seemingly limitless potential for growth. And although some nervous types in the press and academia fretted about the future availability of water in one of the driest regions on the planet, that didn't stop the construction of thousands of new houses and businesses throughout most of the valley.

Most, but not all. On the predominantly black Westside, a generational drought of investment and economic growth had turned the community to tinder. Attempts to draw attention to the area's many maladies by Joe Neal and other dedicated civil rights leaders, as ever, had been met with tepid concern and only grudging acknowledgment.

Historian Michael Green summarized the elusiveness of rights versus reality in his modern history of the state: "Hard-fought civil rights victories had yet to produce the investment and jobs that Nevada's African Americans wanted. Civil rights leader Bob Bailey helped as director of the US Commerce Department's Minority Business Development Agency. But in 1990 the Las Vegas Alliance for Fair Banking reported four local home mortgage lenders made only fifty-nine out of more than ten thousand of their loans in West Las Vegas, with African Americans turned down twice as often as whites."

Community complaints were met with sops and shortfall gains, and the Westside continued to simmer even after press reports of extremely suspicious officer-involved deaths occurred.

An event unfolding three-hundred miles west of Las Vegas provided the spark. On April 29, 1992, a California jury acquitted Los Angeles Police Department officers in the brutal beating of unarmed black motorist Rodney King. In a prelude to a world where cell phone video would become omnipresent, the King assault was captured on amateur video and was played over and over again on television news. The issue of police brutality was once again part of America's uncomfortable on-again, off-again discussion of race and civil rights.

In Los Angeles, public protest and civil unrest turned violent and played out on television, and the shockwave was immediately felt in Las Vegas. While juries across the country commonly acquitted cops accused of brutality, and rarely found verdicts against officers even in fatal shootings involving unarmed suspects, the King case was particularly egregious. He was beaten with fists, feet, and clubs after he was on the ground. And, most of all, the event occurred on camera and allowed viewers to judge for themselves whether those in armed authority had gone too far. West Las Vegas, with its own ugly history of tumultuous race relations and incidents of police brutality and fatal shootings, was suddenly a Los Angeles suburb.

"Violence began in West Las Vegas, where relationship with the police had long been spiky," Green wrote. "The police cordoned off large portions of the area, especially after learning that rioters had designs on moving toward downtown. Miller sent in the National Guard but, hoping to avoid confrontations, provided ammunition only to officers."

As Miller described it in his memoir, *Son of a Gambling Man: My Journey from a Casino Family to the Governor's Mansion,* he relied on his longtime political advisor Billy Vassiliadis for insight and political contacts on the Westside "for an emergency meeting on averting a possible showdown between demonstrators and police and guardsmen."

At the meeting, held at Metro's City Hall headquarters, Miller observed, "The men formed a huge circle. Now I had a brain trust assembled that would help me develop the soundest plan. This was the best possible solution." He implored everyone to remain calm, then "started with the Westside leaders, who included not only Frank Hawkins and Jesse Scott but state senator Joe Neal and state assemblyman Wendell Williams. One of the other men in the Westside group was a reputed gang leader, but I was willing to hear him out, too. I wanted to restore order, and was willing to listen to anyone who could help bring that about."

Neal recalls the meeting clearly, as well as the well-trodden subject matter. The civil rights abuses and lack of economic progress in the community were among the topics raised. Three decades after the historic and highly publicized meeting of community leaders at the Moulin Rouge, some activists were still trying to see appreciable gains in Strip hiring practices. Of even greater concern was the black community's troubled relationship with local police to consider, and the law enforcement dinosaur, Sheriff John Moran, had only exacerbated matters when he rushed to slap a curfew on the neighborhoods, most of which weren't involved in any of the rioting.

"I recall asking a question as to whether an intelligence assessment had been done on the area where the riot had occurred," Neal said. "Apparently, Moran had never heard a black person use such a phrase as 'intelligence assessment' before. He asked me, 'What did you say?' I repeated what I'd said, with an explanation that if an assessment was done they would probably find that many of the stores that were burned were probably by the owners. I observed the wonderment on Moran's face as if to say, 'Who is this guy?' I do not believe that 'guy' would have been his term of reference to black people at the time."

But as the meeting progressed, it became clear to Miller and Neal that those present were focused on restoring order and preserving life and property. Miller recalled being "pleased that the tone of each group's summaries was even-keeled and to the point, even though anxiety and antagonism roiled below the surface." And later, "When the meeting resumed, I was relieved that both sides seemed eager to reach a middle ground, a moderate position, a compromise."

Neal knew that a heavy hand by police and the National Guard would likely lead to an exchange of gunfire and the loss of life. He also knew that few members of Metro, and certainly not the sheriff's men, held a scrap of credibility in the minority community.

That left it to elected leaders and members of the clergy to step away from the lectern and into the street. And so they went. It was a decision that clearly impressed Miller, who called it "a proposal that was as bold as it was intriguing." Not to mention courageous.

"They said they'd recruit responsible leaders in the Westside community, including church ministers, elected officials, and business owners, to hit the streets, calm residents, send angry youths home, and restore order," Miller recalled. "They would stay out all night, walking every street as citizen monitors. They would light up the streets with any available illumination, even lanterns and flashlights, since the power lines had been cut off in the previous rioting. They would disperse restive groups and counsel any unruly characters against bringing ruin to the Westside, by telling them to get back in their homes, that, 'We're not going to have this happen tonight.' They would create an all-night community and take responsibility for the actions of their residents."

Miller at length agreed with the plan. And it worked thanks in large part to some enlightened cooperation and dedication from the black community's oft-maligned leadership.

For the most part, the trouble emanated from the Westside's growing infestation of drug-dealing street gangs. Young thugs, many of them with access to arms, terrorized local homeowners and brought trouble in the form of the police and National Guard into the neighborhoods. Nucleus Plaza, one of few strip malls in the area, was burned.

But when shots were fired at police, one officer was struck in the leg, and an eleven-square-mile area was cordoned off. A rumor of a violent march toward downtown caused what many believed was an overreaction to the unrest. Police cruised the streets in armored carriers to protect from occasional sniper fire attributed to street gangs.

Although they followed orders and limited the constitutionally protected movement of law-biding citizens, department veterans understood that the trouble was coming from "criminals, doing what they always do . . . under the cause of social justice." When the violence was tallied, one person was dead and 37 were injured.

It had taken more than a week, but peace, along with electricity, was eventually restored. When the smoke cleared in the light of day, it was clear Southern Nevada had been fortunate. The rioting resulted in a just $6 million in damage and sixty-five arrests. In Southern California, fifty-two people died in the public rioting in the wake of the King verdict with destruction topping $800 million.

"In the end, the forces that threatened to rend the city instead pulled Las Vegas a little closer together," Nevada's former governor wrote. Although neither Miller, Neal, or any other community leader would endorse it as a strategy, the civil unrest had a positive effect on the Westside. It finally focused attention on the dire need for job training and the necessity of allowing the minority community to have a forum to voice its challenges and discontent with a system that historically had at best ignored them. Billionaire casino mogul Kirk Kerkorian's Lincy Foundation contributed $1 million toward the creation of the Nevada Partners jobs and community service program. The Culinary Union began a concerted effort to build its new training center in the community of need. Las Vegas Mayor Jan Jones, stepped up to help design and implement the Multi-Jurisdictional Community Empowerment Commission with the high-minded goal of "addressing the root causes of urban unrest in the Westside."

Some of the plans would succeed, others would fall away, but for a change it could be said with certainty that the inertia had ended in some of Southern Nevada's poorest neighborhoods. It was also true that the community at large didn't need a commission to determine what ailed the Westside and other poor and minority constituencies in the valley. All they had to do was to finally start listening to Neal and other experienced officials and activists. The "root causes of the urban unrest," as Miller called them, may have been challenging to solve, but they were painfully easy to spot. Generations of poverty and poor police relations had created a toxic dump that wouldn't be cleaned up with proclamations and committee reports. It would take substantive and continued investment, the kind rarely tried in Southern Nevada's poorest neighborhoods, to ensure what was essentially a race riot never returned to the streets of Las Vegas.

In the wake of the riots, other rhetoric had entered the collective conversation. Metro brass, rarely accused of being forward-thinkers, began to implement a new strategy in troubled neighborhoods in in the form of a style of law enforcement known as "community policing." It called for more time spent in neighborhoods, taking time to get to know residents.

Given the chasm that separated the cops and the black community, it seemed like a long shot for success. But as time passed it showed signs of success.

Longtime West Las Vegas civil rights activist Elgin Simpson called the rioters "mean, stupid people," but added that many of the protesters who assembled did so "over an injustice involving police, and the local police would not allow that to happen.... When you have a pot simmering and you do nothing but cover it with a lid, it will blow over, and that's what happened that night."

He catalogued some of the many challenges black residents had with Metro police, issues Neal had been battling for two decades in the Legislature. Simpson told a reporter, "When you have a situation where, on a daily basis, police stopped black people for no reason in their own neighborhoods and made them kneel on hot pavement in the summer, an incident like the Rodney King verdict is something that makes people stand up and say 'I've had enough. It's time for change.'"

As Neal himself said, "Metro has gone some distance to make improvements, but there are still some cowboys who want to be prosecutor, judge and jury, and they have to be weeded out." He knew that community policing would only be successful, "if police are mindful of the constitutional rights of black folks.... Right now what the area needs most is jobs. In that area, development has been very slow. People need to be employed and they want good jobs close to their homes."

Battling Artful Tax-Dodgers, and Raising the Stakes

JOE NEAL LEARNED EARLY in his legislative career to expect to encounter roadblocks from the state Senate's conservative Republicans, but over time he found that some of Nevada's greatest handmaidens to power and opponents to progress came from his own Democratic Party. Most of the denizens of the Silver State's "citizens' Legislature" knew well how their political bread was buttered. When it came to protecting the powerful from taxation, there was rarely a shortage of volunteers for duty. With mining's protected status guaranteed in the Nevada Constitution, that left the casino industry, at least in theory, as a prime source of revenue.

All that stood between Neal and the fount of additional revenue was a legislative process so beholden and controlled by special interests that it often resembled more a glass menagerie than a lawmaking body. In the Senate, powerful Majority Leader Bill Raggio's career was intricately woven with the casino industry. He even sat on the board of a gaming company. On the Assembly side, Speaker Joe Dini was a casino licensee in Yerington, a small town south of Reno. Many legislators on both sides of the aisle had direct connections to the industry, and most benefited from gaming's calculated political largess.

To take on the industry in a state under its heavy influence was to court political calamity. Casino executive Mike Sloan once admonished Neal that money was not a factor in his races because, if it were, he'd have been beaten. That notion, however, applied only in a single Senate seat in working-class North Las Vegas. The cynical insight fully applied once Neal decided to step out of his comfort zone and run for higher office—in large part to antagonize the casino industry and compel it to increase its lowest-in-the-nation tax contribution to the state.

Privately, Neal well recognized he was little more than David with a slingshot and little chance of slaying the giant. But if Nevada's myriad societal shortcomings were ever to be meaningfully addressed, increased revenues were essential to the process. That meant once again taking on big gaming.

He had plenty on his mind. Unbeknownst to many in the political establishment, Estelle Neal's health had taken a grave turn. Diagnosed with breast cancer in 1995, she fought with the vigorous strength of character friends and family had come to expect from her. But she was losing ground as the cancer spread.

"Usually when he started a session, he'd start out driving home every weekend, but by April it was every other weekend because the Legislature was so busy," daughter Withania Neal recalled. "In her last six months, he drove home every weekend. He made sure he was home every weekend. He was back on Friday. She was in a separate room in a medical bed then. He would sit with her and always stayed awake. I don't know when he slept. It was their private time together. They spent a lot of time together those last few months."

As her condition worsened, Joe cut back on his schedule. They'd talked for years about doing more traveling and less working, but that was in the past now. As the cancer spread to the lungs, and eventually to the brain, she grew weaker and less conscious of her surroundings. The trained dietician, who possessed a great deal of knowledge about medicine, had waited through trouble signs before finally seeing a doctor. She clung to faith and family and died on November 27, 1997, with her family at her bedside. She was fifty-seven years old.

"After our mother died, he would disappear into his room," Withania recalled. "He was so quiet. I'd never seen him cry that much, or at all, actually, until then."

During the 1997 session of the Legislature, Assembly Speaker Dini sponsored a bill authorizing a full exemption for high-dollar art collectors from the state's 7-percent sales tax law if they agreed to display their works publicly. He shouldn't have been surprised when a member of his own party supplied the ammunition. It was an intriguing choice of bill draft for a man from a farming and ranching area of rural Northern Nevada. Not exactly intended to benefit the workingman, the tax exemption was specifically written to give a break for art valued at $25,000 or more.

The bill was a bouquet to casino king Steve Wynn, an avid art collector who planned to use multimillion-dollar paintings to help market his upscale Bellagio resort on the Strip. The legislation quickly became known as the "Show Me the Monet" bill, as one of Wynn's own acolytes labeled it, and was escorted through the process by top gaming lobbyist Harvey Whittemore, who was never shy about touting his close relationships with legislative leadership.

In interviews, Wynn downplayed his relationship to the bill as a multimillion-dollar tax avoidance for a $300 million art collection paid for with approximately $160 million in corporate assets. He argued in part that changing the law would help make Nevada a tax haven for art and, as the *Los Angeles Times* breathlessly put it, "to encourage others to follow his lead, to buy and display." To *The New York Times* Wynn himself enthused, "I had an interest in the matter, but not a burning one because it couldn't affect me...I didn't need the exemption: me or the company."

Wynn told another interviewer, "This can't be about money. It has to be about the pictures! This is a dicey thing still, introducing fine art in this environment." Although he assured a reporter the paintings wouldn't be hanging over a bank of slot machines, following the Bellagio's opening, those who dined at the ritzy Picasso restaurant couldn't help noticing the modern master's original works on display.

When pressed about wanting the tax break while also charging $12 for admission to the resort's gallery—Wynn also received millions from the company to "lease" his collection—he offered a variety of replies. In his best salesman's mode, he promoted the art-marketing plan as an opportunity for Nevada schoolchildren to be inspired by priceless work. At times he made it seem like the purchase of nearly $300 million in paintings by Van Gogh, Monet, Cézanne, Renoir, Picasso, and others wasn't part of a grand marketing plan for his new resort, but essentially a gift to the community.

Thanks in large part to Whittemore's efforts and Wynn's own powers of persuasion, the bill was rammed through the process and signed by Governor Bob Miller. A state that had never provided sufficient revenue for public education or indigent health care managed a backbend for an art tax break for a billionaire.

Just seven months after Wynn had successfully lobbied for the tax break, according to the Nevada Tax Commission, he was poised to take advantage of it.

Outmuscled and marginalized during the debate, Neal was not amused. But the passage of the bill gave him an opening to once again raise his voice for a tax increase on the casino industry—this time as a million-to-one-shot candidate for governor.

Neal's reputation as a thorough taskmaster and stickler for the rules on the Senate floor had become legendary by the time future Nevada congressman Mark Amodei joined the Legislature in the late 1990s. Although their politics were very different, Amodei considered Neal an honest broker whose word was solid. He rarely had to guess where the senator from North Las Vegas was coming from and considered him "good people," and "the protector of this house of the Legislature." Amodei watched as Senator Mark James, who chaired the Judiciary Committee, sparred with Neal. "They would go at it debating what decisions had come out of Judiciary. I would sit back and be thankful that there were people from Las Vegas to do the arguing. I was just happy to be here and not be one of them."

But Amodei wasn't able to avoid Neal's gaze forever. "I made the mistake of introducing a bill my first session that had to do with the Nevada Day holiday that a relative of mine had introduced in a similar bill sixty years ago. The day the bill was introduced, Senator Neal rose from his desk and headed toward mine. I hoped he was coming my way to fight with Mark James, who sat next to me. But, he stopped, leaned over my desk and said, 'You think because your uncle did something on this bill, that you have the right to have a bill on it?' I thought, 'Okay, I will withdraw the bill.'"

When it came time for Republican Amodei, an attorney, to move up in responsibility, the chairmanship of the Judiciary Committee seemed like an ideal fit. But that meant he'd be the one who had to joust on a regular basis with Neal, the master of the rules. "I pointed out there are many senior people available for that job," Amodei would recall years later. "The whole time we were discussing this, I was thinking the reason Mark James is not in the Senate anymore is Joe Neal." His colleagues smiled and said, "You chair Judiciary. You deal with Joe Neal on the floor." Amodei thought to himself: for a guy who just wanted to mind his own business from Carson City, to have to deal with the 'Bear' from North Las Vegas, it was quite a cultural experience in terms of 'You better learn on the fly, and if you make a mistake, it is big trouble.'"

At home during short breaks Neal constantly fielded calls from constituents—an occasional blast from Wynn and other gaming figures included. Neal took pains to shield his family from some of the heat he regularly received, but everyone had his phone number and knew his home address. At times the calls came almost nonstop with some of the conversations loud and salty. "That's how I found out that Daddy could curse," Tania Neal Edwards recalled. "Oh, Daddy can curse all right." The kids could hear Wynn's voice "all the way downstairs."

One day, Tania picked up the phone and heard the voice of South African social rights activist and Anglican archbishop Desmond Tutu asking to speak to her father. It was a reminder that, while Joe Neal's booming voice on the issue of apartheid wasn't always appreciated in Nevada, it was highly respected elsewhere. The Neal family welcomed visitors from Congo and South Africa to its home, and when the bishop toured Las Vegas he spoke at the family's church, Saint James.

A year after receiving Neal's rebuke at the Legislature, Joe Dini was still stinging. "Dini defends his bill giving tax break to Steve Wynn, other art collectors," the Las Vegas Sun shouted in a headline in its July 1, 1998, edition. The article raised the issue of whether public school budgets would suffer from the art tax break.

A scalded Dini assured skeptics, "We are not losing money for schools" in a state that perennially ranked nationally at the bottom of public education funding. In a shining example of the lengths to which some Silver State legislators are willing to stoop to court favor with the power elite, Dini laughably tried to argue that exempting a wealthy casino man's art collection from taxation somehow gave the state a panache previously lacking. "This put Nevada on the map for art in the West," he told a reporter. "It is well worth the money."

Neal could only smile at such rhetoric. He'd been hearing the same kind of equivocation for years, and wasn't about to let this issue rest. The tax break had real consequences in a state with struggling schools and rock-ribbed social services. He countered Dini bluntly, "This is not making Nevada an art center. People aren't going to make special trips to casinos to see art."

While the Tax Commission worked overtime on the art tax issue, Neal suddenly faced new vilification for "grandstanding," speaking out against the House in Nevada—during his nearly penniless gubernatorial campaign. When he pointed out the fact that a percentage of sales tax revenues were earmarked for Clark County's public schools, and thus would be harmed by handing a tax break to wealthy art collectors, he was accused of not playing fair. Neal told *Las Vegas Sun* reporter Larry Henry, "This money was going to our school children. This shows you the arrogance of the gaming industry when they can do that."

Wynn spokesman Alan Feldman countered, "He's an underdog candidate for governor. He's going to make as much noise as he can to generate headlines."

One of Neal's few loyalists with a media megaphone, longtime labor activist and *Sparks Tribune* columnist Andrew "Barbwire" Barbano, roared, "(Wynn) got this bill passed by promising to educate the children of Nevada. Now he is going to be doing for gambling what Joe Camel did for cigarettes."

Although the Wynn art tax break was a recurring theme during the primary, without advertising funding, few people were listening. "This is like a license to print money," Neal chided. "...If we gave him a tax exemption, then the public should not have to pay to see the art. He should show it for free."

Lost on the public and members of the press with limited attention spans was Wynn's relentless effort to reshape the art tax exemption law to make it a better fit for his collection and company. When the Legislature convened in 1999, Senate Bill 521 surfaced with Whittemore leading the way and collecting support for a bill that created more exemptions and alterations. From eliminating the Nevada resident discount and diluting the education program component of the original bill to loosening other requirements of the original law, Whittemore whittled away. Suddenly, the art in question would only have to be publicly displayed "within two years of purchase." In an Assembly Committee on Taxation hearing, Whittemore set a new standard for revisionism. Testifying in opposition to the bill, Neal reminded the group that the Nevada Tax Commission had already determined that the art collection would not be exempt from taxes if an admission fee was charged. The new bill "specifically authorized the owner of a gallery to charge an admission fee..." And, he said, the new legislation "preserved the exemption from both personal property tax and sales tax" through a series of deductions. He reminded the committee, much to the chagrin of Whittemore, that the Congress's repeal of the capital gains tax on art in 1997 meant the Wynn collection was responsible for a 24-percent federal tax that SB 521 would help its owner recoup.

Representatives of citizens groups both liberal and conservative rose to testify against SB 521. But in the end the Legislature heard its master's voice.

By the turn of the new century, there were big changes on the Strip. Wynn was forced to sell his Mirage Resorts Inc. to MGM Grand Inc., headed by billionaire Kirk Kerkorian, a man whose sense of art appreciation didn't extend to using corporate funds to fill a gallery. The collection was sold to Wynn, who was able to receive a multimillion-dollar tax break thanks to the laws he'd helped create. Neal told the *Las Vegas Sun*, "This is the same thing that I argued against, that the public would not benefit (by art sales) being granted those exemptions. You expect some kind of benefit from granting an exemption. There's no benefit by granting this.... You can't get angry with Steve Wynn, because, hell, he wasn't voting. It was the legislators voting. It's up to the public to address this issue if they want to address it."

Several years later, Neal still enjoyed reminiscing about the battle with the billionaire. "Wynn wanted to get an exemption from sales tax on the purchase of art, such as Rembrandts, Gauguins, and Cézannes. I was opposed to the exemption because we already had too many exemptions. See, our exemptions now exceed the tax base. If we got rid of all the exemptions—just reverse them—we wouldn't have a problem within the state. He got it passed, but he made one mistake when he got it passed, which was not in the bill: he wanted to charge the people

$6.50 each to go see his art. Now he already got an exemption from the people from paying taxes, and he wanted to charge them, too." Neal persisted in his opposition, sometimes as a lone voice of dissent attempting to balance the picture being painted.

"I went before the Tax Commission, where he was trying to get this through, and I fought him," he recalled in 2005. "We had four meetings. The first two were just three lawyers across the board and myself; the next two meetings he showed up. He's a very good speaker, and I guess he thought he was going to show me. He's supposed to be the king of Nevada. He went before the Tax Commission, and nobody else was there but me. I guess everybody else was afraid of him. So the Tax Commission moved the fourth meeting to Carson City. I paid my own way up there. I was not going to give up this fight. So I got to thinking this guy has a vanity problem and has probably said something in some major publication about how he wants to use his art. Lo and behold, a friend of mine in Carson City came up with an article from *The New Yorker*, where Wynn said that he wanted to sell the art to the high rollers. But he was telling the Tax Commission that he wanted to improve the culture of the State of Nevada and have something the kids would come to see. He made a mistake because I examined every word.

"My argument was this: we have people go through the casino to see the art. That tells me that he's trying to create gamblers out of our young folks. He responded that he'd have a separate door for them to go through. But he lost that argument! He lost that argument. The tax people ruled against him. I remember telling some folks of ours who were sitting in the audience after that that he would institute that charge anyway because he believes he's the king of Nevada. I said that when he did, he would have a problem coming with that."

Neal told his allies plainly, knowing the word would get back to Wynn, "If he introduces that charge, he's going to wind up paying approximately $15 million for this tax exemption that he got. And he did. Come the end of the year, he introduced that charge and filed for the exemption. He went before the Tax Commission to get it, and the Tax Commission would not allow the exemption. Steve Wynn hired Harvey Whittemore as a lobbyist on it, and Harvey Whittemore got this admission fee put into the law. When the bill came up before the Legislature,

I didn't give a speech like I'd done before, and Harvey wondered why I didn't get upset. I voted against it, but I didn't say a word. Then Wynn applied to get the exemption, but the Tax Commission didn't give it to him because the law couldn't be retroactive, which I knew. I didn't argue the point because he could not get it retroactively; he had to pay. And that—boom—started him going down.... It was kind of funny."

Later, Neal recalled, Wynn responded to a television reporter's question about "Senator Neal."

"He's vindictive," Wynn said.

"Vindictive—no!" Neal retorted later, "I was just up there trying to protect the public from him trying to rob them."

After that meeting in Carson City, University Regent Joseph Foley, a member of a legendary Nevada legal band of brothers, called Neal and asked him for assistance on a bill. The conversation turned to the Wynn tax battle, and Foley inquired who had helped Neal with his legal argument.

Neal, who admired Foley and knew him as the father of his former legislative compatriot Helen Foley, replied, "No one."

"Do you know what you've done to him?" Foley asked.

"Well, yes," Neal replied. "If he goes and institutes an admission fee, he's going to have to pay approximately $15 million for the tax exemption."

Foley laughed and added, "You ought to come work for me."

Neal would keep his day job and his legislative work a while longer. There was more work to do, and more trouble to make.

A Fly in the 'Anointment'

PERHAPS IT WAS the stunning audacity of the Wynn art tax break, or a hundred other examples of the powerful manipulating the process in Nevada. Maybe it was the accumulated frustration that was part of his quarter-century tenure in the state Senate, or the loss of his beloved wife and partner, Estelle, that led Joe Neal to the decision to run for governor against odds so long that no bookmaker would have put it on the board.

His daughters and son are convinced the decision was driven by personal loss, not political gain.

"When my mom passed at the end of November," Withania recalled, "he went into like a cocoon. I was the only one at home at the time. He was just quiet, quiet, quiet for about a month. I was worried about him. We all were. Then he just pops out and says he's going to run for governor. I wondered if he had concocted a master plan in the last four weeks. I knew he was grieving. I figured his decision to run for governor was that he just needed something to do."

Charisse Neal remembered, "it was awesome" when she learned her father was going to run for governor. No one in the Neal house was confused about his chances. Their father was making a statement—one sometimes lost on the press—that Nevada's super-wealthy casino industry bosses paid the lowest gaming taxes in the country.

"When my mom died, my dad went through a little type of depression, because she was the wind beneath his wings," Charisse recalled. "He loved my mother. When she got more sick, he'd take time away from the Legislature and come down and start spending more time with Mama. He told her they would travel and do things, but that didn't happen.... We all tried to pick him up. John Stephens, Spurgeon Daniels, Morse Arberry, they'd all come by and build him up and talk and try to laugh with him, and my dad began to get back on the scene again. I think he had to realize that, wow, I'm a mentor. I watched him go through his depressed state to right back where he was in the swing of things again."

Daughter Dina Neal is even more emphatic: "He had a personal agenda, regardless of what it meant," she recalled. "I took mental notes that the party didn't necessarily stand by him. I learned a lesson. It's one of the things that I understood about the party—you don't put all of your eggs in that basket unless you want to be disappointed.

"When I asked him why he was running, he said, 'Well, I just want to do it.' Later he admitted he was doing it out of grief because my mom had died. He needed something to do to keep his mind off what was happening at home. I said, okay. I understood his emotional detachment. Politics can be that other life that breathes life in you. He was driving in the rurals, and that's where the people always welcomed him. While we were out there, a Republican commissioner said, 'I love your dad. He always stood up for us even though we were from different parties.' I think that's what he needed. I think those embraces are what he needed."

Neal ran for governor against gaming, out of grief, and against all odds.

Stephens, who was Neal's friend, neighbor, and campaign supporter traces their friendship back half a century. When they weren't taking care of their families or talking politics, the two sometimes enjoyed watching ballgames on television.

"Having known Joe all that time, I was still shocked when he told me he was running for governor," Stephens recalled. "You're talking about a black man running for governor in the State of Nevada. Remember, no one even thought about Barack Obama becoming the President. But no Democrat was willing to challenge Kenny Guinn. 'The anointed one,' that's what Joe called him. So Joe decided to take him on."

No one kidded themselves about Neal's prospects of pulling off such an upset—and that included Neal himself. But his anger toward the gaming industry for failing to increase its tax responsibility to the state was high on his list of motivators.

"I'll never forget when we gave his campaign a coming out party," Stephens said. "It's one of the things that I've kept in my memory. He gave it at the Lions Club in North Las Vegas, in their hall. I was working the door for him. It was a gathering of his volunteers, but it was a chance for Democrats to turn out and show their support by contributing twenty-five dollars. About 200 people showed up. We all felt real good. It was a surprise announcement, and that was pretty good support. Congresswoman Shelley Berkley came with her son to congratulate Joe for challenging the governor. But when I looked around the room, I noticed she was the only white elected person present. Many of the elected people who said they supported Joe disappeared."

Neal was not deterred.

Stephens and Daniels often accompanied Neal on his campaign speeches, which rarely strayed from his central theme: that the casino operators, who do business in Nevada by privileged license, have never paid their fair share for the stress they put on the community. Neal, a lifelong union supporter who had stood by the Culinary Union no matter the cost, found organized labor balking at his candidacy. For the Culinary, an embrace of Neal threatened to harm its relationship with the hotel-casino corporations. For the building trades, Neal was considered such a lopsided underdog that it made no sense to spend resources on a losing cause.

The same people who liked to talk about principles and working people were shunning a man whose principled political life had been all about working people. Stephens, a devoted campaign novice, was appalled at the disrespect. But that was politics, and Neal knew the score. Still, his oratorical skills were admired on all sides of the aisle. Decades later, Senator Valerie Wiener, the feisty daughter of renowned Las Vegas attorney, Louis Wiener, and whom Neal mentored with "generosity," recalled a speech he gave on the floor about Martin Luther King, Jr. "His eloquence was immeasurable. I was awed. He spoke, and I thought, 'Here is a natural place to conclude,' thinking he would sit down. He took a breath and continued. When he finally concluded his remarks, I realized I had never heard anything so well stated about such a historic figure."

Those who knew Neal's story would recall him as a freshman legislator challenging Governor Mike O'Callaghan on key social issues—and laughingly adding a threat to run against him if he failed to pay attention to the people's business. That was 1973, back when the race for the state's top office didn't seem quite such a rigged game. But by 1997, with casino licensees ramming through pet legislation and popular Governor Bob Miller preparing to leave office after a decade, there was little doubt as to the identity of the Nevada political machine's candidate.

It was Neal's longtime friend, the former Clark County School District superintendent and longtime gas company and banking executive Kenny Guinn, a mainstream Republican with more political enemies to his right than his left. Guinn, who became even more popular after he helped lead UNLV out of a tempest as a dollar-a-year president, had a Reaganesque likability in one-on-one interactions with the public. He was groomed as a candidate for governor despite never holding an elected office and possessing a decidedly mixed track record in business.

Still, Guinn received the imprimatur of the casino industry and most of Nevada's political insiders in a backroom process that gave him the nickname "The Anointed One" by longtime political reporter and author Jon Ralston. With help from his friends, Guinn banked millions while other potential challengers saw fat fundraising sources go dry on the Strip and elsewhere.

In *The Anointed One: An Inside Look at Nevada Politics*, his book on the 1998 gubernatorial race, Ralston meticulously reported the insider coziness that essentially rigged the political process in Guinn's favor. With the state's powerful interests in Guinn's corner, he couldn't lose. But Neal's entry was an irritating wild card because he insisted on "talking about proposing a casino tax increase in the Legislature and taking it to the ballot if it failed. So the industry could not afford to take chances with the election for governor." But an attack on gaming had a dire consequence when it came to fundraising: a closed door that was bolted and barred as far as Neal was concerned, but then with few exceptions it always had been. "They knew that not only could Neal not raise any money, but that most Democrats wouldn't eagerly embrace an anti-casino platform," Ralston wrote. "In fact, some would distance themselves as fast and as far as they could from the state legislator's theme of assailing the state's most powerful special interest." It was all "sweet music to the Guinnites." And Neal's fellow Democrats also fretted that his casino tax rhetoric would have the effect of making them feel the chill from their traditionally reliable funding sources.

In a poker game strictly for cutthroats and powerbrokers, Neal didn't rate a seat at the table. Lobbyist Pete Ernaut offered the political insider's perspective of the senator from North Las Vegas. Ralston wrote, "Ernaut figured that while state Senator Joe Neal might get in, he was a fringe candidate who would have no impact."

Former Las Vegas City Councilman and political critic Steve Miller observed in an October 25, 2000, column in the *Las Vegas Tribune*, "In 1998, almost every political reporter in Nevada had come to the conclusion that Guinn was certain to win the gubernatorial election by a landslide against longtime state Senator Joe Neal, the then-Democratic hopeful. At the time, Neal was unable to raise a dime in coveted gaming money because of his penchant for wanting to bring the gross gaming tax into parity with the state sales tax. The race seemed over before it began."

Capable former attorney general Frankie Sue Del Papa, who once appeared in line to become the state's first woman governor, found herself hamstrung by a lack of enthusiasm and plentiful sniping in elements of the press. She got the message and decided not to challenge Guinn, who would be tested only rhetorically in the primary from libertarian Hollywood producer Aaron Russo and eccentric surgeon Lonnie Hammargren.

Las Vegas Mayor Jan Laverty Jones, a darling of the casino and banking communities, made for a dynamic and philosophically safe alternative to Guinn on the Democratic side. After overcoming a breast cancer diagnosis, Jones was encouraged to jump into the race by Nevada Democratic Party boss and U.S. Senator Harry Reid and casino titan Wynn, the latter of whom was still stinging from Neal's very public criticism of the "Show Me the Monet" art tax controversy. When Wynn backed Jones, he ensured the noise from Neal would end in the primary.

Reid, meanwhile, looked shallow by damning Neal with faint praise. When the *Las Vegas Review-Journal's* Sean Whaley accurately reported that Reid was among top Democrats essentially shunning Neal, a retraction was demanded and a clarification granted allowing that Reid had "not taken an official position on Neal's candidacy."

Which only made Joe Neal laugh cynically. He knew he was about as likely to receive a warm embrace from Reid and the state's top-of-the-ticket Democrats as he was from the Republican Party. Neal was considered too inflexible on a wide variety of issues and had never been much of a fundraiser. (He had, in fact, been largely shut out of fundraising on the Strip for the better part of three decades.)

Neal had high name recognition in Southern Nevada and was especially well regarded with those rank-and-file union members who appreciated his fierce leadership on labor issues at the Legislature. In his wife's obituary, the *Las Vegas Sun* described him as a former "local civil rights worker in the 1960s, chairman of the Clark County Economic Opportunity Board in the 1970s and a liberal Democratic senator who in three decades is said to have sponsored more controversial bills than any lawmaker in Nevada history." Neal had taken the point on progressive issues and had also managed to infuriate liberals, and the Democratic Party bosses, with his warm embrace of the Yucca Mountain nuclear waste repository project.

Neal's leadership in improving hotel fire safety in the wake of the MGM Grand and Las Vegas Hilton fires was rarely remembered. Nor was his substantial contribution to the protection of Lake Tahoe, or the state's library system. The civil rights issues he'd stood for in the Senate, on many occasions alone, were nationally recognized but often ignored closer to home, where he was just Joe being Joe. Although hundreds of news articles included his name and comment, few if any mentioned that he was the 1992 winner of the prestigious Elijah Lovejoy Award for his courage and contributions to human rights. (Lovejoy was an outspoken abolitionist, Presbyterian minister, and newspaper editor who was murdered in 1837 in Illinois by a pro-slavery mob.) The Lovejoy award was an honor also bestowed upon Martin Luther King Jr., United Nations ambassador Ralph Bunche, soprano Marian Anderson, and U.S. Supreme Court Justice Thurgood Marshall.

That put Neal in good company, but it did little to improve his astronomical odds of defeating Jones in the primary or Guinn in the governor's race as the chief critic of the state's largest and most influential industry.

"I found it very strange that our Legislature did not see gaming as a privilege that the people extended to the gamers," Neal reflected in a 2005 interview. "Wynn and those guys out on the Strip did not own gaming. Gaming is owned by the people of the state of Nevada. The Legislature, in my judgment, did not see it that way. They saw it as a private concern. Of course, the building of the hotel is a private concern, but the gaming was a privileged right extended to the gamers. I always wonder why it was so difficult for our Legislature to see that and tax gaming accordingly. If you let gaming run amok in a state, it will make your community very, very poor because the only product that gaming creates in a community is an empty pocket.

That's why the Mob, when they were operating, operated on Fremont Street and the Strip. They did not allow any gaming houses to get into the communities because the only person who makes money from gaming is the person who actually owns a casino. It's not the individual who goes in there and plays the game. It's just the lottery. They let you win every now and then, but just think about the millions of people who put up their dollars and did not get anything. But they publicize the ones who win and keep you coming back with the idea that maybe you could win, too." Neal's concerns seemed out of synch with changing perceptions of the gaming industry, but he was historically aligned with former governor Carville, who in 1945 warned that becoming tax-dependent on the casino industry would lead to its takeover of the state.

By the late 1990s, Neal's view was considered increasingly antiquated as revenue-strapped jurisdictions across the United States gradually heard the siren song of the casinos as a source of taxation and service-sector job generation. Few in power listened to Neal's history lesson.

"I wasn't against gaming," he insisted. "I was against the way they allowed it to operate. My argument has always been: go back to the history and see what they offered. They said they will take care of our education system, and they will not be a burden on the state. My argument was that gaming has now become like the miners. They take, and they give back nothing. And that's what it is. They said they are the highest contributors to the state. They should be because they also created the social problems that go along with gaming. See, I was talking about gaming addiction long before it was popular. They'd argue that we're infringing upon an individual's right to go out and do whatever he wants to do. But I said that they put it there as an attraction to tell that person he can win money, but once he loses all of his money and becomes a burden on the state, they don't want to help pay for that. And that's where we are today."

Although the industry had received generous news coverage for implementing problem-gambling programs, it was less well understood that state revenues helped fund them. Neal harped on the problems generated by the casino crowd, noting that it was always easier for the small-hearted Legislature to balance the state budget with increases in motor vehicle fees than it was to challenge the powerful gamers.

Gaming's many allies in the Legislature essentially tuned out Neal's constant criticism of the industry.

"Joe was fearless in advocating the tax increase," one legislative veteran observed, but "clearly there were also those who shrugged and thought, 'There he goes again. Now we have to hear more from Joe Neal.'"

And then he insisted on pointing out the most painful contrast of all: Nevada's lowest-in-the-nation gaming tax. After decades of benefiting from the state's liberal and controversial laws providing for casino legalization, the citizenry remained starved for sufficient funding for schools and social services.

Neal's campaign manager, longtime journalist and labor activist Andrew Barbano, didn't lack for pugnacity but was optimistic in the extreme when he asked rhetorically, "Can state senator Joe Neal…become the first African-American governor west of the Mississippi? In a state known until recently as Mississippi West? Yes."

Barbano questioned Guinn's ability to lead and called out his cabal of backers for their Astroturf "grassroots" efforts—most of the favorite's funding came from a handful of casino companies— and compared Neal's underdog battle to other upset candidacies in Nevada history. But he was more hopeful than logical. The fact was, understated and underestimated Chic Hecht defeated a once-powerful, then politically crippled, Howard Cannon in the 1982 U.S. Senate race with support from many top Republicans, and Neal remained little known outside Clark County and the halls of the Legislature. The dream of a come-from-behind victory and the status of being the second black governor since Reconstruction—after Virginia's Douglas Wilder—remained just that.

Predictably, Jones breezed past Neal in the Democratic primary, 59 percent to 15.9 percent, then ran into the bruising machine assembled on Guinn's behalf. Guinn easily prevailed, 52 percent to 42 percent.

Following Guinn's 1998 rout, it would prove even more difficult to find a Democrat willing to challenge the incumbent. For his part, Joe Neal had just begun to scrap. He brushed off the dust of his primary loss and redoubled his effort to see the seemingly all-powerful casino industry pay more for the privilege. It was one last windmill for the Silver State's political Don Quixote.

In the Good Fight, to the Final Bell

JOE NEAL LEARNED something early in his political career that served him through more than three decades in the Nevada Legislature and two fated underdog runs for governor. In the fight for progress in a state historically set against it, important victories can be plucked from defeat's ashes. Neal lost votes many times on the floor of the state Senate on topics ranging from protection of the poor to the restoration of constitutional rights for felons, but history would note many of his cockeyed causes were righteous and struck at the heart of what ailed Nevada.

For those keeping score, Neal took a drubbing in the 1998 gubernatorial primary to a dynamic and better-funded Las Vegas Mayor Jan Laverty Jones. After Jones lost in the general election by a substantial margin to machine candidate Guinn, she focused on a career as a gaming executive with the corporate casino giant now known as Caesars Entertainment. In that election cycle, even the threat of a Neal candidacy at the top of the state ticket was enough to give powerhouse U.S. Senator Harry Reid palpitations, for he had his own incumbency on the line against a fair-haired casino industry creation in Representative John Ensign, a Republican from Las Vegas. Neal, Ralston observed, "could damage the image of the Democratic Party by leading the ticket. Reid would constantly have to distance himself from the state senator, so he needed to get a much less controversial candidate into the contest to knock off Neal." In addition to the outspoken state senator's stance on Yucca Mountain, his criticism of the casino industry made him politically radioactive.

Left unspoken was the fact that the pigment of his skin wasn't likely to be a benefit in a state that had never elected an African American to a constitutional office. And in the late 1990s, there was no groundswell of public support for such a historic moment. A political party that in the near future would show unprecedented enthusiasm for Hispanic candidates wasn't interested in doing the heavy lifting on the liberal firebrand Neal's behalf. He accepted that fact without complaint, but didn't let it deter him.

When the smoke of the 1998 race cleared, he was the one nagging critic who remained. Neal worked on the conscience of the governor with a drumbeat call for a hike in Nevada's lowest-in-the-land casino tax. Neal's realistic goal had never been to cause mass cardiac arrest in the state's political backrooms by pulling off an upset against Guinn. As Neal well knew, this was the state that failed to pass the ERA and waited years before endorsing a celebration honoring Dr. Martin Luther King Jr. This was the state that failed to pass sufficient revenue increases for public education, but was quick to provide a tax break for private art collections.

For political journalists, Neal was the "forgotten man of the 1998 race," but one "determined to find another way to exact a pound of flesh from the gaming industry, which he blamed for squashing his candidacy." It was true in part, for Neal was decidedly determined to see the casino boys pay more.

Called "vindictive" and "unreasonable" by gaming lobbyists and magnates, he was once again attracting media interest in his call for a two percent increase in the gross gaming tax. They could call it the cry of an angry also-ran, or "purely a symbolic act," as some labeled it, but by trotting out the idea on the floor of the Senate he pushed it as far into the daylight as he could. And when it was blocked with help from Harvey Whittemore and fellow big-money lobbyists Billy Vassiliadis and Greg Ferraro, the idea continued to germinate. The state's needs were undeniable to many. The exponential growth of the population, especially in Southern Nevada, had created tremendous quality-of-life challenges that couldn't be addressed with rhetoric alone.

It was something big-gaming's man Governor Guinn also understood. Before he'd become a high-profile business executive, he'd helped guide the Clark County School District through tumultuous integration and bussing issues and understood the communities of need. And he also knew what Neal was doing when the state senator called to put a gaming tax increase on the ballot, an idea that would effectively take the issue away from the rounders dealing Nevada's political poker and hand it to a general public that might prove harder to control. "Even if he thought the industry was paying its fair share," columnist Jon Ralston observed, "politically he could not do what he had to do without the casinos' participation."

Years later, Neal would recall watching his many worthy adversaries consider their options before Guinn at last "decided" that a slight hike in the gross gaming tax was preferable to the potential calamity of a major increase.

"Of course, my last big fight was with gaming," Neal reflected. "Now we've done these guys a great service by passing the retrofit bill. With sprinkler systems in all the high-rise hotels, their customers are safe. But they don't want to pay any taxes. The last time the gaming tax was raised was in 1987, when Don Mello was pushing the tax. I was on the Tax Committee when that was being done. Gaming came in with their lobbyists and said that if we let them go with a quarter percent, they'd check it out and see what they could do next time or in the very near future. The next session came, but they didn't do anything. They lied to us."

More than a decade later, casino lobbyists hadn't yet run out of reasons a tax increase was a bad idea.

"I watched almost sixteen years go by before anything happened in terms of taxes," Neal said. "Finally, after pushing and nudging and talking about them, we finally got a bill passed in my last session. That was when Kenny Guinn—a Republican—was governor. I had built that issue up in the minds of people so that gaming knew that if it ever went to a ballot question—for any type of gaming tax increase, even up to twenty percent—it would pass. Gaming saw that. So they gave a half percent, which took it from 6.25 to 6.75 percent."

Neal was surprised by little after so many years reading Nevada's political tarot cards, but found himself disappointed in the response from the teachers union in a state with such a sorry history of supporting public education. He explained the crush of annual tourist visitors was a heavy weight on a wide range of government services and precious public resources. From health care to water use, tourists had access to everything residents required.

"I said that we should tax gaming for those services; otherwise, that bill falls on the permanent population, which was about two million people," he said. "That argument was beginning to see daylight and make a lot of sense. Guinn bought it, and we increased those taxes by half a percent, which was not enough. I thought it should go up to at least eight percent—maybe to 8.5 percent," where the teachers later unsuccessfully attempted to set it. "By waiting, the educators missed a fleeting opportunity and set themselves back a decade or more." He later added, "I guess in that way it made me a prophet because the teachers continue to fight to increase the gaming tax for their purposes. It hasn't worked very well, but that's Nevada for you."

While 1998 proved politically noteworthy because of Guinn's lack of experience as a candidate for public office and the bruising push by the state's heavyweights to escort him into the governor's chair, by 2002 there was even less in question. Not only did Guinn enjoy the lion's share of the fundraising and endorsements, he had a sober track record as the state's chief executive on which to run for re-election.

Meanwhile, the Democrats again found themselves scrambling for a candidate willing to play the tackling dummy for Team Guinn. Once again, Neal stepped up and was immediately considered no better than a sparring partner for the popular incumbent. That was all right with him.

"My run for governor was to put forth the issue of the gaming tax and to show that I could get enough votes on a statewide petition to pass it," he said. "That was the purpose. It was a simple way of doing that rather than beating my head against the wall to raise and spend the money to try to collect enough signatures for a petition statewide. I could collect votes and send the same message."

Guinn's once-intense interest in deregulating Nevada's electric utility system might have made a potent campaign argument had the race ever been competitive. Neal had been an ardent critic from its emergence in the mid-1990s. He joined fellow Democrats and a few Republicans in opposition to a bill that made it easier for large energy users such as casinos and mining companies to opt out of the system. "It's not competition," Neal roared to a reporter. "It's a matter of control of the electricity supply industry in this country." Neal's outspokenness on the issue gained him an invitation to speak before political leaders in Mexico, which had been shaken to its foundation by energy deregulation. After the scandalized Enron Corp. collapsed into bankruptcy and neighboring California experienced blackouts and skyrocketing power rates, Guinn became a vocal critic of deregulation, assuring skeptics, "I am not going to do anything that would shift that burden to the families of Nevada, nor the businesses of Nevada."

Week after week, often without much notice in Southern Nevada's largest newspaper, Neal banged away at his one-note samba. When the primary came, he defeated three lesser-known Democrats and the "None of These Candidates" option with 35.75 percent of the primary vote. Although almost 32,000 Democrats voted for him, more than 56,000 others had not.

The Democratic Party's lack of strong embrace for Neal transcended the political reality that he was an extreme underdog. Even Neal himself kept his critical rhetoric focused on the gaming industry. But some Nevada political observers believe the state's party of inclusion missed an opportunity to shine.

Former *Reno Gazette-Journal* political reporter Ray Hagar recalled meeting Neal for the first time on the gubernatorial campaign trail at a church in the Northern Nevada city. The candidate appeared to enjoy few of the benefits of his party despite winning the primary. "The Democratic Party didn't seem to help him at all," Hagar said. "They gave him virtually no funding. It was like the fix was in for Kenny Guinn. They should have at least stood behind him. They treated Joe Neal like shit.... It was a bad stain on the Democratic Party."

Even if Neal had no chance to win, Hagar saw the candidacy in its historic context.

"I still have a Joe Neal bumper sticker," he said. "I grabbed one as a memento."

If Neal was disappointed, he didn't let it show publicly. With a Republican president in the White House, Guinn collected more than 97,000 votes in the Republican primary and set his campaign in cruise control. It was a moveable feast for Guinn's inner circle of advisors, a victory lap for a candidate who'd enjoyed first-class treatment even in a state with a history of company men in the Governor's Mansion.

"Again," Neal said, "what I found so devastating in terms of their position was that if you tax them, they can write it off against their federal income taxes. So we tax them at 6.75 now? The way gross gaming tax is structured is if they don't make the money, they don't have to pay the tax. And I sat up there, looking at those suckers, and I said, 'Oh Lord, they just get away with murder, and they're just killing poor folks.' Well, so much for that."

As he looked back, Neal could take pride in the public elementary school and neighborhood park named in his and the late Estelle's honor. The Rawson-Neal Psychiatric Hospital in Southern Nevada was also a reminder of his years spent fighting for the rights and needs of Southern Nevada's mentally ill.

But if forced to count his greatest accomplishments, he would point to his five children, all successful in their own rights. With her election to the Nevada Assembly in 2010, Dina Neal carried on the family tradition of public service. Her dad served as a campaign rabble-rouser and advisor.

Joe Neal, the son of a Louisiana sharecropper, had come a long way from the cotton fields of Madison Parish and left his imprint on history of politics and civil rights in Nevada with 32 years in the state senate. The battles seemed endless. He lost many, but was deterred by none.

Not long after he retired from the Legislature, Neal was asked to return for a ceremony inducting him to that body's Hall of Fame on a cold day in 2005. He attended with his daughters, Cherisse and Dina, and family members. Neal was overcome with pride that his grandchildren were present for the ceremony held in a room that had seen far too few black faces over the previous century.

"One senator got up and said, 'We have not had a gaming tax bill introduced in this Senate since he left,'" Neal recalled. There was some laughter, but Neal was given pause. He later recalled, "what I'm being told now is that a voice like mine has disappeared from the process. That's the sad part. We must have someone to challenge those issues that need to be challenged." Senator Mike McGinness said, "I don't think we will ever see a student of the legislative process better than Senator Neal ... As chairman of the Senate Committee on Taxation, I can say, 'We miss you, and it has been six weeks, and no one has taken a run at the big gamers.'" Neal's view of these "big gamers" and the state's political system was best highlighted in a *Washington Post* interview with reporter Lou Cannon. In the piece headlined "Trying to Beat the Odds in Nevada," Neal offered: "There is really only one party in Nevada, and it's not the Democrats or the Republicans but the Gaming Party."

Following his retirement, political allies and enemies alike at the Legislature acknowledged Neal's fearless advocacy. His friend from the Senate, Dina Titus, was winding down her nearly two decades in the state Legislature with plans to run for Congress. "Senator Neal's legislative agenda has always been an ambitious and aggressive one," Titus later described his efforts. "Whether he was fighting for voting rights or against racial profiling, he has never relented. He has never shied from controversy, and he has never cowered in the face of enormous opposition. Senator Neal is much more than a role model. He is a man who has changed the face of this state. Although he has left the Senate ... he is going to keep calling it as he sees it—unbossed and unbought."

At the Hall of Fame ceremony, Titus, in her quintessential Georgia drawl, called Neal "the greatest orator in the history of this state. His eloquence derives from his academic knowledge, from his vast experience, and from his compassion for those who are about to be affected by the actions that we are about to take. When Joe stands to speak, a hush falls over the room. Everyone, including legislators, staff, the press, the lobbyists in the back, all stop to listen. He speaks from the heart. He fears nothing. He deftly parries any argument, and he does not hesitate to attack those who he believes turn a blind eye to injustice."

Titus said that Neal frequently quoted Abraham Lincoln on the floor of the Senate, but she thought he was more like Benjamin Franklin "with a twinkling eye and always an amusing anecdote." Like Neal's, she said, Franklin's "guiding principle was a dislike of everything that tended to debase the spirit of the common man."

Nevada senator Cliff Young, a future Nevada Supreme Court justice, was a highly respected Republican who found himself impressed by Neal's indefatigable spirit and political tenacity on a variety of progressive issues. "Joe, you're the Westside slugger," Young said. "You get knocked down, but you always get back up, and you never stop swinging."

Taking on the powerful in Nevada came at a cost. It is a price Neal paid without regret.

"You try and protect the public," he said. "...When you come out and challenge someone, you have nothing but your courage. Of course, you're not getting any support that the newspaper's going to write about. They're going to give the facts, but they're not going to give the editorials because this guy you're challenging buys advertisements from them.... All you've got is your courage to go out and try to do the best job you can.

"You fight for the causes you believe in. You get knocked down, but get back up again. And the fight never ends because you're fighting for the rights of people."

Epilogue: Wins and Losses, and a Legacy

EVEN A CURSORY STUDY of Joe Neal's public life and political career would find it inseparable from the battle for civil rights in Southern Nevada. A deeper analysis reveals the influence of the soil of Louisiana sharecroppers and the traditions of Jim Crow on a young black man hungry for education and equal opportunity. It's a hunger that was never sated, and backward Nevada is the better for it.

From the 1960s to the turn of the new century, Neal was omnipresent on issues ranging from minority employment and police relations to the ill-fated push for the ERA and the struggle to squeeze a little more from Nevada's powerful casino industry. Although often portrayed in the role of the loud black man by the press, it is important to note that without Neal and a few others like him, the essential and at times ugly story of race relations in Las Vegas would have largely been a tale left to the majority to tell. And no place in America is better at revising its history and marketing a pretty picture than Las Vegas.

Few might remember some of the needless and arguably racist tough-on-crime legislation that Neal helped knock down. His efforts to help force fire-safety-retrofitting legislation through the process in the wake of the MGM and Hilton fires alone were an important accomplishment by any reasonable measure. And his work, often at odds with the casino industry, to ensure water quality at Lake Tahoe is undeniable.

But it's also true that many of Neal's greatest challenges, on the ERA, restored rights for ex-felons, and protections for sexual minorities, were delayed for years or defeated entirely. There were plenty of losses, some wins, and what can only be called a few draws on his legislative record. But, as colleague Floyd Lamb liked to say, Joe Neal got knocked down, but he always got up again. "I do think he was an effective legislator. He called people out. He took policy and he worked that policy," Giunchigliani said. "Even when he was on the losing end of an issue," she said, "he forced the lawmaking body to consider a minority view. He once compelled a health insurance giant to produce box after box of documents to illustrate a point on how overwhelming the system was for working people and the poor," she recalled. "He demanded that they prove him wrong. He made them work. I totally respected him for that. He wasn't afraid. He didn't allow people to bully him. He spoke the truth. He was never mean, but he was tough…He was the conscience of the Legislature in his time."

After watching Neal work the Legislature for two decades, veteran Nevada political journalist Steve Sebelius concluded, "I think he was ahead of his time on many issues." Jon Ralston, dean of Nevada political journalists who covered the Legislature for more than thirty years, considers Neal's legacy mixed. Although Neal was clearly a man of "deeply held principles" who "believed that his role was to give a voice to the voiceless," his legislative impact was "somewhat limited."

"While I always admired his passion, and some of his speeches really were riveting, you have to ask the question, 'What did he really get done, and could he have done more?'" Ralston asked.

Nevada historian Michael Green counters that a more measured Neal would have been less successful than the at times bombastic genuine article. Neal's public life exceeded that of a mere rabble-rouser. Neal's unwillingness to "play the game" served him well at a time the Legislature wasn't much interested in progressive change. And, Green observes, although Neal's successor Steven Horsford was much more adept, and far better connected, at working the halls of government, "It doesn't seem to have done much to pull West Las Vegas out of its economic status. That suggests to me that the Legislature isn't much interested in the subject, period, and it would take a lot to change that, just as it would have taken a lot for Neal to have been able to change that, considering that for much of his tenure, the Legislature included a lot of less liberal-minded people."

Someone in Nevada's lawmaking choir needed to sing loudly about the state's many inequities on the issues of race and economic fairness.

"His legacy will be partly as a pioneer, partly as a voice in the wilderness," Green said. "In some ways, he is similar to the abolitionists of the nineteenth century, or the people who advocated Social Security and other reforms in the twentieth."

Neal's unrelenting outspokenness reflected an integral and often forgotten part of the history of American social reform. His rhetoric, Green noted, was not so different from that of antislavery newspaper publisher William Lloyd Garrison, who once said, "I do not wish to think, or speak, or write, with moderation...I will not equivocate— I will not excuse—I will not retreat a single inch—AND I WILL BE HEARD."

"Not much legislation or policy bears Neal's name, any more than we say that William Lloyd Garrison passed the Thirteenth Amendment," Green said. "But people like Garrison moved the needle, forced the discussion, forced people to look inside themselves. By coming back each time and fighting, Neal won attention for the causes he believed in, and whatever he did or didn't push through the Legislature, he forced people to look at reality."

For Joyce Woodhouse, a longtime educator and state senator, Neal would forever remain the master of the rules and a legislative pathfinder for minorities. "He is the forerunner of Nevada state legislators who made it possible for others, whether they be African American or Hispanic, to know that they could step into leadership roles as he did," she said. "And the fact that he pursued the civil rights issues and equal rights issues and human rights issues, he was a real trailblazer. He was willing to stand up for what he believed in, even when it wasn't the popular thing." Giunchigliani saw firsthand how he mastered the rules. When she first joined the Assembly in 1991 she approached Neal and asked his advice. He said, 'Baby girl, learn the rules.' He was absolutely correct about that. If you don't know how an institution runs, how proceedings are going, where you can move a bill and also stop bad stuff, how to handle the workflow—you need to know all of that."

Liberal columnist and longtime Nevada political mechanic Andrew Barbano remains Neal's unabashed and unapologetic advance man. "From the first time I met him, through all his years at the Legislature, my first impression has held true: he's a man of absolute principle,"

Barbano said. "In the forty-seven years I've been doing this, Joe Neal has remained in a class by himself and is the best public official I have had any dealings with—because he is a man of high integrity."

Neal's perceived enemies in corporate Nevada and the Legislature's cozy lobbying corps remained remarkably consistent throughout his career. Casino titans and their powerful hired men considered him "a pain in the ass" whose predictable umbrage on the gaming industry's contribution to the state coffers was overcome with patience and an abundance of more reasonable "team players" in the Senate.

Throughout his public life and legislative career, Neal took it upon himself to educate his own community and fellow lawmakers about black history. Session after session in Carson City he rose and gave speeches about the contributions of African Americans to the nation. He sometimes went on at substantial length, lecturing his at times impatient colleagues about the important lives of blacks that were seldom remembered by white society and seldom taught in schools. The efforts of H. A. Johnson, who invented a device to enable trains to switch tracks, to Dr. Daniel Hale Williams, who performed the first open-heart surgery, echoed through the Senate chamber in 1987 as Neal read a lengthy list of inventors and innovators of color. And Neal held a special place for black Nevadans of historical significance.

Looking back on her childhood fascination with the politics that swirled ceaselessly around her father, Dina Neal recalled, "Our house might as well have been a legislative building. People would ring the doorbell and state their problem and ask to see my dad. My mom was focused on cleanliness everywhere in the house, but the living room would have to be spotless—someone was always at our house. Total strangers would say, 'I need to talk to your dad. I have a problem.' I was completely aware that the living room was his office. And when someone was there, it was 'Shoo fly, go away.' The living room was his meeting room. But in a split-level house, the kids were on the bottom floor, you can hear it all. You look out and you could see who he was talking to. I just kind of thought it was fascinating that all of these people needed him."

After Dina was elected to the Assembly in 2010, her first legislative session in Carson City was an emotional mash-up. She was proud of

her father, but wanted to cut her own trail and establish her own political career. But what she didn't initially realize was the fact that, for
some legislators and especially some lobbyists, the latter of which are
not term-limited, Joe Neal hadn't yet left the building.

His framed photograph signifying his membership in the Senate
Hall of Fame hung from a wall. Members of the Legislative Counsel
Bureau had no shortage of Neal stories to tell. It was almost assumed
that Dina Neal, as a chip off the old block, would be as firebrand and
outspoken as her old man with the same allies and enemies. It took an
entire session to prove doubters wrong.

"Life is really weird," Dina recalled. "I met this political science professor when I was in my senior year at Southern University. I was the
pre-law president and taking students around, and the political science professor who taught my dad was teaching pre-law at Thurgood
Marshall School of Law. I introduced myself, and she remembered my
dad. She said, 'I told your dad he was going to move west, and he wasn't
going to be nothing greater than a dogcatcher.' I have a lot of pride in
my dad because I've been able to see the layers of what it means as an
individual in this process. Your individuality, your ability to think, and
remain a thinker, and maintain what you believe in is one of the hard-
fought principles he has taught me. I have a lot of pride about who
he is as a person. He's experienced real pressure. That adversity either
builds your character, or breaks your character down. Politics is such a
human process where people are pulling on you to make you do what
they want. You have to decide who you're going to be."

Even after four sessions she remained in awe of her father's resil-
ience. "He did this for thirty years," she exclaimed. "The battles he had
to fight were philosophical battles, totally philosophical. He had to ask
himself, 'Am I going to be with people, or with lobbyists.'"

"Some of the attachés who had been in the building for twenty and
thirty years would introduce themselves and say, 'I remember your
dad.' I was like he's still there, this presence. It's weird how somebody's
presence can live on in the building." She was proud of her father, of
course, but at times the constant reminders were frustrating. "The first
session, it was like I was 'mini Joe,'" Dina recalled. "The first session
was a challenge. Everyone had an assumption of who I was. They al-

ready assumed I was going to be anti-gaming, anti-whatever. I had no preconceptions. I'm a policy person."

At one point, some women who had worked on the Equal Rights Amendment came up to me to talk about my dad. 'We love your dad,' they said. I thought, your dad, your dad, your dad. Look, I'm me. He's him. I want to do my own thing, but sometimes you find yourself walking in the footsteps regardless of whether you want to or not."

In time, she adjusted to the daily grind of politics and the friendly ghost as well. She was reminded by her Assembly colleague James Ohrenschall, whose mother Genie Ohrenschall was a legislative veteran, that Everything is cyclical. And it was true."

Tania Neal Edwards observed, "He's still the same person he's always been. So many people cave in on important issues because they want to be liked, because they don't have the guts to stand alone. It comes full circle in time. The things he was fighting for are just as important today as they were during his time in the Legislature, and some people see that now. The people he was fighting against, people thought he was crazy. But he was on the right side of history. I admire the fact that my sister is going in his footsteps. She has a different nuance, but she definitely has that strength about her. She will fight for issues even if she's the only one standing."

Knowing that a Neal is still speaking up at the Legislature makes her father proud. "I have great confidence in Dina," Joe Neal said. "She works very hard, understands the issues, and she has a better idea of the law than I did. The only one thing I told her, 'If you have any questions or problems, give me a call.' I am happy to say she has done that time and time again. I'm very proud of her. And she's very much aware that not everyone is going to appreciate that she's my daughter. I once asked her to test the idea by giving Steve Wynn a call and asking him for a campaign contribution."

The answer?

No.

"Some things never change," Neal said, laughing.

The man who fought more than anyone to carve out a place in Nevada politics for African-American residents would watch the man who took his place in the state Senate, Horsford, not only rise to the top of legislative leadership, but go on to serve one term in Congress as Nevada's first minority member of the U.S. House of Representatives. Horsford, a favorite of top Nevada Democrats and the politically potent Culinary Union, was the first successful elected official from a new generation of black politicians. It was Neal who had first encouraged Horsford to run for the state Senate. Neal had watched Horsford win and quickly be taken under the wing of the state's political kingmakers. Horsford would go on to serve as Senate majority leader and then spend a single term in Congress before losing and entering a lucrative partnership in the private sector with R&R Partners, the state's preeminent political and advertising factory.

To Horsford, Neal was a larger-than-life figure who "championed causes and used his position in the state Senate to represent those who had no voice. As the first African American elected to the Nevada Senate, Neal faced challenges that people in my generation have only read about."

By the 2017 session, Democrat Aaron D. Ford would serve as the Senate's majority leader with Kelvin Atkinson as his assistant, and Jason Frierson would be named speaker of the Assembly. Ford climbed out of an impoverished Texas childhood to earn five college degrees. Frierson rose from a tough Compton, California, neighborhood and parlayed a football scholarship to the University of Nevada, Reno into a law degree and political career. Add to that other African-American members and a growing contingent of other minorities, and Nevada's citizen lawmaking body was finally beginning to reflect the state's diverse demographics.

They all owed a debt to Joe Neal. Although his fearless voice no longer boomed from the Senate Chamber or echoed through the long hallways at the Legislature, he helped open the door for a new generation of elected officials of color. The path he cut from the cotton fields of Louisiana to Carson City helped change Nevada and shape its political structure forever.

Acknowledgments

Before I ever met him, I first heard Joe Neal's name at our dinner table. It was in the late 1960s. I was a boy, and we had only recently moved thirteen miles from Henderson, Nevada, to Las Vegas. My mother, Jan, worked in Democratic Party politics and the local court system, and my father, Smitty, was a union painter and future business agent of the local. We attended Saint James the Apostle Catholic Church, then located on H Street on the Westside. Neal was also a congregant, but the first time I recall hearing his name it was being taken in vain by my parents, who were mad about something he'd done inside the county party. Fired up by the civil rights movement and his own life experience, Neal was pushing local Democrats and the building trades unions to be more inclusive of people of color. Some were slower than others to hear his message.

My folks grew to appreciate Neal's persistence and courage. Years later, as a high school teenager, I found myself on a panel on race seated next to state senator Joe Neal, who was never too busy to speak out on the topic of equal opportunity. Looking back, perhaps it was inevitable I would write at length about Neal's life and career. For whatever this project's successes or shortcomings, it has benefited immeasurably from the patience and cooperation of the subject, his family, friends, former political colleagues, members of the press, and some of his critics as well. I owe you all a great debt.

My wife, Sally Denton, provided invaluable editing assistance and the kind of insight gained from her life as a third-generation Nevadan and life's work as an award-winning author and investigative journalist. I can't thank her enough. My daughter, Amelia, long ago learned to be patient with her often-distracted dad during his seemingly endless deadlines, and the rest of my family has more or less forgiven me for my time-consuming pursuit of the craft.

Dozens of people were kind enough to share their thoughts, experiences, and insights into Neal, the civil rights era, and Nevada politics generally. Their voices echo through these pages. Among many: Andrew Barbano, B. Mahlon Brown, Bob Coffin, Sara Denton, Pat Dingle, William Evans, Chris Giunchigliani, Michael Green, Earl Greene, Ray Hagar, William Hernstadt, A. D. Hopkins, Jon Ralston, Karen Siena Rogers, Steve Sebelius, Dina Titus, Harriet Trudell, Joan Whitely, and Valerie Wiener.

The work of several highly conscientious interviewers proved invaluable. The work of Claytee D. White, director of the Oral History Research Center at UNLV, should be celebrated by anyone hoping to capture the Nevada experience. Dana R. Bennett led a remarkable team that interviewed, filmed, and transcribed a lengthy conversation with Neal in 2008 on behalf of the Nevada Legislature Oral History Project. That team included Gwendolyn B. Clancy and Jean Stoess.

I'd also like to thank publishing veterans Don Lamm, Gloria Loomis, and Joanna Hurley for taking time out of their busy lives to read the manuscript and offer their insight and suggestions. Michael Green's keen eye and encyclopedic knowledge of Nevada history greatly improved the working draft and final product.

My special thanks to University of Nevada Press Director Justin Race, Editorial Design and Production Manager Alrica Goldstein, and copy editor Paul Szydelko and proofreader Luke Torn for their faith in the book and their effort to make the story the best it could be. You are real professionals.

One of the joys of this project is the time I was able to spend with Joe Neal. We logged so many hours of interviews, often over doughnuts and coffee at a local Krispy Kreme shop, that I hesitate to tally them all. We should have bought stock in the company, Joe. I can only say I am proud to have been there—although next time perhaps we should choose a place less calorie-laden.

Neal and I have been talking about the issue of race and society a long time. During my research, I came across a yellowed news clipping from 1977 that featured a photo of a civil rights discussion held at Western High School. The panel included an appearance by up-and-coming state senator Joe Neal. Next to him sat a longhaired, woefully underdressed junior who looks an awful lot like my younger self.

Finally, late in his own remarkable life, the groundbreaking African-American attorney Charles Kellar was kind enough to give me one of his scrapbooks, which not only was a source of many news clippings and much perspective, but also provided an unexpected treat: a grainy photograph of a 1968 NAACP meeting as its members planned a memorial rally honoring the late Dr. Martin Luther King Jr., who had been assassinated only a few months earlier in Memphis. I am proud to say my intrepid mother, Jan Smith, then an NAACP board member, was right in the middle of the action.

It is to that generation—struggling but splendid, black, white and blended—that I dedicate this effort.

A Note on Sources

One of the biographer's great advantages, and one the daily journalist can only envy, is the gift of hindsight and the perspective that only the passage of time affords. I was reminded of that fact often during the research of Joe Neal's life. Early articles on Neal's activism were littered with euphemistic language and flawed assumptions about his politics and motives. Neal has always been an unapologetic black man, one who spoke his mind without fear or favor whatever the subject. That didn't always translate into favorable press coverage. Nor was it always the smartest political poker, but after a lengthy study of the subject it's clear Neal was never interested in gathering the most chips at the Nevada Legislature's lobbyist-dominated table.

That nuance was occasionally misunderstood by working reporters early in his career, and written off in later years by more sophisticated journalists who saw him as a perennial outsider who might have been more effective had he swallowed his considerable pride, pontificated less, and "learned to play the game." That, of course, was never his style.

Time has shown Neal to be far more than an outspoken agitator, and his profile in the press grew more nuanced and fulsome with the passing decades. A political career that began with receiving scathing vitriol from *Sun* columnist Paul Price, eventually blossomed into a cover of Southern Nevada's *Desert Companion* magazine in 2016 as one of the state's civil rights icons is a truly intriguing transformation.

As with so many public servants, Neal's career was chronicled in the local newspapers, chiefly in the *Las Vegas Review-Journal, Las Vegas Sun, Las Vegas Tribune, Valley Times,* and *Sentinel Voice.* The *Reno Gazette-Journal, Nevada State Journal,* and *Carson Appeal* also covered Neal's decades at the Legislature with depth on deadline. While sporadic, many other Nevada newspapers also weighed in on Neal's efforts at everything from passing the Equal Rights Amendment (which ultimately failed) to securing millions for new public libraries throughout the state for the first time in years (a major success). When issues such as the water quality of Lake Tahoe or a proposed tax on the powerful gaming industry entered the news, newspapers such as the *Los Angeles Times, Sacramento Bee, San Francisco Chronicle,* and *The Washington Post* provided coverage and valuable outsider perspective.

For the section on Neal's upbringing in Louisiana, I relied on many interviews with the subject, family friends, and some of his lifelong pals he met during his school days at Thomastown School. In addition to the invaluable education I received by reading the histories listed in the Bibliography, I would like to acknowledge Annelise Orleck's remarkable *Storming Caesars Palace: How Black Mothers Fought Their Own War On Poverty.*

Nevada's effort to chronicle the state's black culture has been, to put it politely, sporadic for many years. But that has changed in large part to the attention the subject has received from dedicated historians at UNLV and UNR. Two highly informative oral histories of Joseph M. Neal Jr., were also essential to the research of this project: the first was conducted in 2006 by Claytee White as part of her groundbreaking series on historical figures of West Las Vegas. Dana Bennett, on behalf of the Nevada Legislative Counsel Bureau, conducted the second in 2009. The author is indebted to both professionals. Among other oral histories used in preparing the manuscript include those of Ruby Phillips Duncan, Lawrence Jacobson, Lubertha Johnson, Woodrow "Woody" Wilson, William "Bob" Bailey, Charles Kellar, Dr. James McMillan, and William Raggio.

These days, the effort to chronicle the black struggle in Las Vegas and Nevada history has many champions, not least are academic authors Michael Green, Eugene Moehring, and James Hulse. Documentary filmmaker Stan Armstrong and activist Trish Geran are other contributors to this widening body of work. And everyone who writes about this subject is indebted to the late Elmer Rusco for his relentless pursuit of history and independent spirit.

Information on organized crime's grip on Las Vegas, and the interaction of black entertainers with casino bosses on the segregated Strip, comes to a great degree from the formidable work of Nevada natives Sally Denton and Roger Morris in their 2001 *The Money and the Power: The Making of Las Vegas and Its Hold on America, 1947–2000*. Among other helpful and entertaining works used is *Why Me? The Sammy Davis Jr. Story* by Davis and Jane and Burt Boyer. As ever, no book that touches on Las Vegas history can fail to tip a fedora to the efforts of Ovid Demaris and Ed Reid in *The Green Felt Jungle*.

The work of many journalists writing "the first rough draft of history," as an old reporter once called it, went into every page of the manuscript. Among so many: Lee Adler, Bryn Armstrong, Andrew Barbano, Myram Borders, Bob Brown, George Bryson, Wade Cavanaugh, Foster Church, Jim Coleman, Anjeanette Damon, Ned Day, Bill Deutsch, Ann Ehrenburg, George Franklin, Daryl Gibson, Hank Greenspun, Martin Griffith, Larry Henry, Hugh Jackson, Charles McCabe, Jack McFarrin, Mike McNamara, Jane Ann Morrison, Erin Neff, Mike O'Callaghan, Bob Palm, Vic Pollard, Paul Price, John Pryzybys, Jeff Rabin, Jerry Ralya, the aforementioned Ralston and Sebelius, David Strow, Howard Stutz, David Youngblood, Stacy J. Willis, and Chris Woodyard.

For the section on Neal's emergence on the forefront of the fight for equal opportunity in the workplace in Southern Nevada, his voluminous letters to as the Equal Opportunity Compliance Officer for Reynolds Electrical & Engineering Co. (REECo) provided a look at the case-by-case struggle he fought at his own place of employment. News articles and interviews with Neal fleshed out the at times heartbreaking challenge of helping break through often invisible barriers to good-paying jobs for blacks and other minorities.

In addition to dozens of letters collected in Neal's own personal archives from neighbors, constituents, and public officials, I gathered court documents from early lawsuits involving equal employment issues and infighting with the O'Callaghan administration. With the precious passage of time, I can only conclude that despite hard-fought workplace improvements the battle for equal pay and equal work continues.

It's not exactly breaking news that the eccentric billionaire Howard Hughes was an enigma during his four-year reign as king of Las Vegas. Many volumes have been devoted to understanding his place in the state's history and the city's slow evolution from hoodlum-backed gambling mecca to publicly traded corporate casino industrial complex. But the one thing that hasn't been written about sufficiently is Hughes's virulent racism, which came at a time of great transition and struggle in Las Vegas. Jack Anderson and Daryl Gibson take time to outline it in their informative *Peace, War, and Politics: An Eyewitness Account*, while Michael Drosnin's *Citizen Hughes* lays out the ugliness in graphic detail by using the billionaire bigot's own words. Neal, then focused on equal employment opportunity in the workplace and improving conditions one job at a time, couldn't have known what he was up against—especially because some reporters and Vegas insiders kept quiet about Hughes's racial prejudices.

For the chapter on the ill-fated attempt to pass the Equal Rights Amendment in Nevada, many news articles were used. The work of the League of Women Voters of Nevada was invaluable, most notably the multi-byline effort that composed the moving *The Proposed Equal Rights Amendment: A Brief in Support of Its Ratification*. Neal's oral histories also touched on the subject in substantial detail, and my interview with the late legislator Wilbur Faiss was memorable and insightful.

For the chapter on the MGM fire and its legislative aftermath, I relied on many news sources as well as *The Day the MGM Grand Hotel Burned* by Dee Coakley and Hank Greenspun and his intrepid *Sun* staff. Neal's recollections and an interview with gracious former state senator William Hernstadt were also valuable.

One of the surprises of Neal's political career was his devotion—sometimes in direct opposition to the interests of the casino industry—to protecting the environment of Lake Tahoe. That effort most often placed him in the camp of former California state legislator and current House member John Garamendi, who has spent more than four decades battling to protect the lake. Garamendi provided insight on those important early years in an interview with the author. The *San Francisco Chronicle*, *Sacramento Bee*, and *Los Angeles Times* provided insightful coverage of the political struggles to save Lake Tahoe. The lake is obviously dear to the heart of environmental historian Michael J. Makley, who has devoted two informative works to the subject. *Saving Lake Tahoe: An Environmental History* is essential to understanding the battles that have taken place—some outside the public eye—for control of the lake.

Then there's what some will call the other surprise of Neal's public life: the defiance of the party line in support for the plan to create a high-level nuclear waste repository in Nevada. His alliance with interests at the Nevada Test Site, coupled with his belief that union workers would benefit and the Democratic Party was practicing hypocrisy, set him apart—far, far apart at times—from many of his legislative colleagues. It didn't appear to deter him in the slightest. For real insight into Nevada's atomic schizophrenia, I relied on Dina Titus's essential *Bombs in the Backyard: Atomic Testing and*

American Politics. Titus was also an invaluable source on understanding Neal's importance at the Legislature. The discussion of Neal's efforts to oppose the Guinn administration's pursuit of energy deregulation was augmented by deadline journalism and the
Historic Overview: Nevada Deregulation 1990's compiled by the state's Public Utilities
Commission on behalf of the Governor's Committee on Energy Choice in 2017.

The attempt by casino billionaire Steve Wynn to manipulate the state's tax on art
was well chronicled in the press, notably by Ralston and Sebelius. Along with a few
others such as Ray Hagar and Cy Ryan, they have written much of the modern history
of Nevada politics in newsprint, on the internet, and the airwaves. They were on the
sidelines, and occasionally in the huddle, when Neal mounted his quixotic gubernatorial campaigns. Ralston's *The Anointed One* remains the best book on the selection of
Nevada's governor by the state's power elite.

Keeping up with Joe Neal wasn't easy. In researching Neal's at times controversial, public life and political career, I couldn't help but be amazed by his energy and
outspokenness in the face of a consistent drumbeat of criticism from what passed for
polite society. Whether it was registering voters in Madison Parish, Louisiana, challenging the Sheriff of Clark County, standing alone on the short end of a vote in the
Nevada Senate, or running an against-all-odds campaign for governor, Neal's character
and courage never ceased to impress me. When it came to promoting equal rights for
women and minorities, the mission focus of the former member of the United States
Air Force never wavered. And the fact he was so often unsuccessful didn't appear to
deter him in the least.

Selected Bibliography

Anderson, Jack, with Daryl Gibson. *Peace, War, and Politics: An Eyewitness Account.* New York: Tom Doherty Associates, LLC, 1999.

Archer, Michael. *A Man of His Word: The Life & Times of Nevada's Senator William J. Raggio.* Ashland, Ore.: Hellgate Press, 2011.

Bailey, William H. *Looking Up! Finding My Voice in Las Vegas.* Las Vegas: Stephens Press, 2009.

Barlett, Donald, and James B. Steele. *Empire: The Life, Legend, and Madness of Howard Hughes.* New York: W.W. Norton & Company, (Rev. ed.) 2004.

Bellamy, Blank, Goodman, Kelly, Ross, and Stanley. *The Proposed Equal Rights Amendment: A Brief in Support of Its Ratification.* League of Women Voters of Nevada, undated.

Coakley, Dierdre, with Hank Greenspun, et al. *The Day the MGM Grand Hotel Burned.* Secaucus, N.J.: Lyle Stuart Inc., 1982.

Davies, Richard O., Editor. *The Maverick Spirit: Building the New Nevada.* Reno: University of Nevada Press, 1999.

Davis, Sammy Jr., Jane Boyar and Burt Boyar. *Why Me? The Sammy Davis Jr. Story.* New York: Farrar, Straus and Giroux, 1989.

Demaris, Ovid, and Ed Reid. *The Green Felt Jungle: The Truth About Las Vegas Where Organized Crime Controls Gambling,* paperback ed. New York: Pocket Books, 1964.

Denton, Ralph, and Michael S. Green. *A Liberal Conscience: Ralph Denton, Nevadan.* Reno: University of Nevada Oral History Program, 2001.

Denton, Sally, and Roger Morris. *The Money and the Power: The Making of Las Vegas and Its Hold on America, 1947–2000.* New York: Random House, 2001.

DeRosier, Arthur H. Jr., *The Removal of the Choctaw Indians.* Harper & Row: New York, 1970.

Detter, Thomas. *Nellie Brown: Or the Jealous Wife, With Other Sketches.* San Francisco: Cuddy & Hughes Printers, 1871.

Drosnin, Michael. *Citizen Hughes.* New York: Holt, Rinehart and Winston, 1985.

Elliott, Russell R. *History of Nevada.* Lincoln, Nebraska: University of Nebraska Press, 1973.

Geran, Trish. *Beyond the Glimmering Lights: The Pride and Perseverance of African Americans in Las Vegas.* Las Vegas: Stephens Press, 2006.

Glass, Mary Ellen. *Nevada's Turbulent 50s.* Reno: University of Nevada Press, 1981.

Green, Michael S. *Nevada: A History of the Silver State.* Reno: University of Nevada Press, 2015.

Heller, Dean. *Political History of Nevada 2006.* 11th ed. Carson City: State Printing Office, 2006.

Hopkins, A. D., and K. J. Evans, eds. *The First 100: Portraits of the Men and Women Who Shaped Las Vegas.* Las Vegas: Huntington Press, 1999.

Hulse, James W. *Forty Years in the Wilderness: Impressions of Nevada, 1940–1980.* Reno: University of Nevada Press, 1986.

———. *The Silver State: Nevada's Heritage Reinterpreted.* Reno: University of Nevada Press, 1991.

Kaufman, Perry B. *The Best City of Them All: A History of Las Vegas, 1930–1960.* PhD. dissertation, University of California, Santa Barbara, 1974.

Land, Barbara, and Myrick Land. *A Short History of Las Vegas.* Reno: University of Nevada Press, 1999.

Laxalt, Paul. *Nevada's Paul Laxalt: A Memoir.* Reno: Jack Bason & Company, 2000.

Laxalt, Robert. *The Nevada: A Bicentennial History.* New York: W.W. Norton & Company. 1977.

League of Women Voters of the United States. *In Pursuit of Equal Rights: Women in the Seventies.* 1976.

Littlejohn, David, ed. *The Real Las Vegas: Life Beyond the Strip.* New York: Oxford University Press, 1999.

Makley, Michael J. *A Short History of Lake Tahoe.* Reno: University of Nevada Press, 2011.

———. *Saving Lake Tahoe: An Environmental History.* Reno: University of Nevada Press, 2014.

McMillan, James B. *Fighting Back: A Life in the Struggle for Civil Rights from Oral Histories with James B. McMillan.* Interviewed by Gary E. Elliott and narrative interpretation by R. T. King. Reno: University of Nevada Oral History Program, 1997.

Miller, Bob. *Son of a Gambling Man: My Journey From A Casino Family to the Governor's Mansion.* New York: St. Martin's Press, 2013.

Moehring, Eugene P. *Reno, Las Vegas, and the Strip: Tale of Three Cities.* Reno: University of Nevada Press, 2014.

———. *Resort City in the Sunbelt: Las Vegas, 1930–2000.* Reno: University of Nevada Press, 2000.

———. and Michael S. Green. *Las Vegas, A Centennial History.* Reno: University of Nevada Press, 2007.

Morris, Aldon D. *The Origins of the Civil Rights Movement: Black Communities Organizing for Change.* New York: The Free Press, 1984.

Neal, Joseph M., Jr. *A Compilation of Remarks from the Floor by Senator Joseph M. Neal Jr., 1973–2003.* Presented by Black Elected Officials of Southern Nevada, January 21, 2005. Las Vegas: private printing, 2004.

Orleck, Annelise. *Storming Caesars Palace: How Black Mothers Fought Their Own War on Poverty.* Boston: Beacon Press, 2005.

Ostrander, Gilman M. *Nevada: The Great Rotten Borough, 1859–1864.* New York: Oxford University Press, 1966.

Overstreet, Everett Louis. *Black Steps in the Desert Sands: A Chronicle of African-Americans' Involvement in the Growth of Las Vegas, Nevada.* Las Vegas: private printing, 1999.

Ralston, Jon. *The Anointed One: An Inside Look at Nevada Politics.* Las Vegas: Huntington Press, 2000.

Reid, Harry. *Searchlight: The Camp that Didn't Fail.* Reno: University of Nevada Press, 1998.

Rothman, Hal. *Neon Metropolis: How Las Vegas Started the Twenty-First Century.* New York: Routledge, 2003.

Rowley, Rex J. *Everyday Las Vegas: Local Life in a Tourist Town.* Reno: University of Nevada Press, 2013.

Rusco, Elmer. *Good Time Coming? Black Nevadans in the Nineteenth Century.* Westport, CN: Greenwood Press, 1975.

Sawyer, Grant, and Gary E. Elliott. *Hang Tough! Grant Sawyer: An Activist in the Governor's Mansion.* Reno: University of Nevada Oral History Program, 1993.

Schumacher, Geoff. *Howard Hughes: Power, Paranoia & Palace Intrigue.* Las Vegas: Stephens Press, 2008.

———. *Sun, Sin, and Suburbia: The History of Modern Las Vegas.* Las Vegas: Stephens Press, 2012.

———. *Nevada: 150 Years in the Silver State.* Las Vegas: Stephens Press, 2014.

Sheehan, Jack, Ed. *The Players: The Men Who Made Las Vegas.* Reno: University of Nevada Press, 1997.

Simich, Jerry L., and Thomas C. Wright. *The Peoples of Las Vegas: One City, Many Faces.* Reno: University of Nevada Press, 2005.

Smith, John L. *Of Rats and Men: Oscar Goodman's Life from Mob Mouthpiece to Mayor of Las Vegas.* Las Vegas: Huntington Press, 2003.

———. *On the Boulevard: The Best of John L. Smith.* Las Vegas: Huntington Press, 1998.

———. *Vegas Voices: Conversations With Great Las Vegas Characters.* Las Vegas: NevadaSmith Press, 2014.

Summers, Anthony, and Robbyn Swan. *Sinatra: The Life.* New York: Alfred A. Knopf, 2005.

Swanson, Doug J. *Blood Aces: The Wild Ride of Benny Binion, The Texas Gambler Who Created Vegas Poker.* New York: Viking, 2014.

Titus, A. Costandina, ed. *Battle Born: Federal-State Conflict in Nevada During the Twentieth Century.* Dubuque, Iowa: Kendall-Hunt, 1989.

———. *Bombs in the Backyard: Atomic Testing and American Politics.* Reno: University of Nevada Press, 1986.

Vernetti, Michael. *Senator Howard Cannon of Nevada: A Biography.* Reno: University of Nevada Press, 2008.

Wagner, Sue, with Victoria Ford. *Through the Glass Ceiling: A Life in Nevada Politics.* Reno: University of Nevada Oral History Program, 2005.

Whitely, Joan Burkhart. *Young Las Vegas, 1905–1931: Before the Future Found Us.* Las Vegas: Stephens Press, 2005.

Wilkerson, Isabel. *The Warmth of Other Suns: The Epic Story of America's Great Migration.* New York: Random House, 2001.

Wilson, Earl. *Sinatra: An Unauthorized Biography.* New York: Macmillan Publishing, 1976.

Selected Remarks and Speeches before the Nevada Legislature

(Note: Neal made numerous remarks and speeches during his long career. Some of his oratory was several thousand words in length. Here is a partial list.)

1973: 57th Legislative Session

2/28 SJR 1 Ratifies proposed constitutional amendment relative to equal rights for men and women.

3/27 SJR 12 Memorializes Congress to enact legislation recognizing health care as a right of citizens and to adopt national heal insurance plan.

4/5 SB 545 Defines offenses of capital murder and provides mandatory death penalty therefore.

4/23 AB 319 Permits licensed physicians to perform abortions except where limited by certain conditions.

1975: 58th Legislative Session

2/19 AJR 1 Ratifies proposed constitutional amendment relative to equal rights for men and women.

3/1 SR 17 Adds new Senate Standing Rule which requires, with certain exceptions, all meetings of the Senate and its committees to be open to the public.

4/28 Poem: "The Calf Path."

5/16 AB 320 Prohibits charging fee for use of public toilet.

1977: 59th Legislative Session

2/8 SJR 5 Ratifies proposed constitutional amendment relative to equal rights for men and women.

4/13 SB 220 Provides conditions for imposition of capital punishment.

5/6 Provides safeguards in discipline of public school education personnel.

1979: 60th Legislative Session

5/21 AB 519 Revises procedure for demotion, suspension, dismissal or and refusal to employ certain personnel of public school system.

5/26 AB 503 Changes structure and substantive requirements of Tahoe Regional Planning Agency.

1980: 14th Special Session

9/13 An act relating to the Tahoe Regional Planning Agency.

1981: 61st Legislative Session

3/10 SB 392 Abolishes death penalty.

3/17 AJR 30 Proposes to amend Nevada constitution by prohibiting commutation of sentences of death and life imprisonment without possibility of parole to sentences which would allow parole.

4/23 SB 411 Makes substantial revisions in law relating to governmental finance.

5/30   SB 688 Prohibits houses of prostitution within certain distances of incorporated cities.

6/3   AB 596 Revises requirements for consent and notice in cases of abortion.

1983: 62nd Legislative Session

2/16   SB 88-89 Provides for treatment rather than acquittal for criminal offender, found insane.

2/16   SB 90 Abolishes defense of insanity in criminal proceedings.

2/22   SB 109 Changes method of inflicting death penalty.

5/15   AB 167 Revises laws on driving while intoxicated.

1984: 15th Special Session

3/30   SB 2 Allows acquisition of bank in Nevada by holding company in another state.

1985: 63rd Legislative Session

5/14   Remarks commemorating Dr. Martin Luther King, Jr.

1987 64th Legislative Session

2/13   SCR 8 Commemorates Black History Month.

3/9   Remarks pertaining to bill to consider simultaneously parental fault and best interests of child in proceeding for termination of parental rights.

4/1   Remarks on article titled, "Dreams Don't End with Indiana Loss."

4/19   Remarks on AB 127, attempt to repeal prospective changes to provisions governing of gross revenue of gaming licenses.

4/24   Remarks on AB 116, declaring Martin Luther King Jr.'s birthday and day after Thanksgiving to be legal holidays.

5/21   SB 268, revising restrictions on detention of persons suspected of criminal behavior.

5/22   SB 270, revision of provisions pertaining to forfeiture of property related to criminal activity.

5/27   AB 288, Allowing limited local regulation of use, sale, and possession of firearms.

5/29   AB 289, making various changes relating to restraining costs of medical care.

6/7   SB 301, Repeals Tahoe Regional Planning Compact upon disposition of certain legal disputes.

6/15   AB 417, modifications to mandatory collective bargaining for local government employers.

1989: 65th Legislative Session

2/13   Remarks pertaining to SB 18, creating committee to negotiate with federal government concerning repository for high-level radioactive waste.

3/14   Remarks pertaining to SB 9, increases compensation and allowances for certain expenses of legislators.

5/29 Senate Joint Resolution 18, proposing to amend Nevada Constitution to remove Lieutenant Governor from position of President of the Senate.

6/5 Urges Congress to expedite review by federal courts of state capital cases.

6/7 SB 357, requiring certain appointments by Governor to be confirmed by the Senate

6/15 SB 191, Establishing standards for pupils to exercise freedom of speech and press while on school property.

6/28 AB 222, prohibiting storage in Nevada of high-level nuclear waste.

6/30 AB 935, establishing advisory council on education relating to Holocaust.

1991: 66th Legislative Session

1/21 SJR 1, expressing Nevada's support for actions in Persian Gulf War.

2/5 SJR 5, pertaining to desecration of American flag.

2/26 Regarding Charles Bush case and police violence.

3/28 SB 230, pertaining to additional penalties for criminal offenses by gangs.

5/6 SB 449, pertaining to penalty for intentional killing of wild burro.

6/17 AB 577, pertaining to changes relating to costs of health care.

1993: 67th Legislative Session

1/18 CR 2, commemorating Martin Luther King Jr.

2/1 SJR 4, commemorating African-American History Month.

3/24 SB 316, making various changes governing industrial insurance.

4/14 Remarks on liability of transporting nuclear waste.

4/21 SB 329, making supplemental appropriation to state Distributive School Account.

5/4 SB 23, requiring Governor to impanel economic forum to forecast future state revenue and balanced budget.

5/19 AB 357, clarifying certain provisions of state water law.

5/28 SB 466, prohibiting certain sexual conduct in public.

6/17 SB 440, relating to drug screen tests for state employees.

7/1 SCR 57, supporting efforts of Committee on High-Level Radioactive Waste to clarify compensation and benefits due host state for repository.

1995: 68th Legislative Session

1/16 SCR 1, commemorating Martin Luther King Jr.

1/26 SB 113, expanding aggravated circumstances under which death penalty may be imposed for murder.

2/1 Remarks commemorating Black History Month.

3/29 Remarks pertaining to SR 4, expressing disapproval of certain actions of Governor and Attorney General.

5/5 SB 416, making changes regarding sentencing of persons convicted of felonies.

5/24 SB 400, limiting civil liability of gaming licensees and affiliated employees.

5/31 SCR 45, condemning bombing of U.S. Forest Service office in Carson City.

6/1   SB 445, clarifying that right to work includes right to join labor organization.

6/21   SB 474, regarding civil liability and revising provisions relating to punitive damages.

6/21   SB 428, requiring program for self-sufficiency for applicants for Aid to Families with Dependent Children.

1997: 69th Legislative Session

2/5   Remarks pertaining to SCR 6, commemorating African-American History Month.

4/8   SB 122, pertaining to school employees engaging in sexual conduct with students.

5/6   SB 215, making various changes relating to elections.

6/4   SB 38, amends charter of City of Las Vegas to authorize increase or decrease in number of wards.

1999: 70th Legislative Session

2/10   Pertaining to SJR 4, urging Congress not to enact Nuclear Waste Repository Act of 1999.

2/10   SCR 10, commemorating African-American History Month.

3/17   SB 232, making various changes to provisions governing placement of children.

4/6   SB 285, requiring public schools to provide certain instruction in American government to pupils.

4/23   Remarks pertaining to ACR 49 honoring Dr. James B. McMillan.

5/31   Remarks concerning *Las Vegas Review-Journal* legislative performance ballot.

2001: 71st Legislative Session

2/12   Remarks concerning utility deregulation.

2/28   Remarks commemorating Black History Month.

3/7   SJR 6, providing notice of disapproval to Congress if Yucca Mountain is recommended as site repository for nuclear waste.

4/17   SB 254, establishing a moratorium on execution of sentences of death of certain persons until July 1, 2003.

2003: 72nd Legislative Session

2/6   ACR 2, commemorating victims of September 11, 2001 terrorism attack.

2/13   SB 20, provision making it a misdemeanor for peace officer to practice racial profiling.

3/17   SB 316, revising provisions regarding issuance of search warrants.

2003: 20th Special Session

6/26   Remarks on Governor Guinn's tax plan.

6/29   Remarks on Governor Guinn's tax plan.

6/30   Remarks on Governor Guinn's tax plan.

Index

About the Author

Nevada native John L. Smith is a longtime journalist and the author of more than a dozen books on some of the greatest characters in Las Vegas history. In three decades as a daily columnist with the *Las Vegas Review-Journal,* he garnered many state and national awards for his work. In 2016, Smith was named to the Nevada Newspaper Hall of Fame and was part of a group of reporters to receive the Ancil Payne Award for Ethics from the University of Oregon, the Society of Professional Journalists award for Ethics, and the James Foley/Medill Medal for Courage in Journalism from Northwestern University.

He writes an award-winning weekly column for *The Nevada Independent* news website, offers commentary on National Public Radio station KNPR, and freelances to many other publications.

The father of an adult daughter, Amelia, he is married to the writer Sally Denton and makes his home in Las Vegas and outside Santa Fe, NM.